全球减贫与发展经验分享系列

The Sharing Series on Global Poverty Reduction and Development Experience

东盟减贫与发展年度报告 2024

中国国际减贫中心　编著

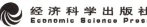

中国财经出版传媒集团

经济科学出版社
Economic Science Press

·北 京·

图书在版编目（CIP）数据

东盟减贫与发展年度报告.2024 / 中国国际减贫中
心编著. --北京：经济科学出版社，2024.7
ISBN 978-7-5218-5867-9

Ⅰ.①东…　Ⅱ.①中…　Ⅲ.①贫困问题–研究报告–
东南亚国家联盟–2024　Ⅳ.①F133.6

中国国家版本馆CIP数据核字（2024）第088800号

责任编辑：吴　敏
责任校对：易　超
责任印制：张佳裕

东盟减贫与发展年度报告2024

DONGMENG JIANPIN YU FAZHAN NIANDU BAOGAO 2024

中国国际减贫中心　编著

经济科学出版社出版、发行　新华书店经销

社址：北京市海淀区阜成路甲28号　邮编：100142

总编部电话：010-88191217　发行部电话：010-88191522

网址：www.esp.com.cn

电子邮箱：esp@esp.com.cn

天猫网店：经济科学出版社旗舰店

网址：http://jjkxcbs.tmall.com

北京季蜂印刷有限公司印装

710×1000　16开　19印张　390000字

2024年7月第1版　2024年7月第1次印刷

ISBN 978-7-5218-5867-9　定价：85.00元

《东盟减贫与发展年度报告 2024》
课 题 组

课题组组长　王怀豫　李　昕

课题组成员　陈虹枢　贾晓薇　徐丽萍　贺胜年

　　　　　　　刘欢欢　姚　远　王巧瑜　范宏琳

　　　　　　　苏志文　杨双全　林　琳　王淏芊

消除贫困是人类梦寐以求的理想，人类发展史就是与贫困不懈斗争的历史。中国拥有14亿人口，是世界上最大的发展中国家，基础差、底子薄，发展不平衡，长期饱受贫困问题困扰。消除贫困、改善民生、实现共同富裕是社会主义的本质要求，是中国共产党的重要使命。为兑现这一庄严政治承诺，100多年来，中国共产党团结带领中国人民，以坚定不移、顽强不屈的信念和意志与贫困进行了长期艰苦卓绝的斗争。自改革开放以来，中国实施了大规模、有计划、有组织的扶贫开发，着力解放和发展社会生产力，着力保障和改善民生，取得了前所未有的伟大成就。党的十八大以来，以习近平同志为核心的党中央把脱贫攻坚摆在治国理政的突出位置，习近平总书记亲自谋划、亲自挂帅、亲自督战，推动实施精准扶贫精准脱贫基本方略，动员全党全国全社会力量，打赢了人类历史上规模空前、力度最大、惠及人口最多的脱贫攻坚战。

脱贫攻坚战的全面胜利，离不开有为政府和有效市场的有机结合。八年间，以习近平同志为核心的党中央加强对脱贫攻坚的集中统一领导，发挥中国特色社会主义制度能够集中力量办大事的政治优势，把减贫摆在治国理政的突出位置，为脱贫攻坚提供了坚强政治和组织保证。广泛动员市场、社会力量积极参与，实施"万企帮万村"等行动，鼓励民营企业和社会组织、公民个人参与脱贫攻坚，促进资金、人才、技术等要素向贫困地区集聚。截至2020年底，现行标准下9899万农村贫困人口全部脱贫，832个贫困县全部摘帽，12.8万个贫困村全部出列，区域性整体贫困得到解决，完成了消除绝对贫困的艰巨任务，建成了世界上规模最大的教育体系、社会保障体系、医疗卫生体系，实现了快速发展与大规模减贫同步、经济转型与消除绝对贫困同步。

一直以来，中国始终是世界减贫事业的积极倡导者、有力推动者和重要贡献者。按照世界银行国际贫困标准，改革开放以来，中国减贫人口占同期全球减贫人口的70%以上，占同期东亚和太平洋地区减贫人口的80%。占世界人口近五分之一的中国全面消除绝对贫困，提前10年实现联合国2030年可持续发展议程减贫目标，不仅是中华民族发展史上具有里程碑意义的大事件，也是人类减贫史乃至人类发展史上的大事件，为全球减贫事业发展和人类发展进步作出了重大贡献。

中国立足自身国情，把握减贫规律，走出了一条中国特色减贫道路，形成了中国特色反贫困理论，创造了减贫治理的中国样本。坚持以人民为中心的发展思想，坚定不移走共同富裕道路，是扶贫减贫的根本动力。坚持把减贫摆在治国理政突出位置，从党的领袖到广大党员干部，目标一致、上下同心，加强顶层设计和战略规划，广泛动员各方力量积极参与，完善脱贫攻坚制度体系，保持政策连续性稳定性。坚持用发展的办法消除贫困，发展是解决包括贫困问题在内的中国所有问题的关键，是创造幸福生活最稳定的途径。坚持立足实际推进减贫进程，因时因势因地制宜，不断调整创新减贫的策略方略和政策工具，提高贫困治理效能，精准扶贫方略是打赢脱贫攻坚战的制胜法宝，开发式扶贫方针是中国特色减贫道路的鲜明特征。坚持发挥贫困群众主体作用，调动广大贫困群众积极性、主动性、创造性，激发脱贫内生动力，使贫困群众不仅成为减贫的受益者，也成为发展的贡献者。

脱贫攻坚战取得全面胜利后，中国政府设立了 5 年过渡期，着力巩固拓展脱贫攻坚成果，全面推进乡村振兴。按照党的二十大部署，在以中国式现代化全面推进中华民族伟大复兴的新征程上，中国正全面推进乡村振兴，建设宜居宜业和美乡村，向着实现人的全面发展和全体人民共同富裕的更高目标不断迈进。中国巩固拓展脱贫成果和乡村振兴的探索和实践，将继续为人类减贫和乡村发展提供新的中国经验和智慧，为推动构建没有贫困的人类命运共同体贡献中国力量。

面对国际形势新动向新特征，习近平总书记提出"一带一路"倡议、全球发展倡议等全球共同行动，将减贫作为重点合作领域，致力于推动构建没有贫困、共同发展的人类命运共同体。加强国际减贫与乡村发展经验分享，助力全球减贫与发展进程，业已成为全球广泛共识。为此，自 2019 年起，中国国际减贫中心与比尔及梅琳达·盖茨基金会联合实施国际合作项目，始终坚持站在未来的角度、政策的高度精心谋划项目选题，引领国内外减贫与乡村发展前沿热点和研究走向。始终坚持将中国减贫与乡村发展经验与国际接轨，通过国际话语体系阐释中国减贫与乡村振兴道路，推动中国减贫与乡村发展经验的国际化传播。至今已实施了 30 余个研究项目，形成了一批形式多样、影响广泛的研究成果，部分成果已在相关国际交流活动中发布。

为落实全球发展倡议，进一步促进全球减贫与乡村发展交流合作，中国国际减贫中心精心梳理研究成果，推出四个系列丛书，包括"全球减贫与发展经验分享系列""中国减贫与发展经验国际分享系列""国际乡村发展经验分享系列"和"中国乡村振兴经验分享系列"。

"全球减贫与发展经验分享系列"旨在跟踪全球减贫进展，分析全球减贫与发展趋势，总结分享各国减贫经验，为推动联合国2030可持续发展议程、参与全球贫困治理提供知识产品。该系列主要包括"国际减贫年度报告""国际减贫理论与前沿问题"等全球性减贫知识产品，以及覆盖非洲、东盟、南亚、拉丁美洲及加勒比地区等区域性减贫知识产品。

"中国减贫与发展经验国际分享系列"旨在讲好中国减贫故事，向国际社会分享中国减贫经验，为广大发展中国家实现减贫与发展提供切实可行的经验。该系列聚焦中国精准扶贫、脱贫攻坚和巩固拓展脱贫攻坚成果的经验做法，基于国际视角梳理形成中国减贫经验分享的知识产品。

"国际乡村发展经验分享系列"聚焦国际乡村发展历程、政策和实践，比较中外乡村发展经验和做法，为全球乡村发展事业提供交流互鉴的知识产品。该系列主要包括"国际乡村振兴年度报告""乡村治理国际经验比较分析报告""县域城乡融合发展与乡村振兴"等研究成果。

"中国乡村振兴经验分享系列"聚焦讲好中国乡村振兴故事，及时总结乡村振兴经验、做法和典型案例，为国内外政策制定者和研究者提供参考。该系列主要围绕乡村发展、乡村规划、共同富裕等议题，梳理总结有关政策、经验和实践，基于国际视角开发编写典型案例等。

最后，感谢所有为系列图书顺利付梓付出辛勤汗水的相关项目组、出版社和编辑人员，以及关心和支持中国国际减贫中心的政府机构、高校和科研院所、社会组织和各界朋友。系列丛书得到了比尔及梅琳达·盖茨基金会的慷慨资助以及盖茨基金会北京代表处的悉心指导和帮助，在此表示衷心感谢！

全球减贫与乡村发展是动态的、不断变化的，书中难免有挂一漏万之处，敬请读者指正！

刘俊文

中国国际减贫中心主任

2024年1月

贫困是当今世界面临的最大挑战，消除贫困是全人类的共同责任。东盟是全球人口最密集的地区之一，也是发展程度差异最大的区域之一，推动东盟国家减贫进程对于全世界消除贫困具有重要意义。新冠疫情（以下简称"疫情"）对东盟国家发展产生了不同程度的影响。疫情过后，各国积极谋求经济复苏，但地区内复苏并不均衡；同时，气候变化、营养健康及教育等因素给可持续增长和消除贫困带来不确定性。

中国和东盟山水相连、血脉相亲，友好关系源远流长。习近平总书记指出，中国东盟合作的成就，得益于双方地缘相近、人文相通得天独厚的条件，更离不开双方积极顺应时代发展潮流，作出正确历史选择。30多年来，中国与东盟携手前进，战略伙伴关系内涵不断丰富，政治安全、经济贸易、社会人文三大领域合作硕果累累，成为规模最大的贸易伙伴、最富内涵的合作伙伴、最具活力的战略伙伴。

为落实全球发展倡议，在中国—东盟合作框架下持续推进中国与东盟国家减贫交流合作，推动构建更为紧密的中国—东盟命运共同体，中国国际减贫中心组织撰写了《东盟减贫与发展年度报告2024》，全面回顾疫情前后东盟国家减贫进展。本报告采用描述分析和对比分析，根据世界银行、联合国粮食及农业组织、联合国开发计划署以及东盟秘书处等国际机构公布的数据，从多维度、多方面探讨东盟减贫成就、实践和前景。

报告认为：

1.疫情前东盟国家减贫成效显著。根据世界银行国际贫困标准和东盟各国国家贫困线，疫情前东盟国家贫困发生率均有不同程度的下降。人类发展指数平均值由2012年的0.698上升到2019年的0.733。多维贫困问题得到缓解，在收入、教育、健康和生活水平等多个维度已取得较好进展。然而，各国发展水平和减贫进展仍存在差异，城乡基本公共服务还存在差距。

2.疫情减缓了减贫进程。疫情加剧了东盟国家低收入群体和落后地区的脆弱性，部分国家返贫人口和脆弱人口增加。2020~2021年东盟人类发展指数年均增速为负，部分国家多维贫困问题仍然较为严重。受收入减少、学校关闭等因素影响，部分国家营养不良、教学中断等风险上升，减贫进程有所放缓。为应对疫情影响，东盟及各国积极采取多种措施，国际社会加大援助力度，确保减贫工作向前推进。

3.疫后经济复苏推动减贫与发展。国际机构估算，2023年东盟实现4.9%~5.2%的经济增长，展现出较为强劲的复苏势头。东盟国家间深化经贸联系，扩大贸易往来，提升货物自由流动、供应链互联互通及服务效率，采取各种措施吸引外国投资，支持中小微企业发展。东盟国家数字技术发展迅猛，互联网基础设施发展较快，各国出台政策措施推动数字经济发展，促进充分就业，为实现减贫与发展打下更加坚实的物质基础。

4.减贫与发展主要议题取得新进展。粮食安全展现出较强韧性，2021年以来东盟粮食安全指数持续上升。营养健康水平得到改善，东盟成员国全球饥饿指数降到中等水平。教育体系建设不断加强，包容性教育程度不断提升。通过科学推进能源转型和减排，刺激技术创新，创造就业和经济增长机会，减少贫困并促进公平。加大科技创新和人才培养力度，不断提高减贫成效。

5.东盟国家减贫与发展前景广阔。疫后经济复苏，贸易投资自由化和便利化，数字经济快速发展，区域内合作加强，为东盟实现减贫与发展提供了良好的发展机遇。面向未来，通过减贫经验国际分享、减贫项目合作、开展能力建设，促进东盟国家与包括中国在内的发展中国家交流合作，一道落实全球发展倡议，构建更为紧密的中国—东盟命运共同体，为地区和世界和平稳定、繁荣发展注入新的动力。

本报告共有五章。第一章是东盟基本情况及疫情影响下的东盟国家减贫进展；第二章是东盟国家减贫主要议题实施进展；第三章是推动东盟国家减贫的国际发展援助与合作；第四章是中国—东盟减贫合作；第五章是东盟减贫发展展望。

目录

Contents

第一章
东盟基本情况及疫情影响下的东盟国家减贫进展

一、东盟基本情况

东南亚国家联盟是一个以经济合作为基础的政治、经济、安全一体化合作组织。为促进本地区的和平与发展，建立一个繁荣、稳定的东南亚国家共同体。1967年8月8日，印度尼西亚（以下简称"印尼"）、泰国、新加坡、菲律宾和马来西亚发布《曼谷宣言》，正式宣告东南亚国家联盟（以下简称"东盟"）成立。文莱（1984年）、越南（1995年）、老挝（1997年）、缅甸（1997年）和柬埔寨（1999年）先后加入，东盟成员国扩大到10个。2022年11月，东盟原则上同意东帝汶成为第十一个成员国①。根据《东南亚国家联盟宪章》②，首脑会议是东盟最高决策机构，主席由成员国轮流担任；设立在印尼首都雅加达的东盟秘书处是服务于各成员国的行政机构，东盟秘书长由各成员国轮流派人担任，任期5年。现任东盟秘书长是柬埔寨政治家高金洪，任期到2028年。

东盟③**地理位置关键，矿产资源丰富**。东盟国家均分布在亚洲东南部，北与中国接壤，并与日本隔海相望，西与印度和孟加拉国相邻，东部和南部则与大洋洲国家隔太平洋相望，整体处于太平洋与印度洋、亚洲与大洋洲的交汇区，地缘位置非常重要。缅甸、老挝和越南是中国的陆上邻国，菲律宾、马来西亚和印尼则与中国隔南海相望。东盟地区石油和锡矿资源丰富，拥有世界最

---

① 由于2022年及之前东盟统计数据基于东盟十国汇总，为保证统计口径一致，全书东盟相关指标仍以东盟十国为基础，同时单独补充东帝汶的情况。

② 2008年12月《东南亚国家联盟宪章》正式生效，这是东盟第一份具有普遍法律意义的文件，对各成员国都具有约束力。

③ 文莱和新加坡为高收入国家，本报告重点关注东盟区域新兴经济体和发展中国家，因此后文关于贫困的分析中不涉及文莱和新加坡。

大的锡矿带，其中马来西亚的锡矿砂产量居世界首位；印尼是重要的石油、天然气出口国；泰国钾盐储备世界第一；越南矿藏资源种类多样，拥有 50 多种矿产资源①。

东盟是全球受气候变化影响最严重的地区之一②。2020 年，泰国每 10 万人中有 14768 人直接或间接受到气候灾害的影响，这一数字是 2019 年的 2 倍。菲律宾每 10 万人中有 8723 人直接或间接受到气候灾害的影响。在印尼和缅甸，每 10 万人中分别有 2388 人和 2494 人直接或间接受到气候灾害的影响③。

东盟农作物资源丰富。 水稻是东盟的主要粮食作物，种植历史悠久。泰国、缅甸和越南是世界重要的稻米生产国和出口国。该区域也是世界上橡胶、棕油、椰子和蕉麻等热带经济作物的最大产区。其中，泰国是世界上最大的橡胶生产国，马来西亚的棕油生产和出口居世界首位，菲律宾是世界上最大的椰子生产国。

东盟成员国间国土面积相差较大。 东盟总面积约 449 万平方公里④。其中，印尼国土面积为 192 万平方公里，是东盟国土面积第一大国；缅甸和泰国的国土面积分别为 68 万平方公里和 51 万平方公里；马来西亚、越南、菲律宾、老挝、柬埔寨的国土面积都在 18 万~33 万平方公里。老挝是区域内唯一的内陆国。

东盟国家间发展水平和产业结构存在差异。 2022 年东盟 GDP 总额为 3.6 万亿美元⑤，占世界总量的 3.6%⑥；人口约 6.7 亿，占世界总人口的 8.4%⑦。其中，马来西亚和泰国经济发展水平较为领先：马来西亚人均 GDP 为 12448 美元，泰国人均 GDP 为 7494.4 美元⑧；两国 GDP 增速较为平缓，2013~2022 年马来西亚的 GDP 年均增速⑨为 4.2%，泰国为 1.9%；两国服务业产值在其 GDP 中的占比均超过 50%，农业产值占比都在 10% 之下⑩；两国政府治理能力得分领先其他东盟国家（见表 1–1）。印尼、菲律宾、越南和老挝的经济发展水平在东盟国家中处

---

① 参见《对外投资合作国别（地区）指南：东盟（2022 年版）》《对外投资合作国别（地区）指南：马来西亚（2022 年版）》《对外投资合作国别（地区）指南：印度尼西亚（2022 年版）》《对外投资合作国别（地区）指南：泰国（2022 年版）》《对外投资合作国别（地区）指南：越南（2022 年版）》。
② 参见《2023 年世界银行年度报告》。
③ 数据来源于东盟秘书处。
④ 根据中华人民共和国商务部发布的《对外投资合作国别（地区）指南：东盟（2022 年版）》整理。
⑤ 数据来源于《2023 年东盟统计年鉴》，不包括东帝汶。
⑥ 基于世界银行统计数据，2022 年全球 GDP 为 100.88 万亿美元。
⑦ 基于世界银行统计数据，2020 年世界总人口为 79.5 亿人。
⑧ 数据来源于《2023 年东盟统计年鉴》。
⑨ GDP 增速指标为 2013~2022 年年均增长率。
⑩ 数据来源于世界银行公开数据库（https://data.worldbank.org）。

于中等水平；GDP增速较快，如印尼的GDP增速为4.3%，菲律宾为5%，越南为6%；这四个国家的服务业产值占其GDP的比重为30%~40%，农业产值占其GDP的比重为10%~17%[①]；这四个国家的政府治理能力得分在东盟国家中处于中等水平（见表1-1）。柬埔寨和缅甸经济发展水平最低，人均GDP不足1800美元，但GDP增速快，柬埔寨的GDP增速达到5.7%，缅甸为5%；这两个国家的服务业产值占其GDP的比重为30%~40%，农业产值占其GDP的比重保持在23%左右[②]；这两个国家的政府治理能力得分相对较低（见表1-1）。

表1-1　　　　2017~2021年东盟国家政府治理能力情况

国家	2017年	2018年	2019年	2020年	2021年
新加坡	89.03	89.22	88.82	88.82	89.22
文莱	70.06	71.84	70.72	74.62	74.62
马来西亚	59.75	63.96	63.48	63.25	62.53
印尼	46.31	46.83	46.11	47.70	48.91
泰国	43.00	41.46	43.84	43.85	43.76
越南	40.18	39.75	39.76	42.25	42.25
菲律宾	40.88	39.90	40.13	40.03	38.36
东帝汶	31.91	33.03	34.42	35.29	38.00
老挝	27.16	24.25	23.68	25.18	27.58
柬埔寨	24.82	25.48	25.11	25.04	24.87
缅甸	19.87	19.61	18.57	19.14	8.56

数据来源：根据WGI数据库整理得到。

农业是东盟国家重要的支柱产业。 农业是东盟大多数成员国国民经济发展的重要支柱。2022年，东盟农业生产总产值占GDP的比重为16.4%[③]，对经济增长的贡献较大，为东盟国家创造了大量就业岗位。2022年，泰国的农业产值占GDP的比重仅为8.8%，但为全国创造了31.9%的就业岗位；印尼和越南的农业产值占GDP的比重分别为12.4%和11.9%，创造的就业分别占28.3%和29.1%；菲律宾的农业部门以9.5%的产值提供了全国24%的就业岗位；柬埔寨和缅甸

---

① 数据来源于世界银行公开数据库（https://data.worldbank.org）。
② 同上。
③ 参见 *ASEAN Key Figure 2023*。

的农业产值占GDP的比重分别为22.2%和22.6%[①]。农产品贸易是东盟国家重要的外汇来源。东盟农产品，特别是热带作物，在国际市场具有较强竞争力，贸易总额始终呈顺差状态，2022年贸易顺差额为493亿美元[②]。

东盟区域内贸易依存度高，与中国互为最大贸易伙伴。2012~2022年，区域内贸易是东盟国家对外贸易的重要组成部分，2022年东盟区域内货物贸易额占贸易总额的22%。自2020年起，中国成为东盟第一大贸易伙伴，2022年中国东盟贸易总额占东盟贸易总量的18.8%，其次是美国和欧盟，占比分别为10.9%和7.7%[③]。

东盟各国基础设施持续改善。截至2022年，印尼、马来西亚、泰国和越南的电力普及率达到99%以上。[④]老挝、菲律宾和柬埔寨的电力覆盖率分别为94%、96%和98%。尽管缅甸在电力供应领域取得了进展，从2016年的33%上升到2022年的62%，但仍低于其他东盟成员国。东盟各国道路长度年增长率为5.6%。其中，泰国的年增长率为12.7%，马来西亚、越南和缅甸的年增长率超过7%，柬埔寨和老挝的年增长率低于4.5%，印尼和菲律宾的道路设施增长缓慢，年增长率仅为1%左右。

数字化水平明显提升。总体上东盟各国互联网覆盖率显著提升。东盟互联网普及率从2013年的26.1%上升至2022年的72%[⑤]，每百人拥有移动电话数量增长较快，从2016年的88部上升到2022年的99.6部。大多数东盟国家已经基本完成4G网络的全面覆盖，2022年新加坡、泰国的4G网络覆盖率超过98%，其他东盟国家也都在80%以上。[⑥]东盟国家发展5G网络的积极性较高，部分国家已经通过小规模商用、建立实验网络等方式逐步推进5G落地。菲律宾通过中菲4G/5G通信基站项目，成为东盟第一个实现5G商用的国家[⑦]。新加坡、越南、印尼、老挝、马来西亚以及柬埔寨也陆续在其国内部署5G网络。

东盟国家年龄结构呈年轻化，人口主要分布在农村。多数东盟国家的人口年龄结构较为年轻，仅泰国和越南进入老龄化社会。大多数东盟国家的人口主要分布在农村。缅甸的农村人口占比接近70%，越南、老挝、柬埔寨、菲律宾

---

① 数据来源于《2023年东盟统计年鉴》。
② 同上。
③ 同上。
④ 数据来源于 *ASEAN Key Figure 2023*。
⑤ 数据来源于《2023年东盟统计年鉴》。
⑥ 数据来源于中国移动研究院2021年发布的《东南亚和南亚信息通信基础设施发展现状和趋势》。
⑦ 参见：新华网，"'一带一路'发展学：全球共同发展的实践和理论探索"，2023年10月19日。

也有超过一半的人口生活在农村①。此外，柬埔寨的成人识字率和净入学率均不到90%。

区域内种族多样，社会文化多元。东盟人口空间分布不均，多集中在平原和河口三角洲地带。区域内多民族聚集，印尼和缅甸有100多个民族，菲律宾有超过90个民族②，其余国家的民族数量也都在20~50个③。东盟官方语言是英语，但其成员国语言种类繁多，多语种并存。东盟成员国宗教信仰多元，泰国、缅甸、老挝和柬埔寨以信仰佛教为主，马来西亚和印尼主要信奉伊斯兰教，菲律宾是信仰天主教的国家，越南主要信奉儒家文化④。文化多元使东盟各国价值观存在差异，增加了区域内一体化的复杂性。

总的来看，大多数东盟国家仍处于发展中国家阶段，但区域内部发展差异较大。马来西亚发展水平相对较高，但GDP增速较低，产业结构以服务业为主，农村人口比重低，互联网覆盖率和政府治理能力位居区域前列。柬埔寨和缅甸发展水平较为落后，但经济增速较高，农业是支撑国家发展的基础产业，农村人口占比高，政府治理能力、教育水平和基础设施等领域尚有不足。老挝是唯一的内陆国，经济正在高速增长。印尼和菲律宾的人口已经超过1亿，资源丰富，但易受气候变化影响。越南和泰国资源丰富，货物贸易发达，人口增速放缓，老龄化程度较高。泰国是区域内受气候变化影响最严重的国家。

二、疫情对东盟经济社会发展的影响

疫情前经济快速发展。2012~2019年，东盟整体GDP从2.2万亿美元上升到3.1万亿美元，年均增长率为5%；人均GDP从3575美元增长至4641美元，年均增长率为3.8%。疫情前东盟经济增速高于全球平均水平，经济快速发展，与全球平均水平的差距缩小，绝对贫困发生率显著降低。然而，区域内差异较大，泰国、马来西亚和印尼属于中等偏上收入国家，菲律宾、缅甸、越南、柬埔寨和老挝则属于中等偏下收入国家。

---

① 数据来源于《2023年东盟统计年鉴》。

② 周建新.东南亚各国的民族划分及相关问题思考［J］.贵州民族研究，2018，39（2）:1-7.

③ 根据中华人民共和国商务部发布的《对外投资合作国别（地区）指南：越南（2022年版）》《对外投资合作国别（地区）指南：老挝（2020年版）》《对外投资合作国别（地区）指南：柬埔寨（2020年版）》整理。

④ 刘金光.东南亚宗教的特点及其在中国对外交流中的作用：兼谈东南亚华人宗教的特点［J］.华侨华人历史研究，2014（1）:28-33.

　　疫情造成经济负增长，增加经济脆弱国家的返贫风险[①]。受疫情影响，2020年东盟整体 GDP 和人均 GDP 年增长率分别为 –3.6% 和 –4.5%，均低于全球平均水平[②]。2020年，印尼被列入中等偏下收入国家[③]，菲律宾、马来西亚和泰国的人均 GDP 年增长率分别为 –11%、–6.7% 和 –6.4%。2020~2022年，东盟经济逐步复苏，东盟整体 GDP 和人均 GDP 年增长率分别为 4.6% 和 3.7%（见图1–1）。除文莱和缅甸外，其余东盟国家的人均 GDP 年增长率为正，其中新加坡、菲律宾和印尼的年增长率最高，分别为 6.7%、5.1% 和 4.8%。总体来看，受疫情冲击，东盟部分国家经济波动明显，减贫事业面临较大挑战。

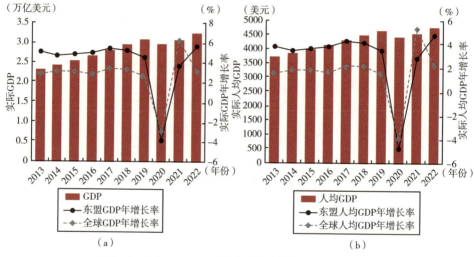

图1–1　2013~2022年东盟经济发展的变化趋势

数据来源：世界银行公开数据库（https://data.worldbank.org），按2015年不变价计。

　　疫情对东盟各国产业的影响存在差异，对服务业占比较高国家的负面影响较大。由图1–2可知，整体来看，东盟产业结构中农业占比较大，高于全球平均水平。与东盟其他国家相比，缅甸、柬埔寨和老挝的农业占比最高，均超过15%[④]。文莱的制造业占比为62.7%，远高于其他东盟国家，印尼和越南的制造业占比也相对较大，分别为 39.9% 和 37.5%。新加坡、菲律宾、泰国和马来西

[①]　文莱和新加坡为高收入国家，本报告重点关注东盟区域新兴经济体和发展中国家，因此后文关于贫困的分析中不涉及文莱和新加坡。

[②]　2020年，全球 GDP 和人均 GDP 年增长率分别为 –3.1% 和 –4.1%。

[③]　数据来源于世界银行公布的基于收入的国家分类。

[④]　数据来源于世界银行公开数据库（https://data.worldbank.org）。

亚的服务业占比均超过50%。受疫情影响，2020年新加坡、泰国、马来西亚和菲律宾的农业出现负增长，年增长率分别为–4.2%、–3.5%、–2.4%和–0.2%。疫情对菲律宾、马来西亚、泰国、印尼和柬埔寨的制造业影响较大，2020年年增长率分别为–13.1%、–6.1%、–5.4%、–2.8%和–1.4%；同年，老挝、缅甸和越南的制造业产值仍保持4%的年增长率。2021年，除文莱的制造业年增长率为–4.2%之外，其余国家的制造业均恢复正增长，其中新加坡、柬埔寨、菲律宾和老挝恢复最快，年增长率分别为13.3%、9.4%、8.5%和7.6%。除缅甸和越南外，疫情对其余东盟国家的服务业均产生了负面影响。其中，菲律宾、泰国和柬埔寨受影响更大，2020年的年增长率分别为–9.1%、–7.0%和–6.3%。2021年，除了缅甸、柬埔寨和老挝外，其余东盟国家的服务业均逐渐复苏。到2022年，所有东盟国家的服务业均恢复正增长。

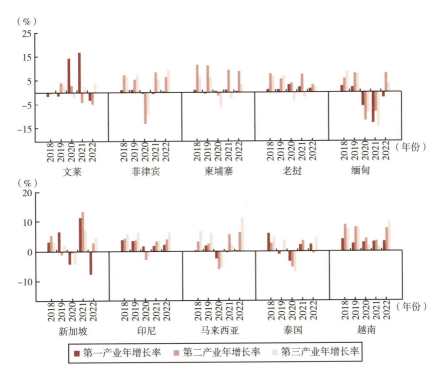

图1-2　2018~2022年东盟国家三次产业年增长率

数据来源：世界银行公开数据库（https://data.worldbank.org）。

疫情加剧了人口增长率下降的趋势。2012~2019年，东盟人口年增长率为1.1%，低于全球平均水平0.06个百分点（见图1-3）。疫情前，人口增长率年均下降约0.04个百分点，2020年和2021年人口增长率年均下降0.06个百分点和0.13个百分点。与疫情前相比，人口增长率下降速度加快。2021年，除新加坡之外，其余东盟国家人口增长率的下降幅度放缓。从城市化发展的角度来看，大多数东盟国家农村人口占比超过世界平均水平，其中柬埔寨的农村人口占比超过3/4，越南、老挝、缅甸、菲律宾和泰国也有超过半数的人口位于农村地区，仅马来西亚的农村人口占比较低，不足1/4。结合各国农村人口的绝对数，东盟国家中印尼凭借庞大的人口基数，拥有超过1亿的农村人口；越南、菲律宾、缅甸和泰国居于其后，农村人口也都超过了3000万人；马来西亚和老挝的农村人口则不到1000万人。

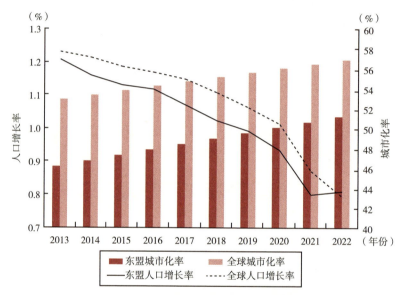

图1-3　2013~2022年东盟人口增长率和城市化的变化情况

数据来源：世界银行公开数据库（https://data.worldbank.org）。

疫情改变了东盟国家的年龄结构，部分国家劳动年龄人口下降。 在人口年龄结构的划分方面，一般将15~64岁的人口视为劳动年龄人口，将65岁及以上视为老年人口，0~14岁视为未成年人口。2017~2022年大多数东盟国家的劳动年龄人口占总人口的比重达到60%~70%，没有明显的差别，各国未成年人口和老年人口占比则有所不同（见图1-4）。根据联合国最新确定的标准，65岁及以上人口占比达到7%以上即为老龄化社会。泰国和越南的老龄人口比重均超过7%，其中泰国已经超过10%，属于老龄化程度较深的国家。未成年人口占比可以体现一国的劳动力资源潜力。在东盟各成员国中，老挝、柬埔寨、菲律宾和东帝汶四国0~14岁人口比重平均超过30%，高于其余成员国，表现出更为年轻的人口结构。与2017~2019年相比，2020~2022年东盟各国0~14岁人口占比均有所下降，其中，东帝汶的下降幅度最大，为2个百分点，马来西亚、菲律宾和老挝的下降幅度较大，约降低1个百分点。东盟各国65岁及以上人口占比则均有所增加，其中新加坡和泰国的增幅最大，分别增加了2.9个百分点和1.9个百分点。另外，疫情使新加坡、泰国、越南和文莱的劳动力人口占比下降，与疫情前相比，分别下降了2.5个、1.1个、0.5个和0.1个百分点。

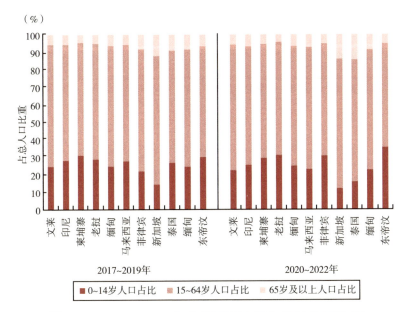

图1-4　2017~2022年东盟国家人口年龄结构平均值

数据来源：根据世界银行公开数据库（https://data.worldbank.org）的数据计算得到。

东盟国家人类发展水平[①]**增速趋缓，疫情期间持续下降。**2012~2019年，东盟国家居民教育、健康情况不断改善，收入水平不断提高，人类发展指数平均值由0.698上升到0.733，处于中等人类发展水平[②]，与全球人类平均发展水平差距逐渐缩小（见图1-5）。疫情期间，东盟各国人类发展情况持续下降。2020年，东盟人类发展指数较2019年下降0.27%；2021年，东盟整体人类发展指数平均

---

① 联合国开发计划署从健康长寿的生活、教育以及体面的生活水平三大基本维度评估人类发展水平。
② 根据联合国开发计划署人类发展指数分类标准。

值年增长率为 –0.64%，低于全球平均水平。除新加坡的人类发展水平保持不变外，其余东盟国家的人类发展均出现负增长，其中菲律宾、印尼和马来西亚受疫情影响较大。2022 年，东盟整体人类发展指数年增长率为 1.32%，高于全球水平 0.37 个百分点。

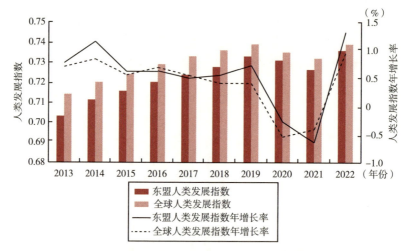

图 1-5　2013~2022 年全球及东盟人类发展指数及年增长率

数据来源：《2023 年人类发展报告》。

疫情使健康、教育和收入水平受到不利影响。2021 年，大多数东盟国家平均受教育年限并未出现明显变化，但预期寿命和预期受教育年限都明显下降（见图 1-6）。印尼和菲律宾的预期寿命降幅最大，分别为 –2.1% 和 –1.8%。老挝和菲律宾的预期受教育年限降幅最大，年增长率分别为 –1.6% 和 –1%。疫情期间，缅甸、菲律宾、泰国、马来西亚和柬埔寨的人均国民总收入负增长，缅甸、菲律宾和泰国受到较大影响，年增长率分别为 –8.3%、–4.5% 和 –2.1%。疫情期间，东帝汶的预期寿命、预期受教育年限没有太大变化，平均受教育年限出现上升，人均国民总收入下降速度放缓。总之，健康、教育和收入受到的不利影响进一步加剧了东盟各国的人口脆弱性，增加了脱贫人口返贫的可能性。

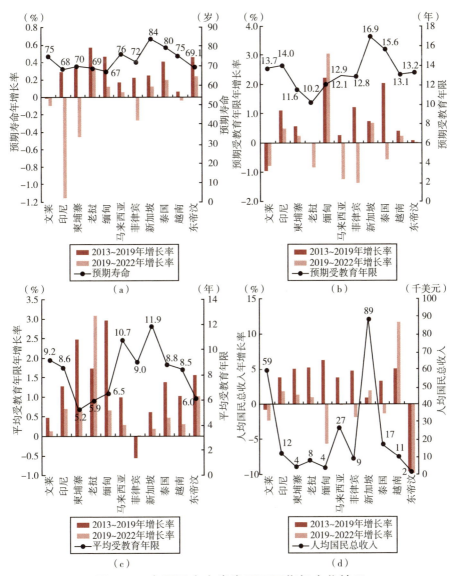

图1-6　东盟国家人类发展不同指标变化情况

注：人均国民总收入按照2017年PPP指数平减。

数据来源：《2023年人类发展报告》。

数字鸿沟在东盟成员国中差异明显，可能加重区域不平等。2012~2019年，东盟固定宽带覆盖率、互联网宽带覆盖率和每百人拥有移动电话数持续上升（见图1-7）。2022年，东盟固定宽带覆盖率和互联网宽带覆盖率分别达9.5%和65%，但各国之间差异明显。2022年，马来西亚、文莱和新加坡的互联网覆盖率超过95%，泰国和越南的覆盖率分别为88%和79%，东帝汶的互联网覆盖率最低，为39.5%。2022年，除新加坡和文莱，越南的固定宽带覆盖率最高，为21.7%，其次是泰国和马来西亚，分别为18.5%和12.4%，菲律宾、印尼分别为7.6%和4.9%，柬埔寨、老挝、缅甸和东帝汶的宽带覆盖率最低，均不足3%。然而，疫情阻碍了数字化进程。2020年东盟每百人拥有移动电话数较2019年下降3%，2021年该指标有所回升。泰国和菲律宾的数字化进程受影响较大。2020年，菲律宾和泰国每百人移动电话拥有量较2019年分别下降12%和11%。2021年，除柬埔寨、缅甸、越南外，其余东盟国家移动电话数有所回升。2021年，泰国每百人拥有的移动电话数最多，达到169部，老挝是区域内每百人拥有的移动电话数最低的国家，为65部，其他东盟国家每百人拥有的移动电话数均为125~150部。疫情期间，尽管大多数国家尝试远程教学，但显然无法覆盖所有家庭①。2020年，东盟配备计算机的小学占比为45.3%。其中，马来西亚全部小学均配备计算机，越南配备计算机的小学的比例为84.6%，菲律宾为70.5%，印尼为40.4%，缅甸仅为1.1%。②学生无法参与在线教育可能导致其未来年收入减少3.8%③。数字鸿沟的存在可能进一步加剧区域内的不平等。

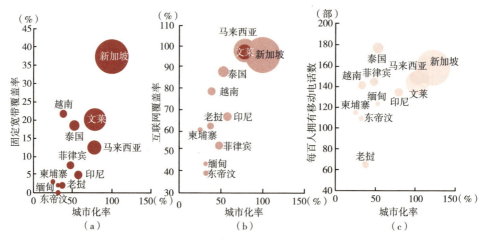

图1-7　2022年东盟数字化发展情况

注：圆圈大小与人均实际GDP成正比。老挝的固定宽带覆盖率和每百人拥有移动电话数为2021年数据，文莱、柬埔寨、老挝、缅甸、菲律宾和越南的互联网覆盖率为2021年数据。

数据来源：世界银行公开数据库（https://data.worldbank.org）。

---

① 根据联合国教科文组织发布的"远程学习中令人担忧的数字鸿沟"整理。
② 数据来源于东盟秘书处发布的 *The 2022 ASEAN SDG Snapshot Report*。
③ 数据来源于世界银行2021年10月发布的东亚与太平洋地区经济半年报。

　　疫情在客观上催生了新业态新模式，数字经济带来更多脱贫机会[①]。虽然疫情导致东盟各国经济负增长，但疫情前东盟各国数字化、信息化已初具规模，这为疫情期间新业态新模式的发展奠定了基础，数字经济为中小企业、妇女和青年等弱势群体带来更多脱贫致富的机会。2019年，东盟数字经济规模为1020亿美元，2020年达到1160亿美元，同比增长14%。自2021年以来，东南亚数字经济收入以27%的增速增长。其中，2023年东南亚数字经济收入估计达1000亿美元[②]。疫情期间的封闭政策使零售商纷纷转向在线销售，2019年东盟地区零售行业电子商务规模为30亿美元，2020年增长超过1倍，达到70亿美元，电子商务的快速增长为女性赋权提供了机会。同时，电子商务的快速发展使快递服务需求激增，2020年Ninja Van在泰国的配送量增长了300%，同年东南亚地区的外卖业务增长了183%[③]。冷链运输和物联网为中小企业发展中游食品供应链提供技术基础，同时还可以支持健康膳食消费，为小规模生产者提供就业机会[④]。大量互联网"独角兽"企业诞生[⑤]，在网约车、电子商务、电子游戏和在线旅游方面表现突出。新加坡、印尼、泰国和越南被认为是东盟地区数字经济规模较大、潜力较大的四个主要市场[⑥]。当前，数字经济已经为东南亚地区直接创造了16万个工作岗位，间接创造了3000万个工作岗位[⑦]，为弱势群体带来了更多的减贫增收的机会。

三、东盟地区减贫进展

　　绝对贫困[⑧]**得到有效缓解**。越南绝对贫困发生率由2002年的29.9%下降到2020年的0.7%，是东盟成员国中降幅最大的。在泰国和马来西亚，绝对贫困人口基本消除（见表1–2）。印尼的绝对贫困发生率虽然下降至2022年的2.5%，

---

　　① 新业态新模式具体表现为电子商务、移动支付、在线医疗、在线教育、在线旅游、外卖配送、网约车等线上线下融合的消费模式。

　　② 数据来源于《东南亚数字经济报告（2022）》和《东南亚数字经济报告（2023）》。

　　③ 数据来源于Momentum Works和SIIA。

　　④ 根据2023年联合国粮食及农业组织发布的世界粮食安全和营养状况整理。

　　⑤ Garena、GOTO、Grab、Lazada、Shopee、Traveloka、VNG等互联网公司被认为是东盟最具影响的"独角兽"企业。

　　⑥ 根据新加坡国际事务研究所（SIIA）发布的*Charting ASEAN's Digital Future: Emerging Policy Challenges*整理。

　　⑦ 间接就业是指数字平台业务创造的就业机会，包括运输司机合作伙伴、外卖骑手、内容创作者和支持电子商务的第三方物流公司岗位等。

　　⑧ 按照联合国发布的《2022年可持续发展目标报告》，绝对贫困线为每人每天2.15美元。

但由于人口基数大，仍有约680万人处于绝对贫困中。与2018年相比，菲律宾的贫困发生率没有明显变化，人口总量增加使绝对贫困人口有所上升。根据各国设定的国家贫困线来看，泰国的贫困发生率从2000年的42.3%下降至2021年的6.3%，在东盟成员国中降幅最大[①]。2012~2017年缅甸和菲律宾的贫困发生率下降最快，其中，缅甸从2015年的42.2%下降到2017年的24.8%，约有350万人摆脱贫困；菲律宾从2012年的25.2%下降到2018年的16.7%，约有660万人实现减贫。越南的贫困发生率稳步下降，从2002年的28.9%下降到2022年的4.3%。东帝汶虽然人口较少，但绝对贫困发生率高，贫困问题突出。

表1-2　　　　各年东盟国家绝对贫困发生率和绝对贫困人口

国家	绝对贫困发生率（%）			绝对贫困人口（百万人）		
	2002年	2017年	2022年	2002年	2017年	2022年
越南	29.9	1.2[b]	1	24.1	1.1[b]	0.98
印尼	26.8	6.6	2.5	59.0	17.5	6.89
老挝	25.4	7.1[b]	—	1.4	0.5[b]	—
菲律宾	13.6[a]	3[b]	3[c]	11.3[a]	3.3[b]	3.4[c]
缅甸	6.2[d]	2	—	3.2[d]	1	—
泰国	1.8	0	0[c]	1.2	0	0[c]
马来西亚	1.6[a]	0	0[c]	0.4[a]	0	0[c]
东帝汶	40.9[e]	24.4[f]	—	0.37[e]	0.3[f]	—

注：（1）2022年世界银行调整国际贫困线为每人每天2.15美元。
　　（2）柬埔寨未披露相关贫困率和贫困人口数据。
　　（3）a、b、c、d、e、f分别为2003年、2018年、2021年、2015年、2001年和2014年的数据。
　　数据来源：世界银行公开数据库（https://data.worldbank.org）和《2023年东盟统计年鉴》。

疫情前大部分东盟国家底层人口的收入和消费增长较快，共享繁荣[②]进程持续推进。近年来，东盟各国底层40%人口的平均消费或人均收入水平显著提升。除越南和老挝外，其余东盟国家底层40%人口的平均消费或收入水平年增

[①] 数据来源于世界银行Povcalnet（在线分析工具，http://iresearch.worldbank.org/PovcalNet/）和东盟统计数据库（ASEANstats database）。
[②] 世界银行将共享繁荣定义为每个国家最贫困40%人口（底层40%人口）年均收入或消费的增长，参见https://www.shihang.org/zh/news/feature/2013/05/08/shared-prosperity-goal-for-changing-world。

长率均高于全国平均水平。其中，缅甸底层40%人口的平均消费或收入水平增长最快，2015~2017年的年均增长率达到9.5%，远高于1.3%的全国平均水平。2011~2015年，马来西亚底层40%人口的平均消费或收入水平年均增长率为7%，高于全国平均水平2个百分点。2015~2018年，菲律宾底层40%人口的平均消费或收入水平年均增长率为6.1%，高于3.3%的全国平均水平。泰国和老挝的年均增长率最小，分别为2.2%和1.9%。越南和老挝底层40%人口的平均消费和收入年增长率分别低于其全国平均水平0.7个百分点和1.2个百分点。

专栏1-1 贫困线与多维贫困

贫困线。贫困线是世界银行用于衡量绝对贫困的国际标准，通常反映一国贫困人口为满足营养、衣着和居住等基本生活需求所需的最低货币数量。世界银行宣布，自2022年秋季起，将国际绝对贫困线从每人每天1.90美元上调至每人每天2.15美元；同时，将中等偏下收入国家和中等偏上收入国家贫困线标准分别调整为每人每天3.65美元和每人每天6.85美元[a]。

多维贫困。多维贫困通常采用多维贫困指数（Multidimensional Poverty Index，MPI）衡量，该指数是联合国与牛津贫困和人类发展研究中心共同开发的指标体系，包括健康、教育和生活标准三个维度，综合反映个人或家庭同时存在多个维度福利被剥夺的情况[b]。

共享繁荣。世界银行采用收入分配中底层40%人口的消费或收入年增长率衡量一个国家的共享繁荣情况，并定义共享繁荣溢价为底层40%人口消费或收入年增长率与全国总人口消费或收入年增长率之差[c]。

资料来源：

a.World Bank, Fact Sheet: An Adjustment to Global Poverty Lines。

b. 联合国开发计划署，《2022年全球多维贫困指数》。

c. 世界银行贫困与不平等数据平台（Poverty and Inequality Platform）。

疫情减缓了减贫进程。根据各国设定的国家贫困线，2020年之后，柬埔寨、菲律宾、印尼和泰国的贫困发生率和贫困人口均有所上升。其中，柬埔寨和菲律宾的贫困发生率上升最为明显，柬埔寨的贫困发生率从2017年的13.5%上升到2021年的17.8%；菲律宾的贫困发生率从2017年的16.7%上升到2021年的18.1%，新增贫困人口248万人；印尼的贫困发生率降幅相对较小，从2019年的10.6%下降到2021年的9.4%，新增贫困人口231万人；泰国的贫困发生率由2019年的6.2%上升为2020年的6.8%，新增贫困人口50万人（见图1-8）。

但若按中等偏上收入国家的国际贫困线标准（每人每天6.85美元）来看，泰国的贫困发生率由2019年的13.1%上升到2020年的13.2%，新增贫困人口超过93万人。

图1-8　各年部分东盟国家处于国家贫困线下的人口占比

注：（1）新加坡和文莱已成功实现减贫，两国停止公布贫困人口数据，故未纳入统计。

（2）柬埔寨为2003年、2012年、2016年和2020年的数据；老挝为2016年和2018年的数据；缅甸为2005年、2010年和2017年的数据；泰国为2002年、2012年、2017年和2021年的数据；马来西亚为2015年和2019年的数据；菲律宾为2003年、2012年、2018年和2021年的数据；东帝汶为2001年、2007年和2014年的数据。

数据来源：世界银行Povcalnet和东盟统计数据。

多维贫困有所缓解，但各国多维贫困的表现不同。除东帝汶外，其他东盟国家的多维贫困指数均低于0.2。其中，缅甸、柬埔寨和老挝的多维贫困指数最高，与其他东盟国家差距较大[1]。缅甸的多维贫困人口占比超过37%，柬埔寨和老挝的占比超过15%[2]。与之前年份相比，东盟各国多维贫困指数均有所下降（见表1-3）。其中，东帝汶、老挝和柬埔寨的多维贫困指数分别下降0.14、0.101和0.1，降幅最大，但这几个国家的指数水平相对较高，多维贫困问题仍较严重。缅甸、泰国、越南和老挝的多维贫困主要受教育水平的影响，教育贫困占比分别为48%、45%、41%和40%。柬埔寨、菲律宾和东帝汶受生活水平

---

① 数据来源于《2023年全球多维贫困指数报告》。

② 按国家贫困线标准计算。

的影响较大,生活水平贫困占比为45%~50%。与其他国家相比,健康对印尼和泰国的多维贫困的影响相对较大,健康贫困占比超过30%(见图1-9)。

表1-3 东盟国家多维贫困指数及其变化情况

国家	多维贫困指数		多维贫困指数的变化	
	调查年份	数值	时间区间	变化
柬埔寨	2022	0.070	2014~2022年	−0.100
印尼	2017	0.014	2012~2017年	−0.014
老挝	2017	0.108	2011~2017年	−0.101
菲律宾	2017	0.028	2013~2017年	−0.009
泰国	2019	0.002	2012~2019年	−0.003
越南	2020/2021	0.008	2013~2021年	−0.012
缅甸	2015/2016	0.176	—	—
马来西亚	2019	0.011	2016~2019年	−0.004
东帝汶	2016	0.222	2010~2016年	−0.140

数据来源:《2023年全球多维贫困指数报告》,以及世界银行公开数据库(http://data.worldbank.org)。

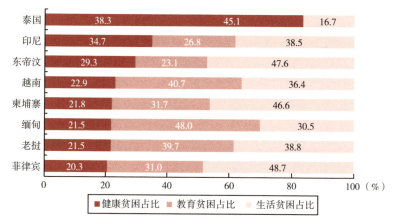

图1-9 部分东盟国家各维度贫困在多维贫困中的占比

数据来源:《2023年全球多维贫困指数报告》。

生活水平不断提高,但城乡基本公共服务还存在差距。2012~2022年,东盟国家生活水平得到较大改善①（见图 1-10）。文莱、新加坡、马来西亚、泰国基本实现用电、基本饮用水和基本卫生在城市和农村的全覆盖。缅甸和柬埔寨的生活水平相对较低，用电人口占比、基本饮用水覆盖率和基本卫生覆盖率均低于全球平均值，且城市和农村生活水平差距相对较大。2022年，缅甸城市用电人口占比高出农村用电人口占比31个百分点，柬埔寨城市基本卫生覆盖率比农村高22个百分点。老挝的用电人口占比较高，且城乡无差别，但基本用水覆盖率和基本卫生覆盖率的城乡差距较大。城乡基本公共服务差距使贫困地区在基础设施、教育培训和基本卫生等方面存在短板，可能增加当地的脱贫压力及难度。

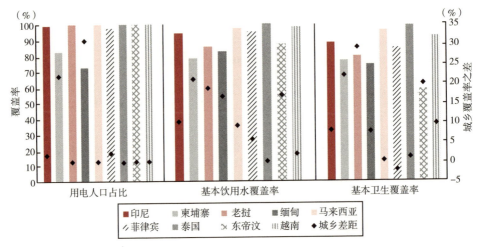

图 1-10　2022 年部分东盟国家生活水平及城乡差距

注：用电人口覆盖率为 2021 年数据。
数据来源：世界银行公开数据库（https://data.worldbank.org）。

四、东盟各国减贫进展

在东盟成员国中，文莱和新加坡属于高收入国家，主要关注社会中处于较低收入水平人口的生活情况。例如，新加坡社会和家庭发展部社会支持/服务提供司通过 ComCare 支持低收入家庭包括学费在内的基本生活费用，并对因疫情失业的家庭提供补助（COVID-19 Recovery Grant）②。除文莱和新加坡外，其余东盟国家面临不同程度的贫困问题。

---

① 数据来源于世界银行公开数据库（https://data.worldbank.org）。
② 根据新加坡社会和家庭发展部公布的信息整理。

（一）马来西亚

马来西亚减贫取得显著成效，减贫速度逐渐趋缓。马来西亚已基本消除绝对贫困。2019年，马来西亚人均国民总收入为27607美元，属于中等偏上收入国家。2018年，该国贫困发生率为3.4%[①]，家庭月收入低于国家贫困线的家庭占5.6%。疫情对马来西亚减贫产生了不利影响。2020年，根据国家贫困线衡量的贫困率上升至8.4%，根据基尼系数衡量的收入不平等从2019年的40.7%小幅上升到2020年的41.1%（见图1-11）。

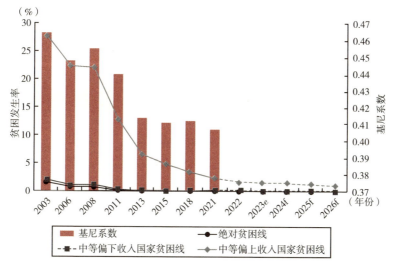

图1-11　马来西亚贫困的发生率和基尼系数变化情况

注：e=估计，f=预测，虚线为估计值或预测值。
数据来源：世界银行贫困与不平等数据平台（Poverty and Inequality Platform）。

与城市地区相比，马来西亚农村地区的贫困和不平等问题仍较严重。按照中等偏上国家贫困线标准，马来西亚不同群体的贫困人口占比均小于10%，其中农村人口、0~14岁人口以及16岁以上未受过教育的人口中贫困人口占比相对较高，分别为8%、6%和7%，且农村贫困发生率为城市贫困发生率的4倍（见图1-12）。马来西亚收入或消费处于最低40%水平的人口主要为农村人口、儿童和未受过教育的人。农村处于底层40%的人口占比为63.4%，接近城市平均水平的2倍。在儿童和16岁以上未受过教育的人口中，一半以上人口的收入或消费处于最低水平，这些人的减贫难度相对较大，面临较高的贫困风险。为防止城乡差

[①]　世界银行将中等收入偏上国家的贫困线标准划为每人每天6.85美元。

距进一步扩大，马来西亚政府采取了一系列措施，如改善农村医疗教育等公共基础设施、发展数字基础设施、增加部分企业和住房租金的优惠力度并延长租金期限、实施农村企业家在线外联计划、实施贫困家庭和土著居民的食品篮子援助计划，以及减免部分幼儿园费用等。这些措施可以有效促进农村包容性发展[①]。

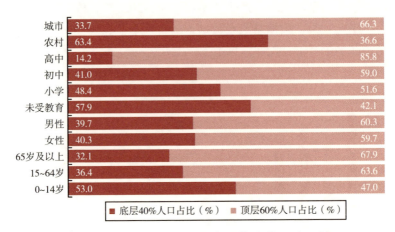

图1-12　马来西亚不同群体消费或收入分配情况

注：（1）未受教育以及接受了小学、初中或高中教育的群体均指16岁以上人口。
　　（2）底层40%人口占比和顶层60%人口占比分别指的收入或消费水平处于最低40%和最高60%水平的人口占比。
　　数据来源：世界银行贫困与不平等数据平台（Poverty and Inequality Platform）。

疫情后马来西亚经济强势复苏，但贫困人口恢复较慢。受疫情影响，2020年马来西亚的实际GDP出现负增长，2022年经济复苏势头强劲，经济增长8.7%，比2021年提高5.6个百分点。根据世界银行预测，按照中等偏上收入国家贫困线标准，2024~2026年马来西亚的贫困发生率分别降至1.4%、1.2%和1%。然而，马来西亚粮食不安全风险依然存在。2019~2021年，因中度或重度粮食不安全的患病率为15.4%，约500万人[②]。同时，疫情进一步恶化了马来西亚的粮食安全问题，世界银行关于疫情对最贫困家庭[③]的影响调查报告指出，约有20%的家庭在过去30天内食物已耗尽。对此，马来西亚第十二个五年计划指出将拨款4000亿林吉特，主要聚焦重振受疫情影响的经济，增进社会福

---

① 参见中国国际扶贫中心，"马来西亚农村发展部战略规划司副司长阿卜杜勒·卡哈尔发言"，2022年。
② 数据来源于世界银行2023年发布的*Macro Poverty Outlook in Malaysia*。
③ 月收入为2000林吉特或以下。

祉、安全和包容性以及推动环境可持续发展，以期实现建设"繁荣、包容、可持续的马来西亚"的目标[①]。

（二）泰国

泰国基本消除绝对贫困，但疫情阻碍了泰国的减贫进展。 泰国的绝对贫困发生率从2012年开始低于0.1%并持续降低。自2015年起，泰国的减贫进展有所放缓，2016年、2018年和2020年的贫困发生率和贫困人口均有所增加。2019年贫困发生率的显著下降得益于社会援助的持续扩大[②]。受疫情影响，泰国的贫困率从2019年的6.2%小幅上升到2020年的6.8%，然后在2021年下降到6.3%。按中等偏上收入国家的贫困线标准，2019年和2020年泰国的贫困发生率为13.2%，基本保持稳定，2022年下降至11%。2014~2019年，泰国底层40%人口的收入或消费水平年增长率高于全国平均水平1.17个百分点，共享繁荣取得进展。受疫情影响，泰国的基尼系数从2019年的0.348小幅上升到2021年的0.351（见图1-13）。

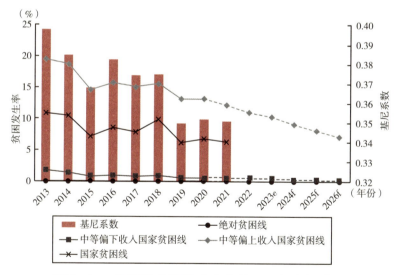

图1-13　泰国的贫困发生率和基尼系数变化情况

注：（1）e=估计，f=预测，虚线为估计值或预测值。
　　（2）2021年为真实数据，2022~2023年为短期估计值，2024~2026年为预测值。
　　（3）2020年，泰国国家平均贫困线为每人每月2762泰铢。
数据来源：世界银行贫困与不平等数据平台（Poverty and Inequality Platform）。

---

① 参见："马来西亚推出新规划聚焦疫后复苏"，《人民日报》2021年10月28日。
② 数据来源于世界银行2023年发布的 *Poverty & Equity Brief in Thailand*。

在泰国，儿童和未接受过教育的人口的贫困发生率较高。2021年，泰国16岁以上未受过教育人口的贫困发生率最高，为25%，其中61.4%人口的收入或消费水平处于底层40%水平，返贫风险较高；16岁以上接受过小学、初中、高中教育的人口的贫困发生率分别为14%、9%和1%，处于最低40%收入或消费水平的人口占比分别为48.6%、31.6%和7.9%。不同年龄段中，儿童和65岁及以上老年人的贫困发生率较高，分别为20%和13%。收入或消费处于最低40%水平的人口占比分别为55.6%和44.5%（见图1-14）。

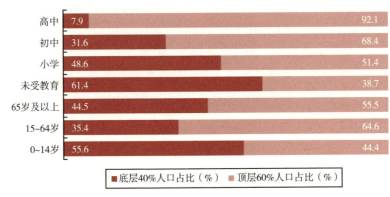

图1-14 泰国不同群体的消费或收入分配情况

注：（1）未受教育以及接受了小学、初中或高中教育的群体均指16岁以上人口。
（2）底层40%人口占比和顶层60%人口占比分别指的收入或消费水平处于最低40%和最高60%水平的人口占比。
数据来源：世界银行贫困与不平等数据平台（Poverty and Inequality Platform）。

泰国政府采取积极措施应对疫后减贫挑战。根据世界银行的预测，未来泰国的绝对贫困发生率将降为0，按中等偏上收入国家贫困线标准，贫困发生率会持续下降，2024~2026年贫困发生率分别为9.1%、8.1%和7.1%。尽管疫情后泰国经济复苏，但一些救济项目已经停止，不断上涨的商品价格给低收入家庭带来了更大的负担。相比之下，经济复苏带来的劳动收入增加不足以让低收入家庭应对不断上升的通货膨胀[①]。为此，泰国政府拨款600亿泰铢用于全国1700万处于贫困线下的人口纾困解难，并于2022年初批准14.8亿泰铢的预算，在全国76个府以及曼谷及其周边地区的便利店、商场、市场、公共区域或加油站等至少3000个销售点出售价格低廉的商品[②]。泰国在《农业发展规划（2017—2036年）》中指

[①] 数据来源于世界银行2023年发布的*Poverty & Equity Brief in Thailand*。
[②] 根据中华人民共和国商务部发布的《对外投资合作国别（地区）指南：泰国（2022年版）》整理。

出，要坚持"农民稳定、农业富余、农业资源可持续发展"理念，培养智慧农民，把新发明和现代科技运用于农业。同时，泰国积极学习中国脱贫攻坚过程中机制体制建设相关经验，成立减贫以及可持续性终身发展中心，构建包括国家中心、省级中心、区级层面、分区层面以及家庭层面共五个层次的减贫体制。

（三）印尼

疫情使印尼减贫进程放缓。2019年，印尼人均国民收入水平为11498美元，达到中等偏上收入水平。受疫情影响，2020年经济和人均收入水平出现明显负增长，重新回到中等偏下收入水平，印尼经济和社会脆弱性凸显。根据印尼国家贫困线，2020年和2021年贫困发生率持续上升，分别为9.8%和10.1%。按国际贫困线标准，印尼的贫困发生率虽未出现回升，但下降速度明显减慢。2022年，随着经济复苏，印尼的贫困发生率下降至9.5%，比2021年低0.6个百分点，2023年继续下降至9.4%。据世界银行估计，未来印尼的贫困发生率会继续下降。根据中等偏下收入国家贫困线标准，2024~2026年印尼的贫困发生率分别为16.3%、14.7%和13.2%（见图1-15）。

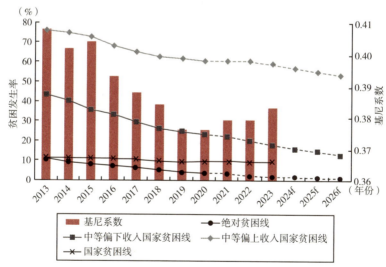

图1-15　印尼的贫困发生率和基尼系数变化情况

注：（1）e=估计，f=预测，虚线为估计值或预测值。

（2）2024~2026年为预测值。

（3）印尼国家统计局（BPS）将贫困线定义为每天获得2100卡路里所需的钱，以及少量用于其他基本非食品项目的花费。印尼国家贫困线是按67个地方贫困线的人口加权平均值计算的。

数据来源：世界银行贫困与不平等数据平台（Poverty and Inequality Platform）。

城乡之间消费和收入差距相对较大，不平等现象加剧。2021年和2022年，印尼的基尼系数维持在37.9%，较2018~2019年提高0.3个百分点。农村人口、受教育水平较低的人口以及儿童和老人中处于底层消费或收入水平的人口占比较高。2017~2022年，底层40%人口的收入或消费年增长率为3.44%，高于全体居民平均年增长率1.04个百分点，共享繁荣进展持续推进。农村和城市底层40%人口的占比分别为46.7%和35%，城乡差距为11.7个百分点。从受教育水平来看，16岁以上接受过小学教育和未受过教育的人口中处于底层40%人口的比例最高，分别为48.1%和47%（见图1-16）。面对农村地区高度贫困问题，印尼政府采取基于扶贫框架下的农村经济复苏战略，主要包括为非正规部门、乡镇企业融资，向贫困家庭提供现金直接援助计划，强化村企带动农村经济发展，通过电子商务实现村庄数字化的战略。然而，印尼国内不平等现象的加剧表明其在扩大社会援助覆盖面和识别目标人群方面仍需要改进。

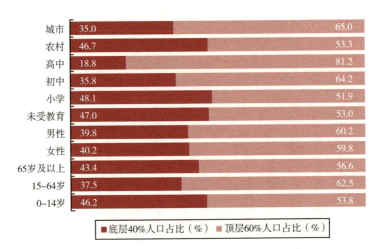

图1-16　印尼不同群体的消费或收入分配情况

注：（1）未受教育以及接受了小学、初中或高中教育的群体均指16岁以上人口。
（2）底层40%人口占比和顶层60%人口占比分别指的收入或消费水平处于最低40%和最高60%水平的人口占比。
数据来源：世界银行贫困与不平等数据平台（Poverty and Inequality Platform）。

（四）菲律宾

疫情期间，菲律宾经济出现负增长，对其减贫和不平等方面取得的成果产生负面影响。2020年，受疫情影响，菲律宾人均GDP年增长率下降超过10%。生活在国家贫困线^①以下的人口占比由2018年的16.7%上升到2021年的18.1%，新增贫困人口约230万人（见图1-17）。疫情期间，菲律宾的贫困发生率和贫困人口与其他东盟国家相比上升较为明显。尤其是当地经济发达地区受到的负面影响更大，菲律宾南部地区、吕宋岛中部和维萨亚斯中部地区的贫困发生率上升3~10个百分点，首都地区的贫困发生率上升1.2%。2018~2021年，菲律宾最贫困的棉兰老岛邦萨摩洛穆斯林自治区（BARMM）的贫困率则从61.2%下降到37.2%^②。

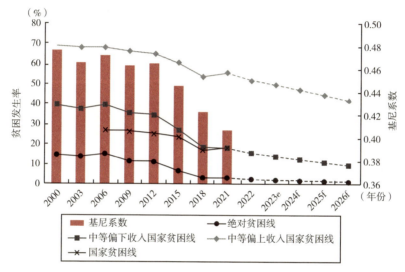

图1-17　菲律宾的贫困发生率和基尼系数变化情况

注：（1）e=估计，f=预测，虚线为估计值或预测值。
　　（2）2021年为真实数据，2022~2023年为短期估计值，2024~2026年为预测值。
数据来源：世界银行贫困与不平等数据平台（Poverty and Inequality Platform）。

菲律宾不同群体之间收入和消费水平差距明显。自2012年起，菲律宾不平等水平持续改善，基尼系数由46.5%下降至2021年的40.7%。尽管如此，菲律宾仍是东盟国家中基尼系数最高的国家之一。菲律宾农村和城市人口中收入或消费处于最低40%水平的人口占比分别为52.9%和27.7%，城乡差距达25.2个百分点。农村贫困人口占比为5%，城市贫困人口占比仅为1%。在菲律宾，教育对于提高消费或收入水平、减少贫困表现出显著的正向影响。在16岁以上未接受过教育的人中，贫困人口占比高达12%，远高于其他群体的贫困人口占比。该群体

---

① 2018年，菲律宾政府将国家贫困线调整为25813菲律宾比索。
② 数据来源于世界银行2023年发布的*Poverty & Equity Brief in Philippines*。

中约有69.9%的人处于最低40%收入或消费水平，而在接受过小学、初中和高中教育的人中这一比例分别为50.6%、29.2%和11.2%（见图1-18）。

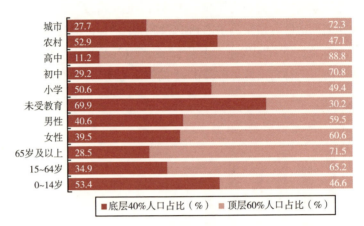

图1-18 菲律宾不同群体的消费或收入分配情况

注：（1）未受教育以及接受了小学、初中或高中教育的群体均指16岁以上人口。
（2）底层40%人口占比和顶层60%人口占比分别指的收入或消费水平处于最低40%和最高60%水平的人口占比。
数据来源：世界银行贫困与不平等数据平台（Poverty and Inequality Platform）。

（五）缅甸

疫情前缅甸减贫取得显著进展，但疫情和政变阻碍了其减贫进程。2002~2010年，缅甸的GDP年增长率始终保持10%以上，人均GDP年增长率保持8%以上。根据国家贫困线标准，缅甸成功地将贫困人口比例从2005年的48%降至2017年的25%。2015~2017年，缅甸的绝对贫困发生率从6.2%下降至2%，中等偏下收入贫困发生率则从30%降至20%。在此期间，缅甸制造业和服务业的快速增长对减贫贡献较大，城市贫困人口下降较快。受疫情影响，估计2023年缅甸的GDP增长3%，但产出远低于2019年水平[1]。2020年4月27日，缅甸政府为应对疫情出台经济政策《新冠肺炎疫情下经济救援计划（CERP）》，包括七大目标、10个战略和各项行动计划，其中七大目标包括：通过货币刺激政策改善宏观经济环境，通过改善投资、外贸和银行服务缓解对私营企业的影响，缓解疫情对劳动者的影响，减轻疫情对家庭的影响，促进创新产品和电子商务平台发展，改善医疗卫生体系，以及增加疫情应对资金和应急基金[2]。

---

[1] 数据来源于世界银行2023年发布的 *Macro Poverty Outlook*。
[2] 根据中华人民共和国商务部发布的《对外投资合作国别（地区）指南：缅甸（2022年版）》整理。

缅甸城乡差距较大。在缅甸，70%的人口居住在农村地区，而1/3的农村人口生活在贫困线以下。根据中等偏下收入国家贫困线标准，农村贫困发生率为24%，是城市贫困发生率的2.7倍。从消费和收入分配情况来看，缅甸农村最底层40%人口占比为47.3%，是城市同期水平的2.2倍。缅甸政府目前采取全方位全覆盖的农村转变战略，推动乡村发展和减贫进展，坚持以人为本的策略与跨领域的农村发展战略深度融合，打造智慧乡村，在促进绿色发展的同时提高民众的生活和收入水平。具体措施主要包括通过农村基础设施发展提高农村人口的生活水平，通过资本输入、财政服务以及技术协助来促进乡村经济发展，促进环保以及提高乡村人民的发展能力，实现可持续发展[①]。

未接受过教育群体的收入和消费水平较低，贫困问题严重。根据中等偏下收入国家贫困线标准，16岁以上接受过高中教育的人中贫困人口占比最低，仅2%。16岁以上未接受过教育的人中，贫困发生率高达32%，远高于接受过教育人口的贫困发生率。从消费和收入分配情况来看，16岁以上未接受过教育和仅接受过小学教育的人中，消费或收入水平处于最低40%的人口占比分别为55.4%和40.5%，在未接受过教育群体中有一半以上的人的消费或收入处于社会最低水平（见图1-19）。

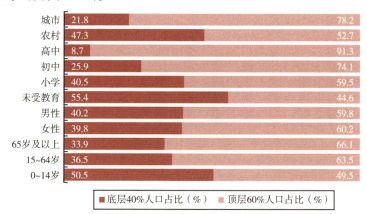

图1-19 缅甸不同群体的消费或收入分配情况

注：（1）未受教育以及接受了小学、初中或高中教育的群体均指16岁以上人口。

（2）底层40%人口占比和顶层60%人口占比分别指的收入或消费水平处于最低40%和最高60%水平的人口占比。

数据来源：世界银行贫困与不平等数据平台（Poverty and Inequality Platform）。

---

① 参见中国国际扶贫中心，"缅甸合作与农村发展农业发展处处长助理赛·密·海因·梭发言"，2022年。

（六）越南

越南减贫取得显著进展，但疫情期间减贫速度趋缓。疫情前，越南经济快速发展，实际GDP从2012年的6210亿美元增长到2022年的11190亿美元，人均国民收入从2012年的6738美元增长到2021年的10085美元[①]。按中等偏下收入国家贫困线标准，越南贫困发生率从2010年的14%下降到2020年的3.8%，贫困人口从2010年的1230万人降至2020年的500万人。2022年越南的GDP恢复8%的年增长率，估计2024~2026年GDP年增长率仍将保持在5.5%~6.5%，预计贫困发生率分别为3.6%、3.3%和2.9%（见图1-20）。越南实现了大部分家庭减贫脱贫，但这些家庭在面临气候和健康冲击、劳动力市场不确定性等因素时仍存在较大脆弱性和返贫风险。为此，越南政府提出要推进全国共同扶持贫困，同时出台有条件的扶持政策，为无法工作的贫困人口提供社会保障，采取政策鼓励企业和合作社在生产经营产品消费等方面联合起来，发展贫困人口和准贫困人口参与的生产模式[②]。

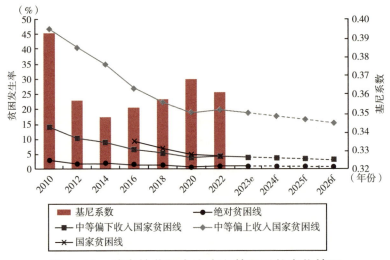

图1-20　越南的贫困发生率和基尼系数变化情况

注：（1）e=估计，f=预测，虚线为估计值或预测值。
　　（2）2020年为真实数据，2022~2023年为短期估计值，2024~2026年为预测值。
数据来源：世界银行贫困与不平等数据平台（Poverty and Inequality Platform）。

越南社会不平等问题持续加剧。自2014年起，越南的基尼系数由34.8%

[①] 数据来源于世界银行公开数据库，按2017年购买力平价（PPP）衡量。
[②] 根据越南驻南宁总领事馆总领事杜南忠在第16届中国—东盟社会发展与减贫论坛上的发言整理。

上升至2022年的36.1%，收入不平等问题逐步加剧。2016~2020年，越南底层40%人口的收入或消费年增长率为4.69%，低于全国平均水平0.91个百分点，社会收入和消费差距逐渐扩大。

越南城乡差距明显加大，农村地区和未受过教育人口可能面临更大的经济和贫困风险。在越南，52%的农村人口的收入或消费水平处于社会最低水平，而在城市，收入和消费处于底层40%的人口仅占城市人口的19%，城乡差距高于其他东盟国家（见图1-21）。16岁以上未受过教育的人中有20%处于中等收入偏下收入国家贫困线标准之下，76%的收入或消费水平处于社会底层水平，即农村地区和未接受过教育的人中约有一半面临较大的返贫风险，经济脆弱性较大。在越南，《2021—2025年国家新农村建设目标计划》旨在与农业结构调整相结合，促进农村经济发展，深化城镇化进程；打造"升级版"新农村、模范新农村和村级新农村[①]。《2021—2025年国家可持续减贫目标计划》基本坚持实施多维度、包容性、可持续减贫，限制贫困复发和贫困产生；协助贫困人口和贫困户达到最低生活保障标准，获得基本社会服务，提高生活质量；支持沿海、海岛地区贫困县和特困乡脱贫脱困。

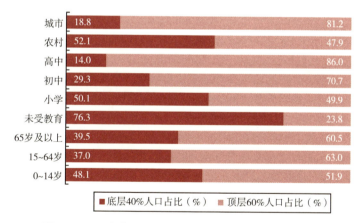

图1-21　越南不同群体的消费或收入分配情况

注：（1）未受教育以及接受了小学、初中或高中教育的群体均指16岁以上人口。

（2）底层40%人口占比和顶层60%人口占比分别指的是收入或消费水平处于最低40%和最高60%水平的人口占比。

数据来源：世界银行贫困与不平等数据平台（Poverty and Inequality Platform）。

---

① 参见：越南共产党电子报，"呈递越共十三大的政治报告草案提出新任期内的六项核心任务"，2020年12月3日。

（七）柬埔寨

疫情阻碍柬埔寨经济发展，增加返贫风险。疫情前，柬埔寨减贫取得了巨大进展，全国贫困率从2003年的50.2%下降到2019年的9.5%（见图1-22）。2020年柬埔寨经济出现负增长，GDP年增长率为-3.7%。2021年，受疫情影响，柬埔寨国际航班大幅减少，旅游业受到较大影响，其贫困发生率与2019年相比提高了8.3个百分点。为此，柬埔寨政府提出要实现包容性发展，针对农村尤其是弱势群体的就业、共享基础设施问题进行干预，努力提高农村地区风险抵御能力[1]。柬埔寨《2016—2025年社会保障国家政策战略》指出，要进一步发展柬埔寨全国性的社会保障系统，以造福全体百姓，尤其是贫困及弱势群体[2]。此外，柬埔寨政府还积极构建乡村网络（Farmer and Nature Net Association, FNN），为小农户农业生产提供资金和技术支持，促进小农户与市场的有效连接[3]。

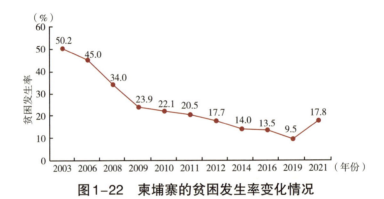

图1-22　柬埔寨的贫困发生率变化情况

数据来源：世界银行贫困与不平等数据平台（Poverty and Inequality Platform）。

柬埔寨政府采取积极措施应对疫情冲击。为应对疫情影响，柬埔寨政府积极鼓励疫苗接种。截至2022年，柬埔寨全程基础免疫接种率达87.3%，加强免疫接种率达62.2%[4]。同时，柬埔寨政府出台了《新冠肺炎疫情新常态下振兴和复苏经济政策框架（2021—2023）》，旨在在2023年底前支持柬埔寨经济增长速度回到其潜在水平，并从长期加强可持续和包容性社会经济发展韧性，关注社会弱势群体发展，降低其经济脆弱性和返贫风险。2021年柬埔寨的经济年增长率恢复到2.4%，低于2017~2019年6.9%~7.5%的年增长率，其中制造业、服务

---

① 根据柬埔寨农村发展部国务秘书韶齐万在第17届中国—东盟社会发展与减贫论坛上的发言整理。
② 根据中华人民共和国商务部发布的《对外投资合作国别（地区）指南：柬埔寨（2022年版）》整理。
③ 根据柬埔寨村官里斯·占塔在2023年中国—东盟村官交流日上的发言整理。
④ 数据来源于中华人民共和国商务部发布的《对外投资合作国别（地区）指南：柬埔寨（2022年版）》。

业、农业分别增长5.7%、0.3%和1.4%。

（八）老挝

疫情前老挝在减贫方面取得了进展，但不平等程度仍在加剧。2012~2018年，老挝的贫困率从24.6%下降到18.3%，降低了6.3个百分点（见图1-23）。按照每人每天3.65美元的中等偏下收入国家贫困线标准，老挝的贫困率从2012年的40.5%下降到2022年的31.9%，降低了8.6个百分点。在这一时期，基尼系数从2012年的36%上升到2018年的38.8%，不平等程度持续加剧。从消费或收入分配情况来看，2012~2018年底层40%人口的消费或收入年增长率仅1.9%，低于全国总人口消费或收入年增长率1.17个百分点[1]，共享繁荣和共享繁荣溢价[2]在东盟成员国中处于较低水平，社会贫富差距持续扩大。截至2022年，老挝仍有6.9%的人口处于绝对贫困。

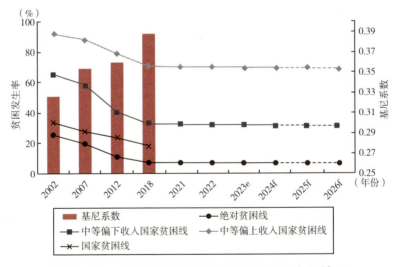

图1-23　老挝的贫困发生率和基尼系数变化情况

注：（1）e=估计，f=预测，虚线为估计值或预测值。

（2）2018年为真实数据，2019~2022年为当前估计值，2024~2026年为预测值。

（3）老挝国家贫困线基于支出和消费调查（LECS）结果，反映每人每天摄入2100千卡的最低消费门槛。2019年，老挝重新划定了贫困计算方法。图中数据根据新的贫困方法，对2012年和2018年的国际贫困估计数进行了修订。

数据来源：世界银行贫困与不平等数据平台（Poverty and Inequality Platform）。

---

[1] 数据来源于世界银行2024年发布的*Poverty & Equity Brief in Laos*。

[2] 世界银行采用收入分配中底层40%人口的消费/收入年增长率衡量一个国家的共享繁荣情况，并定义共享繁荣溢价为底层40%人口消费/收入年增长率与全国总人口消费/收入年增长率之差。

老挝城乡之间和不同受教育群体之间的消费和收入差距明显。在老挝，农村人口的贫困发生率为10%，是城市人口贫困发生率的5倍。老挝农村人口中有一半的消费和收入水平处于社会底层40%，而城市中该群体占比仅为19.3%。在16岁以上未接受过教育的人中，贫困人口占比高达12%，接受过小学和初中教育的人口的贫困占比分别为6%和2%。从消费或收入分配情况来看，未接受过教育的人中有56.4%处于社会底层40%，但在接受过小学、初中和高中的人中，这一比例分别为38.6%、19.7%和5%。总体上，受教育程度越高，贫困发生率越小且消费或收入水平越高（见图1-24）。

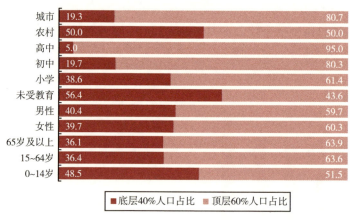

图1-24 老挝不同群体的消费或收入分配情况

注：（1）未受教育以及接受了小学、初中或高中教育的群体均指16岁以上人口。

（2）底层40%人口占比和顶层60%人口占比分别指的收入或消费水平处于最低40%和最高60%水平的人口占比。

数据来源：世界银行贫困与不平等数据平台（Poverty and Inequality Platform）。

疫情后老挝减贫事业面临较大挑战。疫情后老挝经济逐渐复苏，估计2024~2026年GDP的年增长率将恢复至4%的水平。截至2022年5月，老挝就业基本恢复至疫情前水平，但严重的通货膨胀阻碍了其减贫进程。2023年1月，老挝的通货膨胀率达到了40.3%[1]，这使社会底层人口面临较大的下行压力和经济风险[2]，半数以上的家庭选择减少食品消费以及教育或医疗支出以应对高通货膨胀，尤其是农村和贫困地区人口[3]。此外，老挝的社会保护的覆盖面有限，导

---

① 数据来源于世界银行。

② 数据来源于世界银行2023年发布的 *Poverty & Equity Briefs*。

③ 同上。

致疫情后老挝减贫面临较大挑战。据世界银行估算，2024~2026年老挝国内生活在每人每天3.65美元国际贫困线以下的人口占比稳定在31%左右，其减贫进展仍面临较大挑战（见图1-23）。

（九）东帝汶

疫情前东帝汶在减贫方面取得了一定进展，居民生活水平不断提高。 2007年东帝汶有50.4%的人口生活在国家贫困线之下，到2014年已经减少到41.8%。东帝汶政府在粮食安全、教育和营养改善方面持续努力。2014年，东帝汶出台了《消除饥饿和营养不良国家行动计划》，该计划预算资金为1.76亿美元，预计到2025年将实现"零饥饿"目标[1]。针对儿童营养健康问题，在学校和卫生中心建立了供餐计划[2]。当前，国民营养健康水平有所改善，营养不良率从2014~2016年的26.9%下降到2017~2019年的25%，5岁以下儿童营养不良率从2013年的11%下降到2017年的9.9%[3]。在教育方面，截至2022年，东帝汶已有1800多所学校，小学课程体系已经建成，中学课程体系正在建设。东帝汶教育部门通过学校领导定期检查、组织研讨会和颁布教学指导计划等方式，提升教师技能水平[4]。2008~2018年小学净入学率从83%上升到92.3%，中学净入学率从34.5%上升到62.7%[5]。在医疗卫生方面，2013~2020年东帝汶新生儿死亡率下降了41%，孕产妇死亡率从2000年的694/10万下降至2017年的142/10万。

疫情阻碍了东帝汶的减贫进展。 受疫情影响，2019年东帝汶绝对贫困发生率提高了至少5个百分点。根据2020年5月对东帝汶进行的粮食安全调查，81%的家庭的粮食安全受到疫情影响，40%的家庭不得不通过减少日常食物消费以维持生活[6]。为此，东帝汶政府采取措施，积极应对疫情对减贫的影响。截至2020年6月，东帝汶政府计划向每个家庭提供15美元的电费抵免和每月100美元的电费补助以帮助民众渡过难关。为保障疫后发展，东帝汶国家战略计划（2023—2025年）强调要使受疫情影响的居民获得足够的食物，计划到2025年使弱势群体能够获得健康膳食计划支持，同时增强国家防灾救灾能力和供应链

---

[1] 根据东帝汶政府官方发言人2014年7月25发言 "The National Action Plan for a Hunger and Malnutrition Free Timor-Leste" 整理。

[2] 根据 5 Facts About Poverty in Timor-Leste – The Borgen Project 整理。

[3] 数据来源于 ADB Data Library。

[4] Owen, S., Salsinha, A.（2022）. Basic Education in Timor-Leste. International Handbook on Education in South East Asia.

[5] 数据来源于世界银行。

[6] 根据 Timor-Leste – Rapid Food Security Assessment 2020 整理。

管理。据世界银行预测，疫情后东帝汶减贫进程将逐渐恢复，绝对贫困发生率预计从2020年的29.3%持续下降至2026年的24.4%，但仍高于疫情前的贫困水平（见图1-25）。

图1-25　东帝汶的绝对贫困发生率变化情况

注：（1）按照2020年世界银行发布的国际贫困线标准衡量，即每人每天2.15美元。
　　（2）2019年的数据是按每人每天1.90美元（2011 PPP）衡量的。
　　（3）e=估计，f=预测，虚线为估计值或预测值。
　　（4）2014年为真实数据，2015~2023年为短期估计值，2024~2026年为预测值。
数据来源：*TIMOR-LESTE Key conditions and challenges*；*Macro Poverty Outlook for Timor-Leste*。

五、小结

综上所述，**疫情加剧了东盟国家的减贫压力**。马来西亚受疫情影响出现返贫现象。粮食不安全问题制约了马来西亚贫困人口营养健康改善，贫困人口复苏较慢。在泰国，16岁以上未接受过教育人口的贫困问题严重，贫困发生率高达25%。受疫情影响，印尼进入中等偏下收入国家行列，经济社会脆弱性凸显，城乡消费和收入差距加深。在菲律宾，经济较发达地区受疫情冲击明显，贫困发生率上升了1%~10%[1]，且受教育水平低的人口的贫困问题更加严重，贫困人口占比高达12%。在缅甸，城乡差距较大，农村贫困发生率为城市的2.7倍；未受教育人口中，至少一半的消费或收入处于社会最低水平，贫困问题突出。越南在面临气候变化、健康冲击、劳动力市场不确定性等因素时存在较大的返贫风险。柬埔寨因疫返贫风险增加，2021年贫困发生率比2019年提高

---

　① 数据来源于世界银行2023年发布的*Poverty & Equity Briefs in Philippines*。

了8.3个百分点。在老挝，贫困问题集中在农村和未接受过教育人口，高通货膨胀、粮食不安全以及社会保障体系不完善等问题使老挝减贫进展面临较大挑战。虽然东盟各国贫困人口和地区分布存在差异，但总体特征和目标人群基本相同，社会底层人口减贫问题更为突出。

数字经济带来发展机遇。疫情前，东盟各国数字化进程取得进展，这为疫情期间新业态新模式的出现和扩展奠定了基础。数字经济可以提高中小企业生产力和增加就业机会，帮助弱势群体摆脱贫困[①]。例如，马来西亚政府采取了包括发展数字基础设施、改善农村医疗教育条件等一系列措施以缩小城乡差距，促进农村的包容性发展。印尼政府致力于通过电子商务、乡村企业带动农村经济发展。另外，东盟国家积极部署以5G为代表的新型数字基础建设，推动数字化发展。

---

① 参见联合国粮食与农业组织发布的《2023世界粮食安全和营养状况报告》。

第二章
东盟国家减贫主要议题实施进展

为应对疫情对东盟经济社会和减贫进展产生的冲击，东盟成员国加速落实《东盟全面复苏框架》及其实施计划，聚焦受影响最大的行业和弱势群体，以求实现更有韧性、包容和可持续的经济复苏，提高脆弱性人群的风险应对能力，缓解疫情对减贫的阻滞效应。疫情后东盟经济强劲复苏，亚洲开发银行对2024年东盟经济增长的预测为5%。

一、粮食安全

粮食安全和减贫相互依存。联合国粮食及农业组织将粮食安全定义为所有人在任何时候都能从物质上和经济上获得足够的安全和有营养的食物，以满足其饮食需要和食物偏好，过上积极健康的生活[1]。贫困是粮食不安全的根源，穷人无法获取足够的粮食来维持其最基本的生存需要[2]。粮食不安全与贫困相互强化，二者不可分离[3]。一方面，贫困意味着抵御风险和冲击的能力弱；另一方面，粮食不安全导致人们营养不良、健康状况恶化、劳动能力丧失、死亡率上升，最终导致贫困程度加深[4]。随着经济全球化的发展，粮食安全越来越需要全球及地区层面的通力合作，在一定程度上，全球的粮食问题更多地表现为流通问题，而非生产问题。

保障区域粮食安全需要通力合作。 由于历史传统和饮食习惯，东南亚地区

---

① FAO，An Introduction to the Basic Concepts of Food Security，2009.

② Rose，D.，Basiotis，P.P.，& Klein，B.W. Improving Federal Efforts to Assess Hunger and Food Insecurity，1995.

③ Barrett，C.B. Food Aid as Part of a Coherent Strategy to Advance Food Security Objectives，2006.

④ Walingo，M.K. The Role of Education in Agricultural Projects for Food Security and Poverty Reduction in Kenya［J］. International Review of Education，2006（52）：287-304.

对大米的需求较大①。作为世界上人口最为稠密的地区之一，东盟国家在粮食生产方面出现了严重的两极分化，既有泰国、越南、柬埔寨、缅甸等世界主要粮食出口大国，也有印尼、菲律宾、马来西亚等世界主要粮食进口大国。粮食安全问题在地区安全中的地位至关重要。当前，东盟区域内粮食供应链已经开始出现问题②，需要各成员国加强合作，共同应对挑战。

多措并举保障粮食安全。 保障粮食安全，提高粮食供应链韧性，有利于降低饥饿致贫风险，提高可持续农业生产能力，帮助以农为生的人摆脱贫困。为此，东盟及其成员国通过出台一系列政策，加强区域内合作，保障粮食安全。东盟区域内政策包括《东盟粮食安全一体化框架》（AIFS）和《东盟地区粮食安全战略行动计划（2021—2025）》（SPA-FS），以保障东盟国家长期的粮食安全和改善农民生计。此外，还实施了东盟与中日韩大米紧急储备（APTERR），并加强东盟粮食安全信息系统（AFSIS），提出《东盟关于在粮食和农业领域推广数字技术的指针》，以提升区域内粮食供应链韧性。

泰国政府对大米、木薯、玉米等主要农产品实施最低价格补贴，颁布了《国家稻米五年计划战略（2020—2024）》以保证粮食供应，提出用五年时间研发包括软米、硬米、香米、高营养米在内的12种新水稻品种，突出"短、矮、大、优"特质③。柬埔寨农林渔业部正式推出谷种质量认证系统，通过认证标签制度来鉴定谷种质量，以提高水稻的产量和质量。改良和确保谷种质量是柬埔寨政府促进农业现代化的重要举措，旨在提高农业对国家经济的贡献，增加农民收入，降低贫困率④。菲律宾制定了《2021—2030年国家农业和渔业现代化计划》，并推出农业商品体系路线图和土地综合利用计划等，以促进农渔民就业渠道日益多元，不断提升其收入水平，从而实现可持续减贫。2019~2021年东盟国家大米出口贸易额呈现下降态势，而进口额显著增加。2021年进口额为31.01亿美元，相较于2019年增加了9.52亿美元，增长率为44.3%（见图2-1）。疫情期间，东盟增加水稻进口，以保障粮食供给，减少国家饥饿致贫风险。

---

① 姚毓春，李冰.生产、贸易与储备：东南亚粮食安全与中国：东盟粮食合作［J］.东南亚研究，2021，251（2）：38-56，154-155.

② ASEAN Prosperity Initiative, *ASEAN Integration Report 2022*.

③ 孙广勇.泰国多举措促进大米出口［N］.人民日报，2023-11-01.

④ 赵益普.柬埔寨努力发展大米产业［N］.人民日报，2022-06-15.

图2-1 2012~2021年东盟大米进出口贸易额

数据来源：《2022年东盟统计年鉴》。

疫情后东盟国家粮食安全水平逐渐恢复。 2012~2018年东盟全球粮食安全指数总体上逐年上升，2019年下降至60.3。疫情给东盟农产品供应链带来严重影响，东盟内出现粮食供应链中断、粮食和农产品价格波动，影响贫困人口的饥饿改善情况。2020年东盟全球粮食安全指数年增长率为-1%，但各国采取的应对措施起到了显著效果。2020~2022年，东盟粮食安全指数呈现上升趋势，2021年恢复正增长，2022年实现1.2%的增速，在一定程度上展现了东盟粮食安全供应链的韧性（见图2-2）。

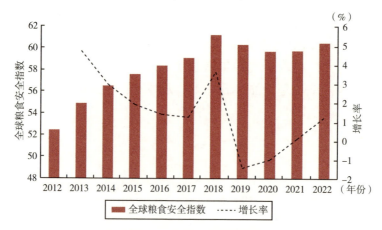

图2-2 2012~2022年东盟全球粮食安全指数

数据来源：《全球粮食安全指数报告》。

专栏2-1　全球粮食安全指数

全球粮食安全指数（Global Food Security Index，GFSI）源于英国《经济学人》智库发布的《全球粮食安全指数报告》，是依据世界卫生组织、联合国粮农组织、世界银行等机构的官方数据，通过动态基准模型综合评估全球113个国家的粮食安全现状，包括粮食价格承受力、粮食供应能力、质量安全保障能力、可持续和适应能力等。

资料来源：《全球粮食安全指数报告》。

东盟成员国之间的粮食安全情况差异显著。水稻是东盟的主要粮食作物，对于保障东盟国家粮食安全有着举足轻重的意义。东盟成员国人均水稻产量呈现出不同的趋势，即除个别年份外，柬埔寨、缅甸、老挝、越南与泰国等国家的人均水稻产量在400公斤以上，印尼、菲律宾、马来西亚与文莱等国家的人均水稻产量在300公斤以下，粮食自给水平存在明显差异（见图2-3）。从人均水稻产量变化来看，柬埔寨的人均水稻产量在2013~2022年整体呈上升趋势，且在2017~2021年远远超过其他东盟成员国。菲律宾、马来西亚、文莱和越南的人均水稻产量比其他东盟国家更稳定。

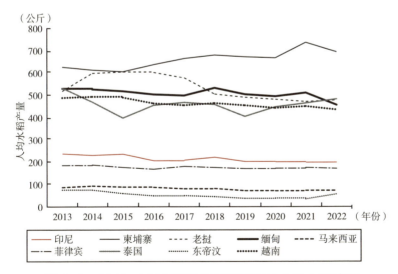

图2-3　2013~2022年部分东盟国家的人均水稻产量

数据来源：世界银行公开数据库（https://data.worldbank.org）和历年《东盟统计年鉴》。

二、经济增长

经济增长是大规模减贫的主要推动力[①]。经济增长的减贫效应主要体现在两个方面：一是经济发展为贫困人口提供就业和增收机会；二是经济增长使政府更有能力帮扶贫困人口。随着经济全球化进程的推进，贸易和投资更加自由化便利化。贸易自由化可以促进经济增长，价值链是发展中国家减贫创新机制之一，能够实现贫困人口和世界市场的连接。数字经济蓬勃发展，对创造就业、优化劳动力需求结构具有积极作用，已经成为引领国民经济增长的重要动能。

加大力度深化经贸联系，贸易恢复增长态势。东盟制定了《东盟数字规划2025》，通过数字服务推动国家间贸易的便利发展。各国政府纷纷出台相应举措，提升货物自由流动、供应链互联互通及服务效率。马来西亚、泰国与欧盟签署了《合作伙伴协定》，积极推动贸易往来。老挝通过中老铁路不断挖掘贸易潜力，积极提升全球价值链参与程度。2020年东盟各国年平均贸易额普遍下降，2021年和2022年贸易额恢复增长态势，贸易占GDP的比重逐步上升（见图2-4），有利于贫困人口享受贸易政策和贸易活动的红利，促进贸易减贫进展。

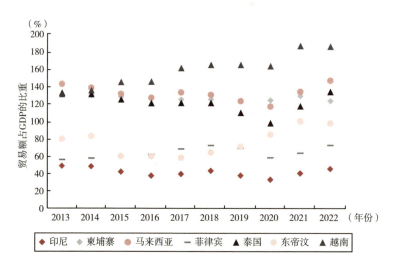

图2-4　2013~2022年东盟部分国家贸易额占GDP的比重

数据来源：世界银行公开数据库（https://data.worldbank.org）。

[①] 汪三贵.在发展中战胜贫困——对中国30年大规模减贫经验的总结与评价［J］.管理世界，2008（11）:78-88.

专栏2-2　泰中罗勇工业园助力周边繁荣，带动当地就业

　　2006年建成的泰中罗勇工业园位于泰国重要的工业基地罗勇府。作为中国首批境外经贸合作区之一，园区的产业主要为汽摩配、机械、新能源、新材料、电子电器、建材五金等，而中国在这些产业领域具有传统优势。经过16年的发展，泰中罗勇工业园已成为泰国产业集群中心与制造出口基地。截至2022年，工业园已吸引180家中国制造企业、30多家配套企业在泰投资，为当地创造超过4.5万个就业岗位。

　　资料来源：

　　a.商务部，"2021年第二季度泰国旅游业55万人失业"，2021年6月30日。

　　b.新华社，"助力周边繁荣 带动当地就业——走进泰中罗勇工业园"，2022年11月20日。

　　持续优化外商投资环境，疫情期间外资逆势增长。2012~2018年东盟国家外国直接投资净流入总体呈现上升趋势；2019年达到1762.78亿美元；受疫情冲击，2020年外国直接投资下降至1264.21亿美元，增长率为-28.3%（见图2-5）。东盟各国采取多项措施吸引外国投资，例如，越南颁布《投资法修正案》，向特殊投资项目提供更多优惠；泰国的《投资促进战略（2023—2027）》为稳定营商环境提供制度保障；印尼推出电动汽车补贴计划，吸引外国投资者建立电动汽车产业链。马来西亚加强与中国的贸易往来，2022年中马双边贸易额为2036亿美元，同比增长15.3%[①]。除缅甸和菲律宾外，疫情之后印尼、柬埔寨、马来西亚、泰国和越南的外资年均增长率均高于疫情前。中国和东盟互为第一大贸易伙伴，截至2023年底，双方累计双向投资总额约3800亿美元[②]。

　　大力支持中小微企业发展，促进充分就业。2019~2022年东盟国家年失业率呈现倒"V"字形走势，2021年以来，大多数东盟国家的失业率均出现不同程度下降（见图2-6）。中小微企业吸收了东盟国家85%~97%的劳动力，在创造就业方面发挥了主导作用。东盟支持落实《东盟中小企业发展战略行动计划（2016—2025）》，鼓励中小微企业参与数字经济，提升其数字技能和市场准入水平，实现可持续、包容和有韧性的增长。东盟商务咨询理事会于2020年推出"东盟韧性和可持续数字创业项目"（Digital STARS），重点推动创业和中小微企业数字化转型，并在2021年继续推出"韧性就业能力数字化影响"项目，为东盟劳动力赋能。

---

① 参见：中华人民共和国外交部网站，《中国同马来西亚的关系》。

② 参见：《中国—东盟经贸合作提质升级》。

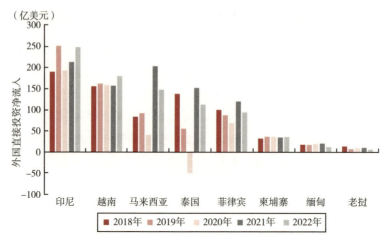

图2-5 2018~2022年部分东盟国家外国直接投资净流入情况

数据来源：世界银行公开数据库（https://data.worldbank.org）。

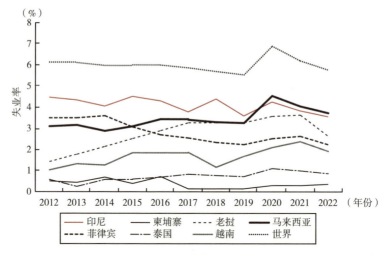

图2-6 2012~2022年部分东盟国家的失业率

数据来源：世界银行公开数据库（https://data.worldbank.org）。

专栏2-3 疫情冲击泰国旅游业

旅游业是泰国服务业的支柱产业，旅游业收入约占泰国GDP的20%。境外游客是泰国旅游业市场的主要力量。以清迈府为例，2019年，大约有1100万泰国本地和外国游客选择去清迈旅游，其中60%是外国游客（The

Nation，2019）。新冠疫情期间，封控措施使泰国入境旅游市场受到重创。2020年全年抵达泰国的外国游客为670万人次，同比下降约83.2%；旅游业总收入为3320.13亿泰铢，同比下降82.6%。泰国旅游委员会表示，2021年第二季度泰国旅游行业共有55万人失业。自2021年4月起，基本没有外国游客入境，严重打击了泰国旅游业。与第一季度相比，几乎所有类型的旅游相关活动临时关停的比例都有所增加，正常营业的酒店比例为59%，水疗保健按摩为27%，只有3%的娱乐场所开放营业。大部分场所只留下51%的员工，其平均工资仅为过去的65%。

资料来源：商务部，"新冠疫情影响泰国旅游业形势不容乐观"，2021年7月7日。

三、营养健康

营养健康是个人和家庭实现脱贫的前提条件。人力资本理论认为，健康是一种重要的人力资本，具备良好的健康状况是个体参与经济社会活动，尤其是参与生产性活动从而创造收入的前提[1]。健康影响劳动生产率，进而影响个人和家庭贫困状况。具体来说，健康通过有效劳动投入和产出水平两个途径发挥减贫作用，即劳动力健康水平越高，患病概率越小，停工时间越少，其寿命和工作年限更长，越能增加有效劳动时间的投入量。同时，健康水平越高的劳动力，其精力越旺盛，认知能力越强，越能承担强度更大的工作，提高劳动力产出效率或经营项目的效益，从而促进减贫。

因病致贫是导致贫困的主要因素之一[2]。健康冲击，尤其是大病风险会直接增加家庭医疗支出，减少家庭可支配收入，从而直接增加居民返贫风险。同时，疾病和照料负担会降低家庭成员的劳动能力，阻碍人力资本和创收能力提升，不利于家庭的长远发展[3]。

东盟国家积极应对疫情对国民营养健康和医疗条件的不利影响。 为减轻疫情造成的经济社会影响，东盟颁布了《东盟突发公共卫生事件战略框架》，建立了东盟公共卫生紧急事件和新型疾病中心（ACPHEED）、东盟抗疫基金以及东盟应急医疗物资储备库（RRMS）等。老挝实施了《2016—2025年国家营养行动计

---

① 张仲芳.精准扶贫政策背景下医疗保障反贫困研究［J］.探索，2017（2）:81-85.

② 汪三贵，刘明月.健康扶贫的作用机制、实施困境与政策选择［J］.新疆师范大学学报（哲学社会科学版），2019，40（3）:82-91，2.

③ 洪秋妹，常向阳.我国农村居民疾病与贫困的相互作用分析［J］.农业经济问题，2010，31（4）:85-94，112.

划》，从国家层面高度支持与关注营养问题，注重多部门协调的方法和行动，以解决营养不良问题。菲律宾制定了《菲律宾营养行动计划（2017—2022）》，同时菲律宾教育部与卫生部于2022年10月联合启动了基础教育部门的健康学习机构，以加强学校健康与营养计划。文莱将《健康饮食国家膳食指南》作为学校食堂指南和学校供餐计划的指南，在成人、婴幼儿膳食以及膳食卫生、安全和食品标签方面提供指导。越南"为贫困儿童助学和加餐"项目为全国各地3万多名贫困儿童提供营养加餐；此外，为保障弱势人群营养健康，制定了相应的医疗保障制度。马来西亚将贫困人口纳入基础医疗健康服务特殊群体。缅甸实施了《国民健康计划（2017—2021）》，针对贫困人口提供基本卫生设施与服务[1]。

东盟整体营养健康状况得到较大改善。 2012~2021年大部分东盟国家的饥饿指数、营养不良人口占比、每10万活产婴儿中孕产妇死亡人数和5岁以下儿童死亡率均呈下降趋势（见图2-7和图2-8）。柬埔寨、老挝和缅甸有效提高了国民营养健康水平，缅甸的营养不良人口占比从2000~2002年的37.6%下降到2019~2021年的3.1%，老挝则从31.2%下降到5.1%[2]。营养不良是威胁贫困人口身体健康的重要因素，东盟各国营养健康状况的改善是其减贫措施有效可行的重要体现。

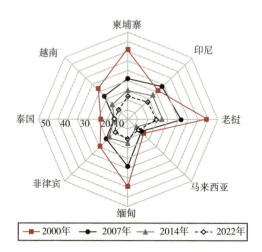

图2-7　2000年、2007年、2014年、2022年部分东盟国家全球饥饿指数变化

注：全球饥饿指数（GHI）严重程度：≤9.9，低；10.0~19.9，中等；20.0~34.9，严重；35.0~49.9，警戒；≥50.0，极度警戒。

数据来源：全球饥饿指数（Global Hunger Index，GHI）数据库。

---

① 崔娟，管竹笋，殷格非.东盟国家减贫议题进展研究［J］.可持续发展经济导刊，2022（7）：60–63.

② 数据来源于联合国粮食与农业组织统计数据和世界银行公开数据库（https://data.worldbank.org）。

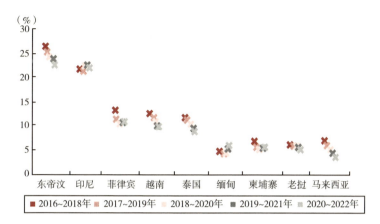

图2-8　2016~2022年部分东盟国家营养不良人数占比（三年均值）的变化情况

数据来源：联合国粮食及农业组织（FAO）统计数据。

专栏2-4　全球饥饿指数

全球饥饿指数（Global Hunger Index，GHI）由国际粮食政策研究所（International Food Policy Research Institute，IFPRI）发布，反映各发展中国家的营养不足率、5岁以下儿童的低体重率、死亡率等的综合指数。

资料来源：全球饥饿指数数据库，参见 https://www.globalhungerindex.org/。

疫情阻碍了部分低收入国家改善营养健康的进程。 与2017~2019年相比，2018~2020年印尼和老挝营养不良人口占比分别提高了5.1个百分点和1.9个百分点。柬埔寨和缅甸营养不良人口及其占比也在2019~2020年有所提高（见图2-8）。东帝汶营养不良人口占比下降缓慢。疫情导致家庭收入减少，从而降低了一些家庭的食物支出[①]。2020年，缅甸11%的家庭至少有一位成年成员在过去30天里吃得比平时少，7%的家庭面临食物耗尽的风险[②]。2017~2019年东盟国家不能负担健康饮食的人口总体呈下降态势，2020年这一指标明显上升（见图2-9）。疫情持续蔓延，给东盟农产品供应链带来严重影响，出现了粮食供应链中断、粮食和农产品价格波动，影响贫困人口的营养健康状况改善。

---

① 数据来源于世界银行发布的报告 *How Hard are Families Hit by the COVID-19 Crisis？ Six Insights from Our Household Surveys in East Asia and Pacific*。

② 数据来源于世界银行发布的报告 *Monitoring COVID-19 Impacts on Households in Vietnam*。

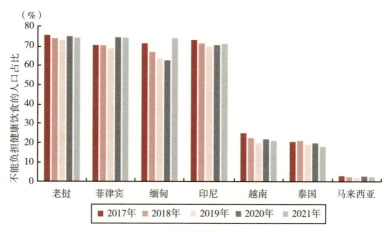

图2-9　2017～2021年部分东盟国家不能负担健康饮食的情况

数据来源：联合国粮食及农业组织（FAO）统计数据。

疫情恶化了医疗卫生条件。 2015~2020年，东盟平均预期寿命总体呈上升趋势。受疫情影响，该指标从2020年的74岁下降至2021年的73岁，而各成员国的预期寿命均在2021年出现不同程度的下降（见图2-10）。疫情影响了正常的医疗服务，使儿童面临更大的早期发育迟缓和消瘦风险[①]，降低了营养健康水平，进而对预期寿命产生影响，尤其是对低收入国家贫困人口的健康状况影响显著。

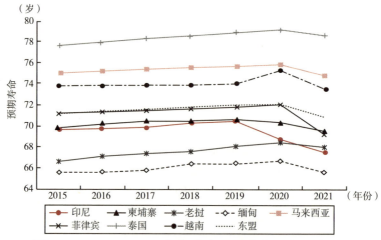

图2-10　2015~2021年部分东盟国家的预期寿命变化

数据来源：世界银行公开数据库（https://data.worldbank.org）。

---

① 参见比尔及梅琳达·盖茨基金会发布的《2020目标守卫者报告》。

四、教育水平

教育是开发和提升人力资本，促进居民脱贫能力建设的重要路径[①]。人力资本积累是提高家庭增收创收能力、阻断家庭代际贫困、缓解相对贫困现状的内生动力，有利于进一步促进地区经济长期增长[②]。儿童是人力资本形成和积累的关键群体，重视早期教育和基础教育也是支持国家长期发展的重要举措[③]。

加强贫困地区教育体系建设，提升教育包容性。东盟教育公平问题突出，儿童教育推进缓慢。《东盟与中日韩合作工作计划（2023—2027）》中《东盟与中日韩教育行动计划（2018—2025）》支持通过包容性学校和替代学习系统、特殊教育和远程教育等其他教育方式，促进包容性教育。东盟国家学前教育参与率从2016年的74.4%上升至2020年的76.2%。2020年，东盟国家45.3%的小学都配备了用于教学的电脑，90.8%的小学老师具有最基本的从业资格[④]。

其中，越南实施"2022~2030年阶段困难地区幼儿教育发展帮扶"计划，争取到2030年实现25%的贫困地区托儿班适龄儿童和95%的幼儿园适龄儿童能够上学，贫困地区100%的幼儿园适龄儿童获得照顾和教育。缅甸制定并启动了《全民教育方案》，教育体系覆盖儿童、偏远地区和少数民族、成人等群体。疫情前东盟整体青年识字率、教育入学率和完成率均有所提升。马来西亚、印尼、泰国和越南的小学、初中和高中完成率较高。缅甸、柬埔寨和老挝教育发展较快，但与东盟其他国家相比，教育完成率仍处于较低水平。2021年东盟各国小学和初中入学率中男女比例基本为1∶1。柬埔寨和老挝在解决教育中性别不平等问题方面取得了显著进展。2017~2019年，在东盟国家中，马来西亚的平均受教育年限达到10.27年，达到了两位数，而菲律宾和文莱两国的平均受教育年限也在9年以上，这三个国家均超过了当时的世界平均水平（8.43年）；印尼、泰国和越南的平均受教育年限为7~9年，而老挝、缅甸和柬埔寨的平均受教育年限则不足6年（见图2-11）。

---

① 程名望，Jin Yanhong，盖庆恩，等.农村减贫：应该更关注教育还是健康？——基于收入增长和差距缩小双重视角的实证［J］.经济研究，2014，49（11）:130–144.

② 蔡昉.如何开启第二次人口红利？［J］.国际经济评论，2020（2）:9–24，4.

③ Heckman，J.J.，Corbin，C.O.Capabilities and Skills［J］. Journal of Human Development and Capabilities，2016（17）：342–359.

④ 数据来源于东盟统计局发布的 *The 2022 ASEAN SDG Snapshot Report*。

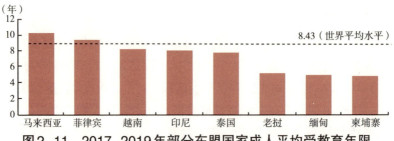

图2-11 2017~2019年部分东盟国家成人平均受教育年限

注：根据《人类发展报告》，该指标计算的是25岁及以上人口的平均受教育年限，根据官方提供的每个教育阶段的时长转换而来。

数据来源：根据联合国开发署历年《人类发展报告》计算得到。其中，"世界平均水平"对应报告中的"世界"一项。

疫情使东盟各国减少教育财政支出，对女性、偏远地区或少数民族群体的受教育情况影响较大。疫情期间，除印尼和越南外，其余东盟国家的教育财政支出占比均小于2017年的教育财政支出占比（见图2-12）。为应对疫情，政府将资金投向实施公共卫生应急措施和加强安全体系建设等方面，投向教育的财政支出相对减少。虽然东盟各国采取多种方式保证教育活动的开展，但由于部分国家经济发展落后，影响教育完成率。在柬埔寨和缅甸，对于在疫情前有子女上学的家庭，疫情期间依然完成教育的家庭不到30%[①]。

图2-12 2014年、2017年、2022年部分东盟国家教育财政支出占比变化

注：（1）教育财政支出占比=政府教育支出/政府财政支出。

（2）由于数据缺失，缅甸2021年数据采用2019年数据代替，印尼2021年数据采用2020年数据代替。

数据来源：世界银行公开数据库（https://data.worldbank.org）。

---

① 数据来源于世界银行新冠疫情检测平台Household Monitoring Systems to Track the Impacts of the COVID-19 Pandemic。

　　受疫情影响，大部分国家的儿童在学校停课期间通过电视、课堂作业、网络等方式参与学习或教育活动。在柬埔寨，疫情期间高中女生与男生人数之比下降较大，从2019年的1.25：1降至2021年的1.03：1。在缅甸，学校关闭影响了约26%的有孩子家庭。在泰国和老挝，仅有不到40%的家庭在学校关闭后儿童仍能参与学习或教育活动。在老挝，来自少数民族家庭的学生在停课期间继续参与教学活动的可能性仅为19.4%，而城市地区的学生在线学习的情况更为普遍。受疫情影响，印尼2020年2月16日至2022年4月30日共停课666天，是有数据的206个国家中停课时间最长的。印尼虽然总体停课天数最长，但有90%以上的家庭在学校关闭后仍能参与学校或教育活动。菲律宾共停课562天，其中仅6天是部分停课（见图2-13）。

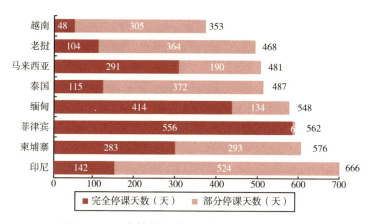

图2-13　疫情期间部分东盟国家停课天数

数据来源：联合国教科文组织发布的各国学校关闭情况的全球分布。

五、科技创新

　　科技创新有助于减少饥饿与贫困。在学术研究中，学者们尝试了各种方法来解决贫困问题，科技创新就是其中之一。尤等（You et al.，2020）强调，缩小与发达国家之间的技术差距有助于帮助落后国家减少贫困。包括东盟在内的亚洲发展中国家和地区的贫困主要集中在农村地区，农业增长被认为是减少贫困的重要手段。科技创新为贫困地区农业生产提供科技支撑，通过优化家庭农业要素配置和提升农业生产效率，降低农业生产经营的交易成本，促进贫困地区家庭农业效益提高和生产成本降低，进而实现贫困家庭的增收减贫。

　　疫情对科技创新产生负面影响。疫情封锁措施导致实验室的研究项目中断、研发人员流动受限以及人员培训中断，进而对科技创新产生负面影响。相较于2019年，东盟各国2020年专利申请量呈下降趋势，其中印尼的专利申请量减少幅度最大（见图2-14）。

图2-14　2013~2021年部分东盟国家专利申请数

注：专利数为非居民专利申请数和居民专利申请数之和。

数据来源：世界银行公开数据库（https://data.worldbank.org）。

专栏2-5　将科技创新转化为支持减贫的现实生产力

中菲农业技术中心于2001年在菲律宾新怡诗夏省成立，主要负责杂交水稻品种的研发与推广。同时，从中国选派杂交水稻专家常驻菲律宾进行指导。经过21年的发展，中菲农业技术中心在菲推广商业化杂交水稻51.44万公顷，水稻栽培与制种技术示范点建设覆盖菲律宾29个省，惠及农户30万余户，促进粮食增收48.21亿公斤。2022年3月，在中菲农业技术中心第三期技术合作项目竣工仪式上，时任菲律宾农业部长威廉·达尔表示，中国杂交水稻种植技术帮助菲律宾水稻产量稳步提高，对保障粮食安全、改善农民生活发挥了重要作用。

资料来源：中国一带一路网，"菲律宾农民：我们相信中国杂交水稻技术"，2022年8月29日。

加大科技创新和人才培养力度，积极推进科技减贫。东盟国家通过有效保护知识产权等措施，营造开放、公平的科技创新发展环境，促进和参加科技创新活动，包括10+3科学英才中心（AGGS）、10+3青年科学家合作创新论坛、青年科技创新营和颁奖等。东盟各国相继实施了相关的战略规划，以促进本国科技创新。

越南颁布《至2030年科技创新与发展战略》，系统规划了越南科技创新发展体系，该战略的具体目标是发挥科技和创新在发展拳头产业中的重要作用，到2030年高科技工业产品价值占加工制造业的比重至少达到45%。柬埔寨颁布《2030年科技创新路线图》，该路线图将是柬埔寨实现可持续发展目标的关键，以增强国家科技创新能力，培育充满活力的创新生态系统，并增加包容性、弹性和可持续性以更好地实现疫后复苏。该路线图有五项政策战略，即加强科技创新系统的治理结构，发展国家科技创新劳动力，加强研究能力和质量，加强不同利益相关者之间的合作和联系，培育有利于创新的生态系统。印尼颁布《国家科技总体规划（2017—2045）》，致力于通过科技创新推动国家经济转型和发展，在农业技术、海洋科学、清洁能源、医药卫生等领域取得显著成就。菲律宾推出《菲律宾创新法案》，旨在促进中小微型企业的快速发展，推动企业创新，提升企业国际竞争力。该创新法案将重点关注粮食安全与可持续农业、"蓝色经济"（海洋资源）、教育、健康、安全、清洁和可靠能源、气候变化、治理、基础设施、数字经济与交通运输等多个领域。总体而言，东盟国家积极提升自身科技创新能力，促进先进适用技术加快转化为支持东盟减贫的现实生产力。

六、气候变化

气候变化被广泛认为是影响贫困的关键因素。莱申科等（Leichenko et al., 2014）通过综述有关气候变化、脆弱性及贫困的文献后发现，虽然气候变化从未被视为贫穷的唯一原因，但研究已经确定了许多直接和间接渠道，通过这些渠道，气候变化可能加剧贫困，特别是在欠发达国家和地区[①]。直接渠道植根于长期建立的影响评估框架，假设生物和物理变化、市场反应和贫困结果之间存在直接联系，而间接渠道则假设气候暴露与贫困之间的因果链是复杂的，并受到个人和家庭特征以及决策过程、社会经济条件、机构和治理质量等其他因素的影响，同时还强调气候变化对健康状况不佳和政治冲突的影响，这些都是影

---

① Leichenko, R., & Silva, J. A.Climate Change and Poverty: Vulnerability, Impacts, and Alleviation Strategies [J]. Wiley Interdisciplinary Reviews: Climate Change, 2014, 5（4）: 539-556.

响贫困的重要因素[1]。但气候变化对于不同人群产生的影响不同。哈勒伽特等（Hallegatte et al.，2017）基于各国际机构的相关报告研究指出，虽然气候变化对非贫困人口的影响有限，但贫困人口可能会受到气候变化的严重影响，即穷人更容易受到环境冲击的影响，并且在受到冲击后从朋友和家人、金融体系和社会安全网获得的支持也较少。东盟各国的地理位置使其更易受到气候的影响[2]。贝尤丹－达屈曲等（Bayudan-Dacuycuy et al.，2019）通过分析强降水与菲律宾长期和短期贫困之间的关系后发现，降水是导致家庭收入减少的原因之一，包括农业收入和非农业收入；此外，降水冲击对企业收入的影响也很明显，特别是服务业和工业[3]。麦克尔威等（McElwee et al.，2017）的研究表明，越南贫困家庭的收入对洪水的影响更为敏感[4]。但是相比家庭的贫困情况，家庭成员的年龄和生计部门的参与程度与洪水影响的关系更为密切。

气候变化增加东盟国家因灾致贫的风险。气候变化增加农业生产的不确定性，导致严重的自然灾害。贫困或脆弱性人口应对气候变化风险的能力较差，因灾致贫或返贫风险较大，阻碍东盟国家的减贫进展。2016~2021年，东盟国家因气候变化而受灾的人口占总人口的比重达20%~30%。部分地区的受灾民众面临饮用水、食品和药品等物资不足的问题。为应对气候变化对减贫进展的不利影响，东盟国家不断加强政策支持。在农业生产方面，各成员国在农村大力发展气候智能型农业，设置可满足未来持续性发展的粮食标准，以有效实现农业粮食系统的转型，减缓和适应气候变化。在灾害风险方面，东南亚灾害风险保险基金提供风险识别、风险控制以及保险等服务，增强金融体系抵御灾害和气候冲击的能力。印尼于2018年启动了灾害风险融资和保险战略，菲律宾发行了地震和台风巨灾债券。2021年，超强台风"雷伊"达到了台风触发等级，巨灾债券向菲律宾政府支付了5250万美元。

① Leichenko R, O'Brien K. Environmental Change and Globalization: Double Exposures [M]. New York: Oxford University Press, 2008: 167.

② Hallegatte, S., Rozenberg, J.Climate Change Through a Poverty Lens [J]. Nature Climate Change, 2017（7）: 250－256.

③ Bayudan-Dacuycuy, C., & Baje, L. K.When It Rains, It Pours? Analyzing the Rainfall Shocks-poverty Nexus in the Philippines [J]. Social Indicators Research, 2019, 145（1）: 67–93.

④ McElwee P, Nghiem T, Le H, Vu H. Flood Vulnerability Among Rural Households in the Red River Delta of Vietnam: Implications for Future Climate Change Risk and Adaptation [J]. Nat Hazards, 2017（86）: 465－492.

专栏2-6　自然灾害导致东盟国家遭受经济损失

2022年5月，自然灾害已使越南国内35人死亡和失踪，15人受伤；24间民房坍塌，738间民房不同程度受损，3078间房屋被淹没；被淹水稻和农作物面积达55725公顷，其他农作物受损面积达2375公顷；49434只（头）家畜禽死亡或被洪水卷走，水产养殖受损面积达1210公顷。自然灾害还致使多段堤坝、渠道、河岸和海岸等受损，经济损失约2100万美元。

受"穆查"的影响，缅甸西部和北部、孟加拉国南部、印度东部先后出现大到暴雨，部分地区出现大暴雨或特大暴雨。据法新社报道，截至2023年5月19日，气旋风暴"穆查"在缅甸已经造成145人死亡，多地受灾民众面临饮用水、食品和药品等物资不足的问题。

资料来源：

a. 越南通讯社，"2022年自然灾害形势严峻复杂和难以预料"，2022年6月2日。

b. 货运全球网，"气旋风暴'穆查'袭击缅甸145人死亡；超级台风'玛娃'登陆关岛，损毁严重！"，2023年5月26日。

气候行动势在必行，为东盟减贫提供新思路。通过科学推进能源转型和减排，刺激技术创新、创造就业和经济增长的机会，可以减少贫困并促进公平[①]。东盟国家积极参与气候行动。在促进能源转型和减排方面，《东盟能源合作行动计划（2021—2025）》提出到2025年将能源强度降低32%，并计划到2025年可再生资源占能源供应总量的23%。大多数东盟国家更新了巴黎气候协定下的国家自主贡献承诺。在可再生能源方面，印尼于2020年底颁布了简化电价、对特定电厂的电价补贴等政策以刺激太阳能和水力发电；菲律宾政府制定政策，计划开放100%外资所有权的新能源发电，以吸引外资投向新能源基础设施建设。但从人均二氧化碳排放量来看，2012~2019年东盟国家总体呈现上升态势，其中马来西亚的人均二氧化碳排放量位居东盟各国之首，而缅甸排在最后（见图2-15）。东帝汶和缅甸的排放量最小。应对气候变化并非朝夕之功，与本国发展阶段、产业结构密切相关。东盟目前有大量燃煤发电厂，正处于从化石燃料转向可再生能源转型的十字路口，为贫困人口创造了大量就业机会。预计到2050年，东盟能够将与能源相关的二氧化碳排放量减少75%[②]。

---

①　参见中国国务院发展研究中心和世界银行2019年发布的《中国减贫四十年：驱动力量、借鉴意义和未来政策方向》。

②　参见国际可再生能源署2022年发布的《东盟可再生能源展望：迈向区域能源转型》（第二版）。

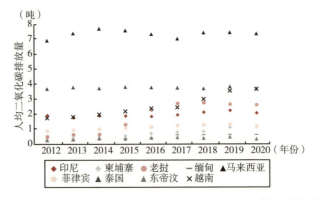

图2-15 2012~2020年部分东盟国家人均二氧化碳排放量变化趋势

注：该指标于2020年更新。

数据来源：世界银行公开数据库（https://data.worldbank.org）。

专栏2-7 马来西亚积极促进能源转型，推动减贫事业发展

为应对全球范围内的能源短缺与环境危机问题，在第26届联合国气候变化缔约方大会（COP26）上，包括马来西亚在内的100多个国家做出了2050年净零排放的承诺。马来西亚政府采取有效的可再生能源举措，促进可再生能源行业发展，这能够创造新的就业机会，同时为减少贫困作出贡献。例如，马来西亚发布的12MP计划中的一项倡议强调碳税抵免，即按碳排放量对采用化石燃料的企业进行征税。净能源计量、智能自动化赠款和绿色投资税等政策对马来西亚清洁能源产业的蓬勃发展非常有帮助。其中，净能源计量政策允许通过采用光伏系统获得电费补偿，智能自动化赠款帮助使用者安装智能AIoT能源解决方案，而绿色投资税为有资格的企业提供高达48%的税收减免。

成本较低的户用光伏有助于减贫。回顾过去十年，光伏系统的成本实际下降了85%，发电效率从1955年的2%大幅提高到现在的20%以上。马来西亚光伏行业厂商正在实施先租后买的计划，该计划使家庭用户可以负担得起安装光伏系统的成本，同时每月节省高达90%的电费。根据相关调查和研究，马来西亚拥有部署320万套户用光伏的巨大潜力。对于家庭用户，节省的电费可以抵消采购光伏系统的成本，这有助于降低电费，从而有助于马来西亚减贫事业的发展。

资料来源："加速实现碳中和！马来西亚'一揽子'政策推进能源转型！"，参见https://news.solarbe.com/202201/18/350105.html。

七、小结

东盟各国在落实联合国千年发展目标和推进减贫进程方面已经取得较好进展，但疫情加剧了东盟国家减贫与发展面临的风险与不确定性。一是东盟国家粮食安全面临严峻考验，各国出台了一系列政策来确保区域内粮食供应链稳定畅通，提升区域粮食供应链韧性。二是低收入国家贫困人口的营养健康问题依然突出，需要精准识别因病致贫、因病返贫人群，完善社会保障体系，提高有限医疗资源的利用效率。三是疫情加剧了受教育机会不均等问题，女性、偏远地区或少数民族群体教育发展出现中断。四是虽然东盟各国的经济增长和充分就业面临挑战，但数字经济和中小微企业发展为推动充分就业带来机遇。五是极端气候条件增加了东盟国家因灾致贫的风险。六是科技创新减少饥饿与贫困的潜力仍有待加强，未来科技合作与科技减贫将成为东盟对外合作的重要内容。

贫困是一种综合性的生活困难现象，具有原因和表现多样化的特征，减贫扶贫需要多方措施共同作用。粮食安全、营养健康、教育水平、经济增长、气候变化以及科技创新六个议题并非孤立存在，抑或单独作用于贫困，各议题之间存在密切联系。对贫困人口而言，粮食安全是其生存的首要目标。在此基础上，人们可获得安全和有营养的食物，改善其营养健康状况，降低患病概率；儿童可以更好地接受教育，降低代际贫困传递的风险；成人可以承担强度更大的工作，提高劳动产出效率，创造更多收入。随着气候变化的加剧，农业首当其冲受到影响，各国积极推动气候适应型和智慧农业发展，这对农业科技创新提出了新的更高的要求。同时，疫情加速推动数字经济发展，电子商务、金融科技、移动游戏等为中小企业发展创造新的机遇，有利于促进充分就业。

第三章
推动东盟国家减贫的国际发展援助与合作

东盟作为区域性多边组织，其社会发展与减贫得到了中国、美国、日本、韩国等多个对话伙伴、发展伙伴的资金援助与支持，如中国政府对东盟的无偿援助、中国—东盟合作基金、日本—东盟合作基金、美国的"通过创新、贸易和电子商务促进包容性增长"项目等。同时，联合国、世界银行、亚洲开发银行等国际组织和金融机构也为东盟及其成员国发展提供支持。为应对疫情冲击，东盟设立了"东盟应对新冠肺炎疫情基金"，多方对话伙伴、合作伙伴和国际机构等也通过不同渠道向东盟及其成员国提供帮助[①]。

一、国际援助总体水平变化情况

国际社会持续提供发展援助。 2013~2022年东盟地区接受的来自国际社会的官方发展援助共计1197.7亿美元，占全世界援助总额的6%。其中，2020~2022年接受的援助总额为364.4亿美元，占比30%，单年援助额明显高于2019年。

从国别视角来看，越南、印尼和缅甸是主要的被援助国。越南已同28个国家（地区）和23个多边组织建立"发展伙伴关系"，主要包括日本、欧盟、韩国等国家和地区，以及世界银行、亚洲开发银行等国际金融机构，自1992年以来，迄今累计承诺向越南提供援助逾956亿美元，年均援助金额达34亿美元[②]。2011~2021年，缅甸共接受88个外国政府或机构提供的1822个官方发展援助项目，援款承诺总额167.8亿美元，援款支付总额84.2亿美元，已经完成项目总额50亿美元，实施中的项目总额95亿美元，储备或立项中的项目总额15亿美元[③]。柬埔寨自1960年以来共接受外国援助承诺总额291.9亿美元，实际援款支出181.6

---

① 根据中华人民共和国商务部发布的《对外投资合作国别（地区）指南：东盟（2022年版）》整理。
② 根据中华人民共和国商务部发布的《对外投资合作国别（地区）指南：越南（2022年版）》整理。
③ 根据中华人民共和国商务部发布的《对外投资合作国别（地区）指南：缅甸（2022年版）》整理。

亿美元，日本、美国、法国、德国、欧盟以及亚洲开发银行、联合国机构等是其主要援助方。自2001年起，柬埔寨接受的官方发展援助以年均10%的速度增长，援助额约占柬埔寨国家发展预算的一半[1]。随着泰国经济社会的发展，泰国已逐渐由发展援助的接受国转变为捐助国，但在科学技术和创新领域，仍接受来自中国、其他发达国家和国际组织关于人才、设施、技术等方面的援助（见图3-1）。

图3-1　2013~2022年部分东盟国家接受的官方发展援助

数据来源：经济合作与发展组织数据库（OECD.Stat），以现价计。

疫情期间，双边、多边和私人部门的援助均明显上升[2]。疫情期间，国际社会加大了对部分东盟国家的援助，越南、缅甸和菲律宾接受的援助仍维持较高水平。菲律宾在2020~2022年接受的国际社会援助明显增加，相较2019年增长了35.7%~37.3%。2022年，柬埔寨接受官方发展援助贷款承诺总额约77.1亿美元，实际支出超过20亿美元，其中基础设施类项目占58%，农业类项目占26%，公共管理类项目占9%，人才开发类项目占7%。同年，菲律宾获得境外官方发展援助总额达306.9亿美元，其中优惠贷款金额290亿美元，占94%，赠款金额16.9亿美元，占6%[3]。2020~2022年，东盟双边援助金额均是2019年水平的1.1倍以上，多边援助金额与2019年相比分别增长了40.1%、15.5%和2.9%。私人部门援助虽然金额较少，但在疫情期间也有所上升，相比2019年，2020~2022年私人部门共增加援助3.7亿美元（见图3-2）。

---

①　根据中华人民共和国商务部发布的《对外投资合作国别（地区）指南：柬埔寨（2022年版）》整理。

②　根据经济合作与发展组织的分类，官方援助分为多边援助和双边援助，其中双边援助包括发展援助国援助（DAC）和非发展援助国援助（Non-DAC）。私人援助单独统计，不包括在官方援助中。

③　根据中华人民共和国商务部发布的《对外投资合作国别（地区）指南：菲律宾（2022年版）》整理。

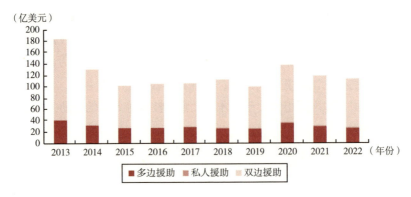

图 3-2　2013~2022年东盟接受的来自不同渠道的援助

数据来源：经济合作与发展组织数据库（OECD.Stat），以现价计。

　　双边援助是疫情期间援助的主要来源。东盟整体接受的双边援助金额占总额的比重超过75%，其中主要来源于美国、日本、韩国三个国家。2013~2022年，美国、日本、韩国对东盟的援助总额占双边援助总额的62%。其中，日本的援助最多，达423.2亿美元，占47%；美国和韩国的援助分别为86.8亿美元和50.4亿美元，占比分别为9.6%和5.6%。多边援助在疫情期间呈现上升趋势，2020~2022年多边援助总额分别为35.1亿美元、29亿美元和25.8亿美元，比2019年分别增长40.2%、15.5%和2.9%。私人援助虽然较少，但一直维持稳定增长的趋势，其中2021年和2022年私人援助分别为1.5亿美元和1.7亿美元，比2019年分别增长30.7%和46.7%（见图3-3）。

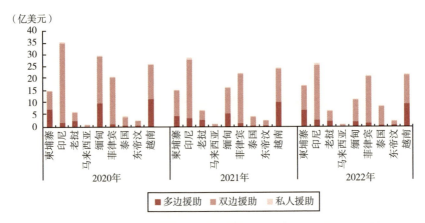

图 3-3　2020~2022年部分东盟国家接受的来自不同渠道的援助

数据来源：经济合作与发展组织数据库（OECD.Stat），以现价计。

　　在疫情期间，以接受基础设施援建为主[①]。柬埔寨主要接受社会基础设施方面的援助，主要涉及教育、供水和卫生，接受的官方援助总额在疫情之后有所增加，从2019年的10.9亿美元增长到2022年的16.9亿美元，2021年接受的援助虽然比2020年有所下降，但同2019年相比仍增长了17%。菲律宾主要接受经济基础设施及生产方面的援助，涉及运输、通信和农业相关基础设施的承建援助。马来西亚主要接受社会基础设施和服务、教育方面的援助。老挝主要接受教育、能源和农业基础设施援建，接受官方援助的总额一直处于3亿~5亿美元的水平，其中2014年接受的援助最多。泰国主要接受运输和通信基础设施方面的援助，所接受的援助总额在2016年出现爆炸式增长，主要增长点仍在经济基础设施和服务下属运输和通信领域方面，分别比2015年增长了4~5倍。此外，相比2019年，泰国在2020年和2021年接受的援助额分别上涨了60.1%和30%。印尼主要接受经济基础设施和服务、交通运输和通信基础设施方面的援助，接受援助的总额经历先上升后下降的趋势，其中2017年接受的援助最多，达36.7亿美元。与2019年相比，印尼在2021年和2022年接受的援助分别增加了12.2亿美元和9.9亿美元。越南主要接受教育、运输和通信方面的援助，所接受的援助总额在2016年之前维持在25亿美元以上，之后逐渐减少至2018年的5.8亿美元，2022年越南接受的援助增长至12亿美元。缅甸主要接受项目和债务减免方面的援助，分别占其全年所接受援助金额（61.9亿美元）的33.1%和42.4%（见图3-4）。

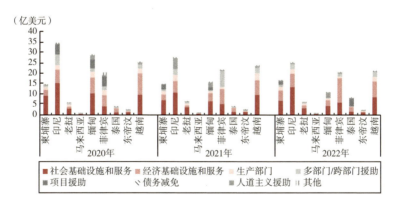

图3-4　2020~2022年部分东盟国家接受的不同领域的援助

　　数据来源：经济合作与发展组织数据库（OECD.Stat），以现价计。

---

　　①　根据经济合作与发展组织数据库的定义，援助领域按用途可细分为：（1）社会基础设施和服务：教育、供水与卫生、其他社会基础设施与服务；（2）经济基础设施和服务：教育、能源、运输与通信、其他经济基础设施和服务；（3）生产、农林渔、工业采矿建筑业、贸易与旅游；（4）多部门援助：环保等；（5）项目援助：粮食援助等；（6）债务减免；（7）人道主义援助；（8）其他。

二、国际机构对东盟国家的援助

世界银行提供低成本贷款融资，缓解减贫资金压力。2012~2021年世界银行对东盟地区的年均援助额为12.4亿美元，占多边机构对东盟的援助总额的40%。2012~2022年，世界银行共向东盟提供资金援助项目313项，支持金额共计1114.7亿美元，其中来自国际开发协会（IDA）和国际复兴开发银行（IBRD）[①]的贷款达1075亿美元，赠款达39.7亿美元。2020~2022年，世界银行共向东盟提供资金支持达462.5亿美元，占41.5%。疫情期间，国际开发协会将贷款发放周期从三年缩短到两年，并承诺提供750亿美元以帮助东盟各国应对紧急需求。世界银行批准向缅甸新冠肺炎疫情应急响应项目提供5000万美元贷款，项目侧重于在选定的医院扩大重症监护病房，同时加强卫生工作人员和官员的能力建设以及在全国开展社区参与活动，共覆盖缅甸八所中央级别医院、43所区级和省邦级医院（见图3-5）。

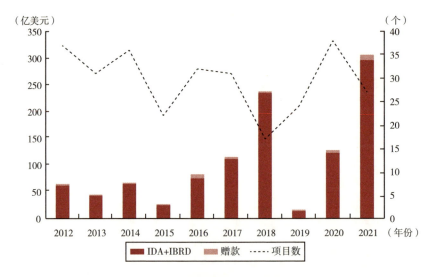

图3-5　2012~2021年东盟接受的来自世界银行的官方发展援助和项目数

数据来源：世界银行公开的援助项目，https://projects.worldbank.org/en/projects-operations/projects-list。

[①] 国际复兴开发银行（IBRD）作为世界最大的开发银行，通过向中等收入国家和资信良好的低收入国家提供贷款、担保、风险管理产品和咨询服务，并通过协调各国应对地区性和全球性挑战，支持达成世界银行集团的使命。虽然根据人均收入水平，柬埔寨、老挝、缅甸符合IDA的援助资格，但对于IBRD的一些借款人来说，其也有信誉，所以可从IBRD贷款并且接受援助。

专栏3-1　国际机构援助促进东盟社会发展与减贫

世界银行助力印尼疫情后的经济复苏[a]：疫情导致印尼经历了近20年来的首次经济衰退。当前，印尼在投资和贸易领域面临巨大挑战，这妨碍了其吸引外商直接投资，限制了其融入全球价值链，并提高了国内粮食价格。世界银行执行董事理事会在2021年批准提供8亿美元资金，用于支持印尼的投资和贸易政策改革，并帮助加快该国的经济转型和疫后经济复苏。这项援助高度符合国家合作伙伴框架（country partnership framework, CPF），旨在支持印尼政府吸引投资和提高经济竞争力的计划，聚焦于获得外商直接投资，增加劳动力市场中的高技能专业人员，并促进可再生能源行业的私人部门投资。

联合国粮食及农业组织和绿色气候基金援助菲律宾发展智慧农业[b]：2020年3月13日，绿色气候基金宣布拨付1.453亿美元资金，与联合国粮食及农业组织在玻利维亚、柬埔寨和菲律宾联合开展三个新项目，以促进这三个国家的小农户和农村社区适应气候变化，增强气候韧性。在菲律宾，3920万美元的投资旨在帮助该国的农业体系适应气候变化，并在七年内直接惠及超过125万人。在柬埔寨，该项目将投资4280万美元，帮助该国洞里萨湖盆地北部的小农户提高备灾能力。联合国粮食及农业组织副总干事玛丽亚·海伦娜·塞梅多表示，创新气候融资或将推动农业粮食体系转型，加强农村地区对气候的适应能力和韧性。

亚洲开发银行支持印尼的财政和投资改革[c]：2018年，亚洲开发银行批准了10亿美元政策性贷款，以支持印尼的公共支出改革，并改善该国的投资环境。第二阶段的财政和公共支出管理计划将获得5亿美元贷款，最后一期的增长加速投资计划将获得5亿美元贷款。第一笔贷款旨在帮助印尼政府完成预算周期并扩大社会援助项目，这符合亚洲开发银行改善该国预算管理和透明度的目标。该计划使政府能够增加目标支出，提高医疗和教育等重点领域的支出。该计划有助于政府提高公共和私人投资的效率，同时也将解决地方层面的投资限制问题。2018年5月，印尼从全球三大信贷评级机构（惠誉、标准普尔和穆迪）获得了投资级评级。

资料来源：

a. ANTARA, "World Bank approves US$800 mln development financing for Indonesia", 2021年6月16日。

b.中国国际扶贫中心，《2023年第11期中外乡村发展信息摘要》，2023年5月19日。

c.华中师范大学中印尼人文交流中心，"来自亚洲开发银行的10亿美元贷款，将用于支持印尼的财政和投资改革"，2018年6月9日。

联合国等国际机构通过多种方式提供发展援助。2021年，联合国粮食及农业组织和联合国开发计划署对东盟的援助分别为0.04亿美元和0.16亿美元，主要用于农业基础设施领域。2023年，联合国粮食及农业组织联合绿色气候基金援助菲律宾发展智慧农业。2012~2021年，亚洲开发银行和欧盟对东盟的援助维持在较高水平，分别占多边援助总额的23.2%和12.2%，并在疫情期间增加了对东盟的援助（见图3-6）。2022年，欧盟通过价值180亿美元的公共和私人融资以支持越南的清洁能源转型。

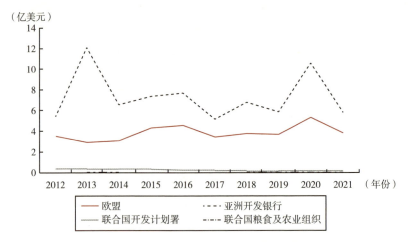

图3-6　2012~2021年东盟接受的来自部分国际机构的援助

数据来源：经济合作与发展组织数据库（OECD.Stat），以现价计。

区域性多边组织通过贷款等方式为东盟国家不同领域的发展提供援助。亚洲开发银行通过贷款等方式对东盟国家提供援助，支持东盟各国不同领域的发展和应对疫情冲击。亚洲开发银行和世界银行是援助菲律宾最大的多边组织，援助额分别占28.52%和20.97%[1]。2019年，亚洲开发银行为"就业培训教育项目"批复了5000万美元贷款，帮助老挝提高入学率和中等教育水平，并批复了三笔价值1.4亿美元的贷款用于帮助老挝发展农业、教育以及公共财政管理[2]。为支持印尼可持续经济增长，亚洲开发银行承诺将为印尼绿色能源发电厂、地热和太阳能项目提供融资支持[3]。疫情期间，亚洲开发银行在

---

① 数据来源于中华人民共和国商务部发布的《对外投资合作国别（地区）指南：菲律宾（2022年版）》。
② 根据中华人民共和国商务部发布的《对外投资合作国别（地区）指南：老挝（2020年版）》整理。
③ 根据中华人民共和国商务部发布的《对外投资合作国别（地区）指南：印度尼西亚（2022年版）》整理。

大湄公河次区域卫生安全项目框架下提供了660万美元，帮助缅甸加强疫情早期应对，同时向缅甸提供3000万美元贷款，帮助缅甸政府对31个地区的乡镇医院进行即时投资，以更好地应对疫情和未来的公共卫生威胁[①]。除亚洲开发银行外，亚洲基础设施投资银行在2020年批准了10亿美元贷款，帮助印尼实施疫情防控，并在2021年为印尼龙目岛曼达利卡城市旅游基础设施项目（MUTIP）提供价值1.7万亿印尼盾（约合1.2亿美元）的全额融资支持，开创了该机构在印尼独立融资以及在旅游基础设施开发领域融资的先河[②]。

三、发达国家对东盟国家的援助

美国、日本、韩国是东盟接受的发达国家援助的主要来源。2013~2022年美国、日本、韩国对东盟的援助总额占双边援助总额的62%。其中，日本的援助额最高，达423.2亿美元，占47%；美国和韩国的援助额分别为86.8亿美元和50.4亿美元，占比分别为9.6%和5.6%。

美国对东盟地区的援助比较稳定，主要援助对象是印尼、菲律宾、越南和缅甸。2013~2022年东盟地区接受的来自美国的官方发展援助共计86.8亿美元，其中2020~2022年为26.4亿美元，占30%，且单年接受的援助额相较于2019年（8亿美元）均增长了至少14%。从国别视角来看，印尼和菲律宾是接受援助最多的国家，接受援助总额远超其他国家，分别为22亿美元和19.2亿美元。此外，在疫情期间，东盟各国接受的美国援助均出现了一定程度的增加（见图3-7）。

日本向东南亚地区提供了大量援助。2013~2022年东盟接受的来自日本的官方发展援助共计422.3亿美元，其中疫情期间接受的援助占30%。此外，2020年、2021年和2022年日本对东盟的援助相比2019年均有所增加，分别增加了33%、5.1%和9.1%。从国别视角来看，越南和缅甸是接受援助最多的国家，接受援助总额远超其他国家，分别为107.3亿美元和99亿美元。在疫情期间，印尼、菲律宾和缅甸是日本的主要援助国，援助额占比均超过20%（见图3-8）。

---

① 根据中华人民共和国商务部发布的《对外投资合作国别（地区）指南：缅甸（2022年版）》整理。
② 根据中华人民共和国商务部发布的《对外投资合作国别（地区）指南：印度尼西亚（2022年版）》整理。

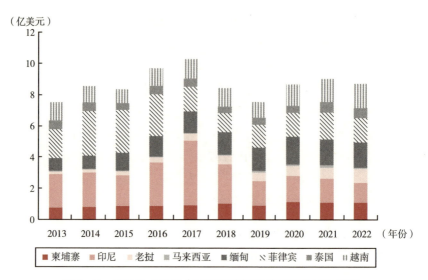

图3-7　2013~2022年美国对部分东盟国家的援助

数据来源：经济合作与发展组织数据库（OECD.Stat），以现价计。

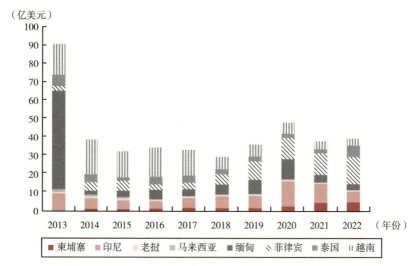

图3-8　2013~2022年日本对部分东盟国家的援助

数据来源：经济合作与发展组织数据库（OECD.Stat），以现价计。

日本主要在基础设施援建领域对菲律宾、印尼和缅甸进行支援。2020年菲律宾接受了来自日本的11.1亿美元援助，是2019年的1.1倍。日本对菲律宾的援助以经济基础设施建设领域的运输和通信援建为主，占比超过40%。与2019年相比，2020年菲律宾接受的运输和通信领域相关的援助有所下降，同比下降了46%。2020年印尼接受了来自日本的13.2亿美元援助，以项目援助和经济基础设施援助为主，占比均超过30%。2021年，日本对印尼的援助总额有所下降，为10.3亿美元，经济基础设施建设仍是主要的援助领域。2020年缅甸接受了来自日本的10.5亿美元援助，以运输和通信领域为主，援助额占比达31%。与2019年相比，2020年缅甸在社会和经济基础设施援助及项目援助领域接受的援助更多，其中基础设施建设援助总额达5.8亿美元，经济领域援助金额为2019年的2倍。2021年，日本对缅甸的援助额减少至3.8亿美元。

韩国持续加大对东盟的援助。2013~2022年东盟接受的来自韩国的官方发展援助达50.4亿美元，疫情期间的援助金额占总援助额的35.8%。2020~2022年，韩国增加了对东盟地区的投资，年援助总额约6亿美元，比2019年增加了至少1.2亿美元（见图3-9）。

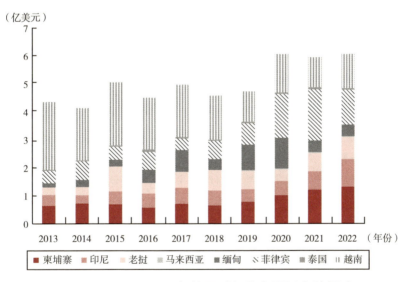

图3-9　2013~2022年韩国对部分东盟国家的援助

数据来源：经济合作与发展组织数据库（OECD.Stat），以现价计。

从国别视角来看，越南是韩国援助最多的国家，援助总额为16.61亿美元，远超其他东盟国家。2020年韩国对东盟官方发展援助总额为1.4亿美元，同比增长26%。韩国只在2015年前对越南提供了高于2亿美元的援助，且以援助公路修建和通信基础设施为主，在那之后，对越南的援助快速减少，到2019年以农业基础设施援建为基础，援助额才开始出现小幅上升。相比2019年，2020年韩国在卫生和人道主义领域增加了对越南的援助，2021年增加了教育方面的援助（见图3-10）。

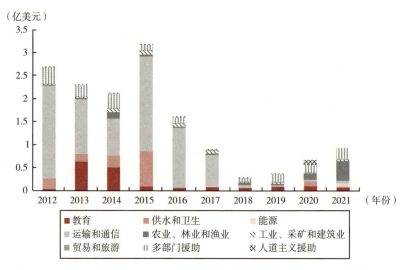

图 3-10　2012~2021 年越南接受的韩国提供的不同领域的援助

数据来源：经济合作与发展组织数据库（OECD.Stat），以现价计。

四、东盟内部减贫合作[①]

东盟作为地区治理实体，各成员国之间通力合作，共同推进减贫进展。东盟各国于 2015 年就共同提出《东盟经济共同体蓝图 2025》，计划 2025 年将东盟建设成高度一体化、竞争力强、创新水平高、充满活力的经济共同体，并强调进一步拓宽东盟各成员之间合作的领域，提高互联互通水平，不断强化东盟经济发展韧性和包容度。为此，澜湄五国在 2018 年提出《澜沧江—湄公河合作五年行动计划（2018—2022）》，旨在促进澜湄沿岸各国经济社会发展，增进各国人民福祉，缩小本区域发展差距，建设面向和平与繁荣的澜湄国家命运共同体。

为应对疫情对减贫的影响，东盟各成员国减贫合作的领域不断扩大。2020 年，《东盟全面复苏框架》指出要进一步完善卫生系统，加强社会保障，最大化东盟内部市场和经济一体化潜力，加快包容性数字转型，促进农业、能源等多个领域的可持续发展。针对粮食安全问题，2020 年颁布的《东盟粮食安全一体化框架》（AIFS）和《东盟地区粮食安全战略行动计划（2021—2025）》（SPA-FS）指出，要通过保障粮食生产、减少灾后损失、促进贸易、确保粮食

---

① 东盟各成员国之间的合作政策、倡议等详见附录 2。

安全等方式确保居民长期粮食安全和营养，改善东盟地区农民的生计。为应对自然灾害对生产和减贫的影响，于2020和2021年先后颁布了《东盟突发公共卫生事件战略框架》和《东盟灾害管理愿景2025》，以提高东盟整体抗灾能力。为强化数字技术的推广和应用，于2021年颁布了《东盟数字规划2025》，目的是将东盟建设成为一个由安全和变革性的数字服务、技术和生态系统所驱动的领先数字社区和经济体。

第四章
中国—东盟减贫合作

　　坚持构建中国—东盟命运共同体。中国和东盟山水相连、血脉相亲，友好关系源远流长。1991年，双方开始对话进程。30多年来，中国与东盟携手前进，战略伙伴关系内涵不断丰富，政治安全、经济贸易、社会人文三大领域合作硕果累累，成为规模最大的贸易伙伴、最富内涵的合作伙伴、最具活力的战略伙伴。[①]在2021年中国—东盟建立对话关系30周年纪念峰会上，双方共同制定并发布《中国—东盟全面战略伙伴关系行动计划（2022—2025）》，宣布建立中国—东盟全面战略伙伴关系，提出共建和平、安宁、繁荣、美丽、友好"五大家园"，为推动构建更为紧密的中国—东盟命运共同体描绘蓝图、指引方向。[②]

一、中国减贫经验总结

　　党的十八大以来，以习近平同志为核心的党中央把脱贫攻坚摆到治国理政的突出位置，实施精准扶贫、精准脱贫基本方略，动员全党全国全社会力量，打赢了脱贫攻坚战，现行标准下9899万农村贫困人口全部脱贫，832个贫困县全部摘帽，12.8万个贫困村全部出列，区域性整体贫困得到有效解决[③]。当前，中国正巩固拓展脱贫攻坚成果，全面推进乡村振兴。

（一）脱贫攻坚经验

　　回顾中国减贫历程，中国减贫战略经历了救济式扶贫、开发式扶贫、综合性扶贫和精准扶贫四个时期，不同时期的贫困特征、减贫驱动力、减贫措施和

---

① 张倪.中国—东盟合作"三十而立"构建更为紧密命运共同体［J］.中国发展观察，2021（12）：31-33，12.

　　② 刘宁，蓝天立.为服务构建更为紧密的中国—东盟命运共同体贡献力量［N］.人民日报，2022-09-15.

　　③ 习近平.在全国脱贫攻坚总结表彰大会上的讲话［M］.人民出版社，2021.

手段存在较大差异。

救济式扶贫阶段（1978~1985年）。改革开放初期，农村贫困发生率超过80%，促进农业收入增长、提高农业生产率成为这一时期中国消除绝对贫困的主要驱动力。在这一时期，国家加大了农村救济式扶贫的扶持力度，积极推进农村土地制度改革，建立以家庭承包经营为基础、统分结合的双层经营体制[①]，激发农民劳动积极性，解放生产力，为促进粮食增产、农民多渠道增收和国家经济增长提供了有力支撑。在这一时期，农村绝对贫困人口从2.5亿人下降到1.25亿人，农村贫困发生率从30.7%降到14.8%[②]。

开发式扶贫阶段（1986~2006年）。开发式扶贫强调依靠贫困地区自身资源和经济开发来解决贫困问题。随着农村改革不断深化，中国扶贫对象逐渐瞄准县级、村级贫困区域。1986年，国务院扶贫开发领导小组成立。1987年颁布的《国务院关于加强贫困地区经济开发工作的通知》确立了开发式扶贫的指导思想。1994年颁布的《国家八七扶贫攻坚计划》通过贴息贷款支持、以工代赈项目、普及义务教育、完善医疗保障体系等方式促进减贫。同时，提出西部大开发、中部崛起战略，通过大规模基础设施投资、财政转移支付和补贴等政策缩小区域差距。在这一时期，中国绝对贫困率从1984年的81.2%下降到2005年的22.1%，约5.53亿人摆脱绝对贫困[③]。

综合性扶贫阶段（2007~2012年）。综合性扶贫主要体现为工业发展和贸易带动的开发式扶贫与社会保障制度相结合。2007年，农村最低生活保障制度在全国迅速推广，标志着中国形成了开发式扶贫与兜底式扶贫相结合的治理体系。在这一时期，政府主要通过社会救助、转移支付等手段为无法参与经济活动的贫困人口提供现金转移。同时，制定了一系列旨在减少农村贫困的社会保障性政策，包括新农村合作医疗保险、农村养老保险制度和农村生活保障制度等。在这一时期，中国绝对贫困率从2008年18%下降到2012年的8.5%，约1.23亿人摆脱绝对贫困[④]。

精准扶贫阶段（2013~2020年）。据2010年国家贫困标准，2013年农村贫困人口比例已降至10%以下，并主要集中在中西部偏远地区。2011年出台的《中国农村扶贫开发纲要（2011—2020年）》标志着中国从区域扶贫向对户精准扶贫的转变。党的十八大提出精准扶贫的基本方略是"六个精准"和"五个

---

① 参见中央农办主任、农业农村部部长韩长赋2018年发表的"中国农村土地制度改革"。
② 范小建. 中国特色扶贫开发的基本经验［J］. 求是，2007，468（23）：48-49.
③ 数据来源于世界银行Povcalnet（在线分析工具，http://iresearch.worldbank.org/PovcalNet/）。
④ 同上。

一批"，对于帮扶谁、谁来扶、怎么扶、如何退以及防止返贫的各个环节作出部署。其中，"六个精准"要求扶贫干预全过程，做到扶贫对象精准、项目安排精准、资金使用精准、措施到户精准、因村派人精准和脱贫成效精准。"五个一批"指具体针对致贫原因的扶贫政策手段，主要包括就业和产业发展、易地搬迁、生态补偿、发展教育以及社会保护五个方面。另外，为保障精准扶贫的顺利实施，《"十三五"脱贫攻坚规划》专门提出针对脱贫攻坚的保障措施，包括创新体制、加大政策支持、强化组织实施等内容。截至2020年底，中国完全消除绝对贫困，精准扶贫有效解决了中国脱贫攻坚"最后一公里"的问题。

（二）中国巩固拓展脱贫攻坚成果同乡村振兴衔接工作进展

守住不发生规模性返贫底线。坚决守住不发生规模性返贫底线是巩固拓展脱贫攻坚同乡村振兴有效衔接的重要前提。习近平总书记在2021年2月25日召开的脱贫攻坚总结表彰大会上的讲话中强调，"脱贫攻坚战的全面胜利，标志着我们党在团结带领人民创造美好生活、实现共同富裕的道路上迈出了坚实的一大步"，"要切实做好巩固拓展脱贫攻坚成果同乡村振兴有效衔接各项工作，让脱贫基础更加稳固、成效更可持续"。脱贫攻坚与乡村振兴战略具有前后相继的衔接逻辑，主要表现在从绝对贫困消除转向相对贫困治理。脱贫攻坚旨在实现农村贫困人口的"两不愁三保障"，聚焦于绝对贫困的消除，瞄准贫困群体的温饱问题。而乡村振兴则关注相对贫困的治理，构筑解决相对贫困问题长效机制，化解城乡发展不平衡、农村发展不充分的主要矛盾，从根本上缩小城乡在生活水平和质量上的差距。相对于绝对贫困，相对贫困是更多维、更深层的贫困问题，中国政府结合数字化技术不断强化防止返贫动态监测，实施针对性帮扶举措，消除返贫致贫风险。

增强脱贫地区和脱贫群众内生发展动力。要从根本上巩固拓展脱贫攻坚成果，必须建立一个基于内生性增长的长效机制。从脱贫攻坚的产业扶贫到乡村振兴的产业兴旺，产业发展始终摆在重要位置。产业发展是巩固脱贫成果、衔接乡村振兴的最大结合点，产业兴旺是解决农村一切问题的前提，要将产业振兴融入脱贫攻坚与乡村振兴的全过程。产业振兴是乡村振兴的根本，也是保障脱贫人口稳定脱贫、增强脱贫地区和脱贫群众内生发展动力的根本之策。2022年，中央财政衔接推进乡村振兴补助资金用于产业发展的比重超过55%，每个脱贫县都培育了2~3个特色主导产业，近3/4的脱贫人口与新型经营主体建立了紧密利益联结关系①。产业扶贫是一种内生性、根本性的扶贫路径，通过融合

---

① 参见http://www.moa.gov.cn/hd/zbft_news/2022nyncjjyxqk/。

一二三产业发展，延长农业产品产业链，提高贫困群众自我发展能力，提升贫困群体的"造血"功能，为乡村振兴注入不竭的动力源泉。比如，贵州省黔东南州榕江县以小香鸡产业为基础，通过"订单养殖"带动贫困户505户2136人，贫困户户均增收3000元人民币以上，小香鸡产业扶贫效果明显。四川省广元市昭化区梅树乡五个村养殖4万羽蛋鸡，养殖户300人，累计销售额达90万元人民币。西藏仁布县康雄乡亚德细褐羊毛织品合作社年销售额达500多万元人民币，带动100多人就业，人均月增收3500元人民币。脱贫劳动力就业形势保持稳定，2022年务工就业规模达到3277.9万人，比2021年底增加132.9万人，超过年度目标任务258.7万人[①]。农村就业创业势头良好，就地就近就业率超过90%。在产业带动、就业拉动下，2022年全国农村居民人均可支配收入达到20133元人民币、实际增长4.2%，城乡居民人均收入比为2.45，比2021年缩小0.05[②]。

不断缩小区域发展差距。稳定帮扶政策是保障脱贫地区稳定脱贫、缩小区域差距的重要举措。中央政府出台有关衔接政策，国家层面确定160个国家乡村振兴重点帮扶县，完善东西部协作结对关系，实施"万企兴万村"行动，保持中央单位定点帮扶工作总体稳定，继续选派驻村第一书记和工作队，促进资金、人才等要素向中西部流动，确保落实各项帮扶举措。发挥好考核"指挥棒"作用，实施巩固拓展脱贫攻坚成果同乡村振兴有效衔接考核评估，促进政策、责任和工作落实。

建设宜居宜业和美乡村。建设宜居宜业和美乡村是当前全面推进乡村振兴和加快建设农业强国的一项重大战略任务。按照党的二十大部署，在以中国式现代化全面推进中华民族伟大复兴的新征程上，中国将全面推进乡村振兴，加快建设农业强国，扎实推动乡村产业、人才、文化、生态、组织振兴，建设宜居宜业和美乡村。构建现代乡村产业体系，促进农村一二三产业融合发展。立足县域统筹规划产业发展，把产业增值环节更多留在农村、增值收益更多留给农民。实施乡村建设行动，统筹乡村基础设施和公共服务体系建设，坚持不懈改善农村人居环境，因地制宜推进农村厕所革命，立足乡土特征、地域特点和民族特色提升村庄风貌。加强和改进乡村治理，创新乡村治理方式方法，推广运用积分制、清单制、数字化等治理方式。推动农村移风易俗，努力培育文明乡风、良好家风和淳朴民风。

---

① 参见http://www.moa.gov.cn/hd/zbft_news/qmtjxczx/wzzb_29371/。

② 参见http://www.moa.gov.cn/hd/zbft_news/2022nyncjjyxqk/。

（三）全面推进乡村振兴

脱贫攻坚向全面推进乡村振兴平稳过渡，是"三农"工作重心的历史性转移。当前，世界百年未有之大变局加速演进，党的十九届五中全会提出要加快构建以国内大循环为主体、国内国际双循环相互促进的新发展格局。"三农"是中国发展的基本盘，是实现危机软着陆，保障经济行稳致远的"压舱石"。2023年中央一号文件指出，"必须坚持不懈把解决好'三农'问题作为全党工作重中之重，举全党全社会之力全面推进乡村振兴，加快农业农村现代化"。加快构建以国内大循环为主体、国内国际双循环相互促进的新发展格局，促进资源要素整合和区域发展联通，建立新型城乡关系，巩固脱贫攻坚成果。

利用数字经济打开就业增收新空间。当前，人工智能、区块链、云计算、大数据、5G等数字技术日益加速向农业农村渗透，为推进乡村振兴提供了很好的发展机遇。中国农村互联网覆盖率进一步提升，根据中国互联网络信息中心发布的《第50次中国互联网发展状况统计报告》，截至2022年6月，农村互联网普及率为58.8%，农村网民规模为2.93亿人。从政策层面看，2019~2022年，国家相关部门陆续出台了《数字农业农村发展规划（2019—2025年）》《"十四五"国家信息化规划》《数字乡村发展行动计划（2022—2025年）》《2022年数字乡村发展工作要点》等诸多政策，支持数字经济赋能乡村振兴。从实践发展看，随着移动互联网在农业的深层应用和在乡村不断普及，众多面向"三农"领域的数字技术产品、数字平台和软件服务赋能农民更高效地进行乡村百业生产经营，为乡村就业和产业高质量发展提供更多机会。2023年中央一号文件指出要推进乡村高质量发展，主要包括做大做强农产品加工流通业、加快发展现代乡村服务业、培育乡村新产业新业态和培育壮大县域富民产业。2022年发布的《数字乡村发展行动计划（2022—2025年）》明确指出要着力发展乡村数字经济，坚持统筹协调、城乡融合。中国各地政府鼓励"数商兴农"和"互联网+"农产品出村进城工程，利用电子商务的力量和强大的国内物流网络将农村融入城市供应链，拓宽农产品销售渠道，有利于农民多渠道增收。

加快发展绿色低碳农业，推进农业绿色转型。中国已明确承诺二氧化碳排放力争2030年前达到峰值，努力争取2060年前实现碳中和。"双碳"承诺推进农业生产方式和农产品全产业链的绿色转型，刺激了技术创新，创造了就业和经济增长的机会，通过农业技术推广促进农业绿色转型，成为农业生产力提高的主要驱动力。

将乡村经济活动与生态环境相结合，激活乡村生态资源价值。2005年，时任浙江省委书记的习近平在浙江省安吉县余村调研时提出"绿水青山就是金山银山"。党的十九大报告强调，"坚持人与自然和谐共生"，"形成绿色发展方式和生活方式"，中国未来生态文明建设和绿色发展必须树立和践行"绿水青山就是金山银山"的理念。在"两山"理念下，生态扶贫和生态振兴具有内在一致性。乡村社会拥有资源、资产、资本"三资合一"的空间生态资源价值，具备成为新动能新增长极的潜力，自然能够成为生态化转型的基础。浙江省安吉县坚持"生态立县"发展战略，推进美丽乡村精品示范村建设和精品观光带提升，探求富而且美的生态富民之路，在改善生态环境的同时提高居民收入和生活水平。

不断提升社会保障治理效能，以高质量社会保障助推共同富裕。未来中国低收入人口特征将发生变化，需要考虑整合精准扶贫和制度化的社会保障政策。中国应有效利用国际组织的专业知识，完善扶贫政策和贫困数据；大量投入精准扶贫的人力资源，利用全面的调查数据确定贫困地区和家庭，根据需要确定政府干预政策，并通过各级官员目标责任来实现政策目标。同时，完善的社会保障系统也有利于更好地保护城市和农村地区的家庭免受冲击。疫情期间，中国为在城市生活和工作的外来务工人员以及低收入群体提供收入支持以弥补工资损失，避免其因收入不足而无法获得医疗卫生服务。

二、中国经验对东盟减贫的启示

强化顶层设计，因地制宜推进减贫进程。减贫是一项复杂工程，需要政策部门统筹全局，把握粮食安全、营养健康、教育水平、经济增长、气候变化以及科技创新之间的关联性，充分发挥本国制度优势。东盟各国减贫进度不同，历史背景、资源禀赋以及现实挑战存在差异，充分考虑当地实际，能够更好推进减贫进程。发展水平较高的马来西亚和泰国已经进入减贫攻坚期，应精准识别致贫原因，巩固减贫成果，防止出现规模性返贫问题。印尼政府对于经济和社会脆弱性问题，需要寻找稳定减贫长效机制。菲律宾、越南政府在解决贫困人群发展机会不均等问题时，可以通过构建开发式扶贫与兜底式扶贫相结合的治理体系，加快推进减贫事业。柬埔寨、老挝和缅甸还处于大规模减贫阶段，可以通过普及教育、完善医疗保障体系以及贴息贷款支持等方式推进减贫进程，同时利用政策缩小城乡差距，实现发展成果人民共享。另外，减贫的复杂性和系统性要求政策保持连贯性，实现精准与稳定的统一。

以科技创新推动农业提质增效。发展农业对于农村贫困人口摆脱贫困具有重要意义。在生产方面，缅甸、老挝可以借助国际合作加强农田基础设施建设，积极开展农田防护与生态环境保护，提升农田输配电等基础设施水平。在农业技术领域，对于越南、印尼和泰国等易受气候变化影响的国家，推广应用节水农业技术，提高农业用水效率，以适应气候变化，引导缺水地区联合开展节水技术攻关，推动建设节水农业技术示范与推广基地。在科技合作方面，越南已率先与中国开展种质资源合作，共建农作物优良品种试验站，通过引进高产优质品种，提升种业发展水平。其他东盟成员国可抓住"一带一路"倡议、《区域全面经济伙伴关系协定》（RCEP）等发展机遇，在农业科技合作领域继续开展务实有效的探索，增强本区域粮食生产能力。在区域粮食安全方面，东盟应增强粮食安全生产能力，加强大米紧急储备与释放合作，提高粮食应急的管理水平和应对能力。此外，东盟各成员国应进一步鼓励科研机构进行跨国合作，尤其是加大研究能力、绿色农业、数字农业和可持续发展等领域的合作。

改善教育和营养困境，重视平等发展机会。发展是解决一切问题的关键。尽管经济增长能够通过"涓滴效应"缓解贫困，但忽视发展机会平等问题，将降低减贫成效。东盟国家发展全面包容社会保障的同时，应推进城市化进程，制定更具有包容性的发展政策，缩小城乡之间收入差距，使生活在农村和城市的人口拥有平等发展的机会。在教育方面，东盟国家，尤其是经济增速较快的国家，比如泰国和越南，可以加大对职业技术教育的关注，特别是数字经济领域，以数字素养框架推动数字化人才培养，强化数字时代人才储备。同时，对于贫困地区适龄儿童要加强教育投资，尤其是加强对低收入国家和地区贫困儿童的营养关注，可通过政府提供营养加餐等方式，确保消除营养不良，提升贫困人口负担健康饮食的能力。在医疗方面，东盟国家经济发展水平差异较大，可进一步推动区域内医疗卫生合作，尤其是不同发展水平区域间的合作与支持，以包容性原则推进东盟国家缩小内部医疗和教育水平差异，增强区域发展韧性。

发展数字经济，提升经济韧性水平。发展是消除贫困的根本和保障。目前部分东盟国家出现返贫问题，应当寻求高质量有韧性的发展，增强抵御风险的能力。疫情改变了人们的生活方式，数字经济快速发展。数字化转型有利于创造和积累社会财富，发展数字经济是当前东盟增强经济韧性，实现高质量发展的应有之义。加速东盟减贫进程，推动东盟各成员国数字发展与合作，将东盟建设成为由安全和变革性的数字服务、技术和生态系统所驱动的领先数字社区和经济体。提升东盟各成员国固定和移动宽带基础设施质量并扩大其覆盖范围，提供值得信赖的数字服务，创建有竞争力的数字服务市场，提升电子政务服务质量并扩大其使用，提供连接商业的数字服务并促进跨境贸易，提高企业和民众参与数字经济的能力，建成具有包容性的数字社会。为中小微企业、未充分就业青年、农村和偏远地区青年提供数据工具和数字技能培训，让发展机会惠及更多的人。

加强与周边国家合作，共同应对气候挑战。应对气候变化需要东盟区域内各国共同努力，加强与周边国家，尤其是新兴国家经济体的合作，这有助于东盟成员国借鉴成功经验，提升应对气候变化能力，减少极端气候对粮食安全和经济发展的风险和不确定性，探索构建生态价值实现的市场机制。对于柬埔寨和缅甸等气候脆弱的低收入国家，可以借助绿色气候基金、全球环境基金等的发展援助，提升应对气候变化的能力。

三、中国—东盟减贫合作总体概况

当前，世界经济复苏乏力，通货膨胀、粮食和能源安全等问题复杂严峻，全球面临诸多挑战。面对复杂的国际形势，中国与东盟国家相互尊重、守望相助，中国—东盟全面战略伙伴关系发展势头良好，树立了地区合作共赢的典范。

东盟是中国重要的国际政治和经济力量之一。2020年中国和东盟互为第一大贸易合作伙伴，2021年中国和东盟的双边关系又进一步提升为全面战略合作伙伴关系。中国—东盟自贸区的建立促使双边农产品贸易频繁往来和快速增长，增强了双方经济发展的相互依赖性，而推进区域经济合作则是发展全球伙伴关系和构建新型国际关系的重要内容[①]。同时，作为松散型的国际组织，东盟各国中有三个国家是中国的陆上邻国，四个国家与中国隔海相望，区域内各国发展水平多样化，资源条件和制度环境不尽相同，而中国通过"一带一路"倡议推动与东盟的合作是有针对性、有区别地与各成员国协商达成一致的[②]。

中国持续加大对东盟援助。进入21世纪后，中国对东盟国家的国际援助总体不断上升，特别是在基础建设、减贫减灾、人力资源开发合作等多方面取得新进展，其中，2016年中国对东盟地区援助的总体规模大幅提升至115.8亿美

① 刘中伟.东亚生产网络、全球价值链整合与东亚区域合作的新走向［J］.当代亚太，2014（4）：126–156，160；钟飞腾.新冠疫情与东南亚经济的U形复苏：一种国际政治经济学的分析［J］.东南亚研究，2020（5）：1–23，154；孙伊然，何曜，黎兵."入世"20年中国经济安全观的演进逻辑［J］.世界经济研究，2021（12）：42–53，132–133.
② 邓启明，刘亚楠，伍湘陵."一带一路"背景下深化中国—东盟合作研究：面临问题与实现路径［J］.福建论坛（人文社会科学版），2018（12）：195–200.

元，较上年增长8倍多[①]。2017年，东亚减贫示范合作技术援助项目在老挝、柬埔寨和缅甸落地试点，首期项目金额为1亿元人民币[②]。近六年来，中国在菲律宾承包工程新签合同额增长近3倍，年度规模突破100亿美元[③]。中国企业积极参与菲律宾路桥、港口、电站、住房、水利等领域工程项目建设，建设了菲律宾最大的电站项目，在建最大的光伏机组。此外，中国还援助了柬埔寨国家交通干线金边至暹粒6号公路以及东南亚最大的光伏项目"越南油汀500兆瓦光伏电厂"等东盟基础设施的建设。

专栏4-1　中国援助东盟的项目成果

雅万高铁助力印尼社会发展[a, b]

雅万高铁是东南亚的第一条高铁，也是中国高铁全方位走出去的第一单项目。它连接印尼雅加达和万隆两大城市，全长约142公里，最高设计时速350公里，将两地间的旅行时间缩短至40分钟。2023年5月，雅万高铁启动联调联试，朝着全线开通运营迈出重要步伐，为印尼加快发展注入新的动力。目前，雅万高铁累计为印尼当地带来5.1万人次就业，开通运营后，每年将为相关配套产业创造3万个就业岗位，成为改善民生的幸福之路。

中老铁路为老挝旅游业注入活力[c, d]

2021年12月3日，中老铁路正式开通，这是中国和老挝两国互联互通共同发展的新通道。截至2022年12月，中老铁路累计发送旅客850万人次，其中中国段720万人次、老挝段130万人次；发送货物1120万吨，其中跨境货物超190万吨。不仅如此，中老铁路还带动了当地的就业。自从铁路开行以来，累计招聘老挝员工3500多人，在物流、交通、商贸、旅游等行业间接增加就业岗位10万余个。老挝驻上海总领事馆领事表示，中老铁路的开通改变了老挝北部地区的出行方式，对贸易、人文交流、运输有所促进，是推动老挝社会经济发展和人力资源提升的重要力量。

柬埔寨进入"高速公路时代"[e, f]

2022年10月1日，柬埔寨第一条高速公路——金港高速正式通车。金港高速是柬中合作以及"一带一路"框架下的重要成果，公路总长187公

---

① 参见AidData数据库。
② 参见https://www.gov.cn/xinwen/2016-10/18/content_5120623.htm。
③ 参见《区域全面经济伙伴关系协定》。

里，耗资20亿美元。建设期间，项目坚持合作共赢理念，持续打造属地化供应链，从柬埔寨当地采购建筑物资、设备及服务，累计金额超过2.46亿美元；大力推行属地化用工，高峰时期当地员工占比超过82.3%，累计带动当地1.1万余人就业。2023年6月，柬埔寨第二条高速公路——金巴高速正式开工。项目建设期内，预计将直接雇佣5000余名柬埔寨员工，为当地累计创造近1万个就业岗位。在50年的运营期内，项目将每年为柬埔寨提供1000余个就业机会。高速公路的建设和运营推动了柬埔寨经济的发展，同时提高了当地员工的专业素养，促进了柬埔寨基建行业的技术进步。

资料来源：

a. 中国一带一路网，"雅万高铁开始试联试调"，2023年5月23日。

b. 人民网，"雅万高铁：擦亮中国高铁'金名片'"，2022年12月7日。

c. 中国政府网，"中老铁路开通一年交出客货齐旺'成绩单'"，2022年12月2日。

d. 根据2023年5月25日外交部发言人毛宁主持例行记者会上的发言整理。

e. RCEP区域全面经济伙伴关系网站，"中企投建的柬埔寨金巴高速公路开关建设"，2023年6月8日。

f. 国务院国有资产监督管理委员会，"中交集团投建的柬埔寨首条高速公路建成通车"，2022年10月9日。

新形势下双方拓展合作领域。长期以来，中国积极在各领域与东盟国家开展合作，重点向东盟低收入国家提供经济技术援助，支持东盟缩小内部差距。面对新的国际形势，双方在制造业、农业、基础设施、高新技术、数字经济等领域投资合作稳步拓展。第19届中国—东盟博览会上，中国与东盟各国现场共签订投资合作项目267个，总投资4130亿元人民币，项目涉及高端金属新材料、绿色环保、轻工纺织、大健康和文旅体育、绿色化工新材料、机械装备制造等产业。截至2021年，中国已为东盟国家举办800余期农业技术培训班，在柬埔寨和老挝建设了农业合作示范区，在越南、老挝、柬埔寨、印尼、缅甸等国实施了农作物优良品种试验站项目[①]。此外，双方在智慧城市、5G、人工智能、电子商务、大数据、区块链、远程医疗等领域也推出了多个合作项目，打造了系列数字化应用创新场景，并共享数字化防疫抗疫解决方案。

中国与东盟共建共同繁荣之路。2023年是"一带一路"倡议提出十周年。十年来，中国对东盟的援助既有雅万高铁、中老铁路、柬埔寨高速和中缅新通道等为地区发展赋能的基建项目，还有聚焦民生的"小而美"项目，提升了区

---

① 参见https://www.mfa.gov.cn/web/wjbxw_673019/202201/t20220105_10479078.shtml。

域内民众获得感和幸福感。截至2023年，中国与东盟成员国均已签署多项共建"一带一路"合作文件。中方近十年在中国—东盟领导人会议上提出重要合作倡议160多项，落实率超过99.5%。中国推动"一带一路"倡议与印尼"全球海洋支点"构想、越南"两廊一圈"、泰国"4.0战略"、柬埔寨"四角战略"等进行战略对接，进一步释放了政策红利。

专栏4-2 "小而美"项目助力东盟国家减贫[a、b]

共建"一带一路"的许多"小而美"项目想当地民众所想、急当地民众所急，接地气、聚人心，有效提升了相关国家民生水平，成为快速提升共建国家民众获得感的重要途径。

喝到干净的水，每天洗澡，这对于以前的柬埔寨民众来说是一个奢侈的梦。2017年，中国援柬埔寨乡村供水项目首期工程开工建设，为柬埔寨六个省新建了846口深水井、近80座社区池塘。2019年，该项目二期工程开始施工，为柬埔寨10个省援建54座社区池塘、964口深水井。中国援柬埔寨乡村供水项目有效解决了当地村民的饮用及生产用水问题，加速了柬埔寨农村减贫进程。

老挝南塔省省立中学位于老挝北部，共有师生2000多人，是南塔省唯一的省立中学。长期以来，学校师生一直被生活污水排放问题所困扰。2018年，中国向该中学捐赠了一套日处理50吨的一体化污水处理装置，并配套建设污水收集系统和中水回用系统。这不仅解决了污水乱排问题，还满足了绿化使用等需求，在校园内实现了雨污分流，切实提升了该校及周边社区污水处理能力。

资料来源：

a. 中国政府网，"聚焦'小而美'促进'心联通'民生工程提升共建'一带一路'国家民众获得感"，2022年1月23日。

b. 中国—东盟环境保护合作中心，"这十年·中国—东盟环境合作：以人民为中心 共建美丽家园"，2022年10月14日。

（一）分享减贫经验

中国减贫经验对东盟发展中国家具有积极作用。中国同东盟多次举办论坛等交流活动，共享减贫经验。2007年10月，首届中国—东盟社会发展与减贫论坛在中国南宁召开，截至2023年，该论坛已成功举办17届（见表4-1）。2005~2020年，中国积极向东盟国家开展减贫培训，共举办了包括澜湄减贫合作能力提升项目研修班在内的54期研修班。此外，中国自2014年起在老挝、柬埔寨、缅甸开展六个东亚减贫示范合作项目，被誉为"减贫合作的标杆"[①]。2019年，泰国学习中国精准扶贫经验，实施"结对子"项目并取得显著成效。2022年11月，澜湄合作减贫联合工作组第六次会议以线上形式召开，各国代表讨论并通过了《澜湄减贫合作指南（2023—2027）》，旨在为促进澜湄区域合作、实现共同发展作出积极贡献。

表4-1　　　历届中国—东盟社会发展与减贫论坛及相关主题

届次	时间	地点	主题
第17届	2023年6月26日~29日	中国广西北海	深化区域合作，促进减贫与乡村发展
第16届	2022年6月28日~7月1日	线上	加强减贫交流，共建繁荣家园
第15届	2021年6月22日	线上	乡村发展与可持续减贫
第14届	2020年7月29日	线上	携手抗击新冠疫情，共同推进减贫进程
第13届	2019年6月26~28日	中国广西南宁	面向联合国可持续发展目标的中国—东盟减贫合作
第12届	2018年6月27~29日	菲律宾马尼拉	深化减贫伙伴关系，构建中国—东盟命运共同体
第11届	2017年7月25~27日	柬埔寨暹粒	中国与东盟：减贫创新与实践
第10届	2016年6月22~24日	中国广西桂林	"一带一路"与中国东盟减贫合作
第9届	2015年7月28~30日	老挝万象	金融创新与减贫
第8届	2014年8月7~9日	缅甸内比都	深化中国—东盟区域减贫合作
第7届	2013年8月21~23日	中国广西防城港	城镇化进程中的减贫与包容性发展
第6届	2012年9月26~27日	中国广西柳州	中国与东盟：包容性发展与减贫
第5届	2011年9月14~16日	印尼雅加达	增长的质量与减贫
第4届	2010年7月13~15日	中国广西桂林	自由贸易与减贫
第3届	2009年9月28~30日	越南河内	全球经济放缓对亚太地区贫困及可持续发展的影响
第2届	2008年11月4~6日	中国广西南宁	为实现千年发展目标、提高食品安全，以及抵御自然灾害的区域合作
第1届	2007年10月30日~11月2日	中国广西南宁	参与和推进区域社会发展与减贫交流合作

[①]　参见中国外交部发布的《中国—东盟合作事实与数据：1991—2021》。

中国—老挝减贫合作社区示范项目[a]

　　老挝万象市金花村是中国—老挝减贫合作社区示范项目中的一个示范村。过去，金花村还是一个默默无闻的贫困小村庄。2016年，该项目在金花村落地实施，瞄准金花村的实际情况和发展需求，因地制宜，开展了大棚有机蔬菜和有机水稻的种植，并提供技术培训，还为当地建设了村级活动中心。该项目的实施改善了金花村公共服务设施，群众生产生活条件明显提高。现在，金花村已经成为小有名气的蔬菜基地，吸引了大批经销商到村里采购蔬菜，打造出了自己的特色产业、支柱产业和致富产业。中国—老挝减贫合作社区示范项目的实施效果得到了老挝各级政府和当地群众的认可和好评，引起广泛反响。

泰国借鉴中国扶贫模式，改善自身减贫道路[b,c]

　　2001年，泰国政府借鉴中国扶贫经验，启动"一村一品"计划，推广传统手工艺品和特色农产品。截至2020年底，该计划已覆盖全国5000多个乡，至少120万农户从事相关的手工业和工业活动。为了推动农业生产，泰国政府从2007年开始推行"农村基金"计划，全国7万多个村庄都能获得约100万泰铢的发展基金。2019年孔敬府官员还专门赴中国参观学习脱贫经验，返回泰国后制定了符合当地实际的"结对子扶贫"项目。截至2020年10月，已有79%贫困户减贫，未来将全部摆脱人均年收入38000泰铢的贫困线。泰国内政部官员表示，该模式全面成功后，将在全泰国推广。

资料来源：

a.中国国际扶贫中心，《澜湄合作减贫示范项目专题》，2021年4月14日。

b.人民网，"泰国借鉴中国扶贫模式取得显著成效"，2020年11月19日。

c.人民网，"泰国加快扶贫步伐"，2020年12月11日。

（二）强化经贸往来

　　中国和东盟持续推进经贸合作。近年来，中国与东盟互为最大贸易伙伴，2022年双方的进出口规模达到6.52万亿元人民币，同比增长15%[①]。中国与东盟都是彼此农产品贸易的重要市场。从中国农产品贸易角度而言，2010~2019年伴随着贸易总量在总体上的增长，中国与东盟农产品贸易占中国农产品贸易比

---

① 参见东盟使团经商处2023年1月13日发布的"贸易快报|2022年中国—东盟贸易增长强劲"。

重始终保持在15%左右，且多数年份有所上升；从不同的贸易方向来看，在出口端，中国对东盟的农产品出口绝对量始终呈现上升趋势，同时占比也有较大幅度的提升，由2010年的15.26%上升到2019年的23.67%，上涨了至少8个百分点；在进口方面，中国对东盟的农产品进口贸易在2012~2017年呈现长期波动，2011~2013年出现了小幅下滑，2014~2019年始终保持在12%~14%（见图4-1）。

图4-1 2010~2019年中国与东盟农产品贸易占中国农产品贸易的比重

数据来源：联合国商品贸易委员会（UN Comtrade），经计算得到。

2010~2019年中国与东盟农产品贸易在东盟农产品贸易中的占比保持在10%~20%。随着农产品贸易总量的增长，其比重由2010年的10.95%上升至2019年的15.97%，上升了约5个百分点，但在2015~2017年有所下降，这与总量变化不完全一致；而出口的比重由2010年的10.45%上升到14.96%，上升了约4.5个百分点；进口的比重由2010年的11.76%上升到17.28%，上升约5.5个百分点（见图4-2）。

图4-2 2010~2019年中国与东盟农产品贸易占东盟农产品贸易的比重

数据来源：联合国商品贸易委员会（UN Comtrade），经计算得到。

（三）共同应对疫情等挑战

携手抗疫，共渡难关。卫生领域一直是中国—东盟合作中的重要领域，自2003年"非典"（SARS）防控合作至今，双方卫生合作稳步发展。疫情发生以来，中国与东盟国家树立了全球抗疫合作的典范，通过加强信息共享、卫生保障和应急响应，促进知识共享及人才培养。疫情期间，中国积极向东盟国家提供疫苗和抗疫物资，并派遣医疗专家团队支援。2020年3月，中国向东盟国家派遣的第一支抗疫医疗队抵达柬埔寨。2021年11月，习近平主席在中国—东盟建立对话关系30周年纪念峰会上宣布，中国将再向东盟国家提供1.5亿剂新冠疫苗无偿援助，再向东盟抗疫基金追加500万美元[1]。此外，中国还承诺自2022年起的三年内向东盟提供15亿美元发展援助，支持东盟抗击疫情及经济复苏。截至2022年，中国已向东盟国家提供超过6亿剂疫苗[2]。

---

[1] 参见https://www.gov.cn/xinwen/2021-11/24/content_5653227.htm。

[2] 参见https://www.yidaiyilu.gov.cn/xwzx/hwxw/270234.htm。

专栏4-4 中国与东盟国家携手抗疫

中国援缅战疫赓续千年"胞波"情谊[a, b]

2020年4月8日,中国政府向缅甸派遣了由国家卫生健康委员会和云南省组建的抗疫医疗专家组,一行12人。同时,向缅甸捐赠了价值434万元人民币的抗疫物资,帮助缅甸抗击疫情。在缅甸期间,专家组分赴仰光和曼德勒,深入两地医院、实验室等40余处开展专题培训和技术指导60余场,与缅甸医疗机构和专家开展经验分享与交流,介绍中国抗疫经验,结合缅方防疫措施和诊疗流程,对缅方病例筛查、传染病防控、病例管理、临床诊疗、社区健康管理和实验室工作等提供指导与咨询。据不完全统计,2020年中国政府、地方政府、驻缅机构等共向缅捐赠835万个口罩,9.3万套防护服,4.1万套隔离衣,18万副医用手套,12.8万个隔离面罩,3471个测温仪,17套成像测温设备,3.8万份检测试剂,35台呼吸机,以及救护车、空调、风扇、床垫、移动厕所等防疫用物资。

中国援助老挝抗击新冠疫情[c]

新冠疫情发生后中国政府及时派出抗疫医疗专家组。2020年3月29日,携带价值417万元人民币医疗物资的中国抗疫医疗专家组抵达万象,通过两周工作,因地制宜协助老挝形成了从外防输入到内防扩散的一整套方案,提高了老挝防控的科学化、规范化水平。同年4月24日,中国人民解放军援老抗疫医疗专家组一行五人抵达万象开展指导工作,并向老挝捐赠了检测试剂、防护服、口罩等抗疫物资。

中国帮助泰国共建疫苗屏障[d]

截至2022年6月,中国共向泰国提供5085万剂疫苗,其中335万剂为无偿援助,帮助泰国建立起有效疫苗屏障。同时,据不完全统计,中国已向泰国提供口罩342.6万个、防护服79400套、检测试剂176000人份、医用手套10.4万副、医用护目镜12000副以及医用防护鞋30000双。

资料来源:

a. 云南省人民政府,"中国赴缅甸抗疫医疗专家组完成任务回国",2020年4月23日。

b. 中华人民共和国商务部,《对外投资合作国别(地区)指南:缅甸(2022年版)》。

c. 中华人民共和国商务部,《对外投资合作国别(地区)指南:老挝(2022年版)》。

d. 中华人民共和国商务部,《对外投资合作国别(地区)指南:泰国(2022年版)》。

（四）提升抗灾能力

开展务实合作，共同提升自然灾害防治能力。中国对东盟的救援目标包括自然灾害和社会性灾害，但以自然灾害救援为主，其中印尼、柬埔寨、缅甸、老挝、菲律宾是中国重点救助的对象。中国先后在老挝、缅甸、泰国、柬埔寨等国开展地震台网项目建设，有力提升当地地震灾害监测预警水平。中国还派遣国际救援队两次赴印尼开展人道主义救援行动，帮助缅甸震后古迹修复，向菲律宾提供100万美元的震后紧急援助等。自2016年起，中国与东盟共同举办了四次灾害管理研讨会、两次科技创新与台风灾害应对研讨会、一次减轻灾害风险管理研讨会和一次减灾与应急管理高官论坛。2021年，双方设立灾害管理部长级会议机制①；10月14日，首届中国—东盟灾害管理部长级会议通过视频方式举行，批准了《中国—东盟灾害管理工作计划（2021—2025）》，并发表了联合声明。

（五）科技合作减贫

加大科技合作，助力实现科技减贫。在技术转移合作方面，中国已和文莱、柬埔寨、印尼、老挝、马来西亚、缅甸、菲律宾、泰国、越南九个东盟国家分别建立了政府间双边技术转移工作机制，构建了覆盖东盟十国的技术转移协作网络，成员数已超过2800家，并推动建立了中国—东盟传统药物研究联合实验室、国际岩溶研究中心等15个联合实验室和研究中心，促进了双方研究机构间长期稳定合作。在科技人文交流方面，广西通过举办"10+3青年科学家论坛"、组织东盟杰出青年科学家"创新中国行"、举办中国—东盟技术经理人国际培训班和专项技术培训班等活动，累计培训东盟国家技术和科技管理骨干1300多名。2021年，中国提出启动科技创新提升计划，并发布了《中国—东盟建设面向未来更加紧密的科技创新伙伴关系行动计划（2021—2025）》②，包括建设农业合作示范区和实施农作物优良品种试验站等项目。中国农业植保无人机助力泰国农业发展，中菲农业技术中心推广商业化杂交水稻51.44万公顷，促进粮食增收48.21亿公斤等③。

1. 国家层面的农业科技合作框架

党的十九大报告提出，加快建设创新型国家，推动形成全面开放新格局，要以"一带一路"建设为重点，加强创新能力开放合作。2012年，中国科技

---

① 参见https://www.mfa.gov.cn/web/wjbxw_673019/202201/t20220105_10479078.shtml。
② 同上。
③ 参见https://www.yidaiyilu.gov.cn/xwzx/hwxw/271921.htm。

部启动首届中国—东盟科技部长会议、中国—东盟科技伙伴计划和首届中国—东盟技术转移与创新合作大会等重大会议和活动。其中，中国—东盟科技伙伴计划提出了中国和东盟国家将开展深入合作的十个重点技术领域，包括政策咨询、技术服务、人力资源开发、合作研究、建设中国—东盟技术转移平台网络等。中国—东盟次区域合作机制包括大湄公河次区域合作机制（GMS）、中老缅泰"黄金四角"计划、澜沧江—湄公河合作机制和泛北部湾经济圈构想[①]。

> ### 专栏4-5 中国—东盟科技合作案例
>
> #### 中国—老挝合作农作物优良品种试验站[a]
>
> 2013年，中国在东盟建设的第一个农作物优良品种试验站——中国—老挝合作农作物优良品种试验站开始运行。该试验站占地40公顷，集农作物新品种试验和示范、新技术推广以及农业培训于一体，能为老挝农业新技术新品种的推广应用提供有力支持。该试验站已试种300多个农作物品种，并从中筛选出适合老挝种植的优良品种67个。这些优良品种在当地推广应用后，产量显著提高。例如，已在万象、占巴塞、沙耶武里等多地推广应用的杂交玉米品种LC188，平均产量为6.26吨/公顷，高于当地的平均产量5.29吨/公顷，增产达18.3%。
>
> #### 中国农业无人机助力泰国农业发展[b]
>
> 农业在泰国经济发展中占有举足轻重的地位，近半数人口从事农业相关工作。近年来，由于农业人口结构调整、老龄化加剧、劳动力成本增加等原因，泰国对现代农业机械的需求快速增长。中国农业植保无人机针对当地核心作业场景不断优化功能，持续为泰国现代农业的发展提供"加速度"。当地居民表示，"使用无人机能帮农民提高工作效率。用人工喷洒农药一天不超过10莱（折合24亩）稻田，用无人机每天能喷洒40~50莱地"。
>
> 资料来源：
> a.中国国际扶贫中心，"农业技术合作结出丰硕成果"，2023年3月31日。
> b.中国一带一路网，"中国农业无人机助力泰国农业发展"，2022年8月11日。

---

① 全毅，尹竹.中国—东盟区域、次区域合作机制与合作模式创新［J］.东南亚研究，2017（6）：15-36，152-153.

在2013年提出"一带一路"倡议之后，中国分别与东盟各国进一步加强了农业科技合作双边对话机制。目前，中国与泰国、越南、菲律宾、马来西亚、缅甸和老挝均已签订农业科技合作协定，并成立农业科技合作联合委员会，形成了多边和双边较为系统完整的农业科技合作机制框架，共建多个国家级联合实验室和技术转移中心。2016年，澜沧江—湄公河领导人首次会议召开，拟设立农业科技合作基金。2017年，"一带一路"倡议国际合作北京峰会启动"一带一路"科技创新行动计划，设立生态环保大数据服务平台等。2019年3月，国家发展和改革委员会印发了《关于支持云南省加快建设面向南亚东南亚辐射中心的政策措施》，中国（云南）与周边国家农业合作、经贸合作是其中的重要内容。

2. 以省级及地方为主的区域合作机制

2014年，广西东盟技术转移中心获批成立，成为推动中国与东盟国家技术需求对接及创新合作的重要载体之一。中国科技部和广西壮族自治区人民政府在中国—东盟博览会框架下主办的中国—东盟技术转移与创新合作大会已成为常态化重要高层论坛，目前已与东盟各国形成覆盖全面的创新网络，落实了双边技术转移合作机制，促进了众多合作项目。2017年，南亚东南亚农业科技辐射中心是由云南省农业科学院倡议，对南亚东南亚国家和地区农业科技交流、合作、创新感兴趣的涉农科研、教育机构及企业等自愿加入并共同发起成立的非政府、非营利的开放性、国际化的合作平台，目前已与40多个国家的相关机构和20多个国际组织建立了长期、稳定的合作关系，尤其与南亚、东南亚国家农业科技合作形成了优势和特色，搭建了大湄公河次区域农业科技交流合作组、中国—南亚农业科技交流合作组等平台，确立了主导地位。然而，该中心的技术输出依托于云南省农业科学院及其下属科研院所，以农业学科向海外扩散技术，合作程度及影响力有限，仍未能在农业区域一体化中形成较强的影响力和辐射效应，缺少"引进来"与"走出去"并重、有针对性地开展创新、主动服务农业"走出去"战略的职责职能[1]。相比云南和广西两地集中于东盟农业科技合作领域，国内发达省份的国际农业科技合作项目以东欧、中东欧、南亚、欧美地区为主[2]。

---

[1]　陈利君.云南省加快建设面向南亚东南亚辐射中心的对策思考［J］.昆明理工大学学报（社会科学版），2015，15（6）：17-24.

[2]　王宇．江苏"一带一路"创新合作与技术转移的实践与思考［J］．科技管理研究，2020，40（7）：104-109.

3. 其他层面的农业科技合作项目

虽然东盟各发展中国家的农业产业和农产品贸易发展对当地经济发展起到重要作用，与中国资源优势形成互补，但国内从事农业科技国别研究的高校和科研院所数量较少，在农业科技国际合作平台与人才队伍建设、多部门资源优势发挥等方面，尤其是通过交叉学科研究强化中国农业技术海外扩散的双赢策略方面十分有限[①]。截至目前，国内最大的国际合作项目"绿色超级稻"虽然引入企业进行技术推广，但以科研合作直接输出和培训为主。中国4.7万家规模以上农业龙头企业中，真正走出国门的龙头企业仅有300多家，且以国有企业为主[②]，而云南农业走出去产业技术创新战略联盟也只有40余家企业参与，且多为小型民营企业。中国与东盟各国的农业科技合作以研究为主，但其发展速度相比发达国家的投入规模和合作深度有待加强。

---

① 倪国华，张璟，郑风田. 对农业"走出去"战略的认识［J］.世界农业，2014（4）：15-18.

② 仇焕广，陈瑞剑，廖绍攀，蔡亚庆.中国农业企业"走出去"的现状、问题与对策［J］.农业经济问题，2013（11）：44-50；王芳，王静，赵文.在开放的视野下再探中国农业"走出去"［J］.世界农业，2014（11）：160-164.

第五章
东盟减贫发展展望

近年来，东盟各国结合自身发展情况制定了减贫目标。印尼政府希望通过向贫困家庭提供援助和发展农村数字经济等措施，计划在2024年将全国贫困率控制在10%以下，并消除所有极端贫困。马来西亚政府明确表示在未来的工作中会持续关注低收入人群，减小区域发展差距。泰国在《第十三个国民经济和社会发展五年计划（2023—2027年）》中指出，要基于"不让任何人掉队"的原则，解决长期贫困和代际贫困。越南明确了在未来五年使绝对贫困发生率年均下降1%~1.5%。菲律宾政府专门为减贫计划的实施成立反贫困委员会，预计在2023年将贫困率降低至16.2%左右，到2028年逐步降至8.9%左右。柬埔寨政府启动了一系列综合计划改善农村经济活动及基础设施，在2023年使全国贫困率降至10%以下。老挝政府承诺在2025年成功帮助20多万个老挝家庭和3104个村（占村总数约36%）实现减贫。缅甸政府在《缅甸可持续发展规划（2018—2030）》中指出要造一个有利的环境，通过包括农业、工业和多元文化的实践来支持多样化和生产性的经济，作为减少农村地区贫穷的基础。

一、减贫与发展面临的机遇

一是疫后东盟国家经济强劲复苏。国际社会对东盟区域经济总体看好。不同国际机构均预测，疫后东盟国家经济强劲复苏。而且，亚洲地区新兴经济体和发展中国家消费品价格持续稳定，通货膨胀指数预计维持在3%左右，反映出包括东盟在内的区域经济韧性和复苏形势向好。比如，越南受益于其在全球供应链中不断提升的重要性，而旅游业的改善将加速柬埔寨和泰国经济发展。

二是贸易投资自由化便利化，提升东盟国家贸易和投资潜力。当今世界经济充满不确定性，而中国—东盟经济日益紧密合作，特别是随着综合性合作机制的建立和完善，如共建"一带一路"、中国—东盟自贸区、《区域全面经济伙伴关系协定》（RCEP）等，中国—东盟贸易自由化便利化水平不断提高，为亚太地区经济增长注入了稳定力量。

三是数字经济成为东盟未来重要的经济增长方向。RCEP中有关电子商务的部分首次就跨境信息传输及数据本地化等议题达成共识，为区域内电子商务合作提供制度保障。农产品跨境电商等贸易新业态将迎来发展新机遇。中国和东盟积极推动RCEP跨境电商行业商协会的对接，中老铁路正探索"澜湄快线＋跨境电商"等发展模式，预计跨境电商等新业态新模式将进一步拓展区域内农业贸易发展空间。

四是区域内合作加强，为东盟减贫提供支持。中国打赢脱贫攻坚战，提前10年实现联合国2030年可持续发展议程减贫目标，为全球减贫事业发展和人类进步作出重大贡献。中国减贫的实践和经验提振了广大发展中国家消除绝对贫困的决心。中国同东盟多次举办论坛等交流活动，中国减贫经验为东盟发展中国家提供了借鉴。

二、减贫与发展面临的挑战

东盟国家也面临着一些挑战。一是区域内经济发展水平差异大，影响地区减贫效果。东盟国家内经济发展水平差异大，加之疫情等多重因素影响，减贫与发展仍面临不确定性。二是国际环境不稳定，影响东盟内新兴经济体和发展中国家经济发展，经济韧性需要增强。全球粮食和能源价格飙升、各国货币对美元下跌以及产出缺口缩小等风险增加了多维减贫难度。三是数字基础设施相对落后，数字鸿沟和人才缺乏影响东盟数字经济的减贫收益。地区发展不协调可能使部分国家难以通过数字技术推动经济增长，全球企业竞争不平等和个体机会不均等可能进一步降低贫困人口减贫的可能性，增强脆弱人群返贫风险。四是气候变化对发展中国家经济转型提出挑战。五是仍需要持续推动性别平等和女性赋权。部分东盟国家女性获得资产、服务和资源的机会还不均等，需要持续推动性别平等和女性赋权。

三、东盟未来减贫重点

区域内减贫协同发展。东盟各国经济发展和贫困水平相差较大，东盟区域内各国应根据当地情况，着力加强能够解决多重不平等且有助于缩小区域差异的干预措施。冲突和不安全仍是粮食危机和粮食不安全的主要驱动因素，实现区域内减贫协同发展是降低系统性风险和实现共同发展的重要内容。

聚焦农业现代化产业。农业粮食体系是主要就业部门。农业产业发展不仅事关粮食安全，也是东盟国家就业和贸易的重要产业，同时也是持续推动性别平等和女性赋权的重要领域。加快推动各国农业产业现代化，构建大食物观系统，有助于推动各国加快实现经济增长、粮食安全和营养健康等多重可持续发展目标。

利用数字化手段减贫。在第四次工业革命迅猛发展的背景下，数字经济是各国支持经济发展和转型升级的新引擎。东盟是全世界互联网发展最快的地区，且人口结构年轻化，数字化生活需求潜力巨大。疫情加快了东盟市场用户行为模式的转变，充分利用数字经济为更多群体和中小企业创造减贫致富机会有助于推动东盟国家的减贫工作。

进一步加强南南合作。虽然东盟国家已经取得较好的减贫进展，但面对当前复杂的国际环境和气候变化带来的不确定性，需要持续加强南南合作，分享减贫经验，在巩固现有减贫成果的基础上，防止发生大规模返贫，加快推进区域内经济可持续性和包容性增长目标。

四、东盟未来减贫合作与展望

一是持续加强减贫经验分享。包括中国在内的发展中国家与东盟在减贫方面存在很多相似的经验，如快速的经济增长和社会转型使很多人摆脱了贫困，而在不平等和农业部门缺乏增长等方面也面临相似的挑战。中国的经验为东盟国家减贫战略的设计和实施提供了经验，通过进一步的交流合作，可促进减贫机制和政策设计沟通、减贫方式方法分享以及减贫策略选择等领域的经验分享。

二是合作实施减贫与发展项目。近年来，中国与东盟有关国家在共建"一带一路"中支持建设的"小而美"民生项目，有效提升了相关国家民众的谋生技能、生产生活条件，以小产业带动减贫事业发展。对于区域内发展差异情况不同的多个发展中国家而言，通过加强统筹谋划，充分利用有限的优势资源，发挥"小而美"项目援外资金四两拨千斤作用，形成更多接地气、聚人心的项目。

三是加强减贫能力建设合作。强化东盟区域内贸易往来，提高区域内价值链参与度。完善交通运输网络，促进东盟成员间互联互通；利用RCEP机遇优化营商环境，吸引其他成员国投资；加强基础设施建设，提升贸易便利度；降低市场准入门槛，为外企提供更多机会；提升政府治理水平与公共部门服务能力。数字经济迅猛发展，文化教育和职业培训国际合作为东盟减贫提供了内生动力。推动东盟数字基础设施建设，提升数字经济对东盟地区经济发展的支撑能力，逐步消除数字鸿沟。发挥数字经济带动就业的功能，大力拓宽就业渠道。通过数字经济让贫困群体实现创业增收，摆脱贫困。提升人力资本水平，在推动数字经济的同时，加强对贫困群体的职业技能培训，实现自我发展。充分发挥中国—东盟数字经济合作机制的作用，促进相对落后国家的数字能力建设。积极推动中国—东盟数字经济人才交流，充分利用中国—东盟科技创新提升计划，有针对性地选择来华交流的东盟青年科学家，建立更加紧密的科技创新伙伴关系。

四是推动构建更加紧密的中国—东盟命运共同体。中国和东盟国家高层交往密切，全面战略合作内涵更加丰富，有力促进了地区共同发展。深化中国—东盟卫生健康领域的合作，升级完善多边卫生合作机制。以实施《中国—东盟全面战略伙伴关系行动计划》为契机，推动务实合作提质增效。推动"一带一路"倡议、RCEP合作机制与印尼"全球海洋支点"构想、越南"两廊一圈"、泰国"4.0战略"、柬埔寨"四角战略"等进行战略对接，以落实全球发展倡议为契机，推动构建更为紧密的中国—东盟命运共同体，为地区和世界和平稳定、繁荣发展注入新的动力。

附录1
东盟各国主要指标概况

主要指标	文莱	柬埔寨	印度尼西亚	老挝	马来西亚	缅甸	新加坡	菲律宾	泰国	越南	东帝汶
经济类指标[1]											
GDP（现价，10亿美元）	16.7	29.5	1319.1	15.5	407.0	62.3	466.8	404.3	495.4	408.8	3.2
GDP（2017年PPP，10亿美元）	26.3	76.0	3418.9	59.8	963.3	230.3	609.0	991.7	1255.2	1119.0	5.3
人均GDP（现价，美元）	37152	1760	4788	2054	11993	1149	82808	3499	6910	4164	2389
人均GDP（2017年PPP，美元）	58670	4534	12410	7948	28384	4250	108036	8582	17508	11397	3943
农业占比（%）	1.1	22.2	12.4	14.9	8.9	22.3	0.0	9.5	8.8	11.9	10.2
制造业占比（%）	67.9	37.9	41.4	34.1	39.1	38.2	24.2	29.2	35.0	38.3	53.8
服务业占比（%）	32.5	33.9	41.8	40.3	50.9	39.4	70.9	61.2	56.2	41.3	37.2
出口额（现值，10亿美元）	14.4	20.2	323.1	7.8	313.2	16.4	870.8	114.8	325.9	384.2	1.8
进口额（现值，10亿美元）	10.1	16.2	275.7	6.1	283.8	16.3	701.6	178.0	337.4	375.1	1.3
社会发展类指标[2]											
用电人口占比（%）	100	83	99	100	100	72	100	97	100	100	100
基本饮用水覆盖率（%）	100	78	94	85	97	82	100	95	100	98	87
基本卫生覆盖率（%）	99	77	88	80	96	74	100	85	99	92	58
每百人拥有移动电话数量（部）	118	116	115	65	141	107	156	144	176	140	110
固定宽带覆盖率（%）	20.1	3.0	4.9	2.0	12.4	2.1	37.4	7.6	18.5	21.7	0.0
互联网用户占比（%）	98.1	60.2	62.1	62.0	96.8	44.0	96.9	52.7	85.3	74.2	39.5
温室气体总排放量（CO_2，千吨）	9588	18653	563197	19179	245139	33875	43705	133471	265479	355323	446

续表

主要指标	文莱	柬埔寨	印度尼西亚	老挝	马来西亚	缅甸	新加坡	菲律宾	泰国	越南	东帝汶
人类发展指数指标[3]											
预期寿命（岁）	74.6	69.6	67.6	68.1	74.9	65.7	69.3	82.8	78.7	73.6	67.7
预期教育年限（年）	14.0	11.5	13.7	10.1	13.3	10.9	13.1	16.5	15.9	13.0	13.2
受教育年限（年）	9.2	5.1	8.6	5.4	10.6	6.4	9.0	11.9	8.7	8.4	6.0
人均 GNI（2017 年 PPP，美元）	644900	4079	11466	7700	26658	3851	8920	90919	17030	7867	2005
贫困发生率[4]											
每天 2.15 美元的贫困人口比率（2017 年 PPP，%）	—	—	2.5	1.2	0	0.3	0.5	—	0	0.1	28.8
每天 3.65 美元的贫困人口比率（2017 年 PPP，%）	—	—	20.3	33	0	20	18	—	1	4	72.9
每天 6.85 美元的贫困人口比率（2017 年 PPP，%）	—	—	60.5	71	3	68	55	—	12	19	—
多维贫困指数	—	—	3.0	10.3	0.1	—	4.4	—	0.1	1.2	—
不平等指标[4,5]											
基尼系数（%）	—	—	37.9	38.8	41.2	30.7	40.7	—	35.1	36.8	28.7
共享繁荣溢价（%）[5]	—	—	1.0	-1.2	-0.4	8.2	2.2	—	1.2	-0.9	—
人均收入消费中位数年增长率（%）	—	—	2.4	2.2	4.5	7.1	1.9	—	1.5	4.9	—

注：（1）经济类指标为 2022 年数据。其中，老挝和缅甸的进出口数据用 2021 年数据替代。

（2）"用电人口比"和"互联网用户占比"使用 2021 年数据，"温室气体总排放量"使用 2020 年数据，其余指标均为 2022 年数据。其中，老拉"每百人拥有移动电话数量"和"固定宽带覆盖率"采用 2021 年数据替代。

（3）人类发展指数指标使用 2021 年数据。

（4）贫困发生率和不平等指标基于世界银行最新发布的数据：印尼为 2022 年数据，老挝、马来西亚为 2018 年数据，缅甸为 2017 年数据，菲律宾、泰国为 2021 年数据，越南为 2020 年数据。

（5）共享繁荣溢价为"最底层 40% 人口的人均实际调查平均消费或收入年均增长率（%）"和"总人口人均实际调查平均消费或收入年均增长率（%）"之差。

数据来源：经济类指标、社会发展类指标来自世界银行公开数据库（https://data.worldbank.org）及 ASEAN Statical Yearbook 2022，人类发展类指标来自《2022 年全球多维贫困指数》，人类发展报告》，贫困和不平等指标数据来自世界银行贫困与不平等数据平台（Poverty and Inequality Platform），多维贫困指数来自《2022 年全球多维贫困指数》。

附录 2
东盟关于减贫主要议题的相关政策

国别	政策	时间	要点	议题
东盟	《2016—2025 年东盟旅游战略计划》	2024 年 1 月	进一步支持旅游业快速复苏，围绕"高质量、负责任的旅游：维系东盟未来"这一主题，强调东盟成员国在各相关领域加强合作的重要性，以确保东盟旅游业的可持续性和韧性	经济增长
	第四届东盟数字部长会议及相关会议联合媒体声明	2024 年 2 月	构建包容可信的数字生态系统	数字经济
	东盟社会文化共同体（ASCC）第 31 届理事会联合声明	2024 年 3 月	在"加强互联互通"方面，确定了四个优先事项：（1）经济一体化和互联互通；（2）打造包容和可持续的未来；（3）数字化转型未来；（4）文化艺术：促进东盟文化艺术在包容和可持续发展中的作用 在"增强韧性"方面，确定了五个优先事项：（1）制定战略计划，以实施东盟共同体 2045 年愿景；（2）加强东盟的中心地位；（3）促进环境合作：气候变化韧性；（4）妇女和儿童：促进妇女和儿童在东盟行为主义转变中的作用；（5）卫生：在新的背景下，转变东盟卫生发展韧性 会议期待老挝担任东盟轮值主席国期间取得成果，加强东盟互联互通和抗风险能力，包括落实《东盟印太展望（2019）》	经济增长、营养健康、气候变化
	第 11 次东盟财长和央行行长会议联合声明	2024 年 4 月	老挝以"东盟：加强互联互通和韧性"为主题，该主题体现了老挝的愿景，即加强东盟互联互通，加强东盟在互联互通和韧性方面的合作，促进基础设施互联互通，加强东盟与外部伙伴的关系，同时保持东盟在不断发展的地区架构中的中心地位。老挝下一阶段的优先发展领域以三大战略重点为基础：（1）经济一体化和互联互通；（2）打造包容和可持续的未来；（3）转型以实现数字未来	经济增长、科技创新

续表

国别	政策	时间	要点	议题
	第 55 届东盟经济部长会议	2023 年 9 月	会议主题为"东盟大事：增长的中心"	经济增长
	东盟 2022—2026 年农村发展总体规划	2022 年 11 月	目标 1：区域粮食安全保障 目标 2：持续丰富区域经济增长点 目标 3：促进高质量包容性增长 目标 4：强化经济韧性，促进减缓和适应气候变化 目标 5：为东盟共同体搭建声明平台 目标 6：持续投资以促进农业粮食系统发展	粮食安全、经济增长、气候变化、科技创新
东盟	《东盟全面复苏框架》	2020 年 11 月	该框架提出东盟疫情应对行动聚焦五大战略领域：一是提升卫生系统，优先方向包括维持现有健康举措，加强关键卫生服务和疫苗安全，提升卫生人力资源水平等；二是强化人类安全，拓加强社会保障，为弱势群体加强食品安全，通过数字技术和教育培训提升人力资本，加强劳工政策对话，维护性别平等，保障人权等；三是最大化东盟内部市场和经济一体化潜力，优先方向包括提升东盟内部贸易投资水平，加强供应链韧性，保持市场开放，减少非关税壁垒，推进贸易投资便利化，提升交通和区域互联互通，促进旅游业和中小微企业发展等；四是加快包容性数字化转型，优先方向包括发展电商和数字经济，提升电子政务服务，数字互联互通和信息通信技术水平，推进中小微企业数字化转型，保障数据和网络安全等；五是迈向更可持续和更具韧性的未来，优先方向包括任东盟各领域实现可持续发展，尤其是投资、能源、农业、绿色基础设施，灾害管理以及可持续金融领域	营养健康、经济增长、气候变化

续表

国别	政策	时间	要点	议题
东盟	《东盟粮食安全一体化框架》（AIFS）	2020 年 10 月	该框架的总目标是确保长期粮食安全和营养，改善东盟地区农民的生计，制定每个时期的粮食安全具体战略行动计划（SPA-FS），创造一个有利的环境，使东盟成员国能够在粮食生产、加工和贸易的各个方面进行整合、运作和合作。为了实现这一总目标，AIFS设置了以下具体目标：一是维持和增加粮食生产；二是减少灾后损失；三是促进有利于农业商品和投入的市场和贸易；四是确保粮食的稳定性和可负担性；五是确保粮食安全、质量和营养；六是促进农业投入物的供应和获取；七是实施区域粮食紧急救济安排	粮食安全
	《东盟地区粮食安全战略行动计划（2021—2025）》（SPA-FS）	2020 年 10 月	为了实现AIFS的目标，SPA-FS制定了九个相应的战略方向：加强粮食保障，包括紧急/短缺救济安排；促进有利的粮食市场和贸易；加强综合粮食安全信息系统，计划和监测、计划和监测主粮的供应和利用；加强粮食安全；促进可持续的粮食生产；识别和解决与粮食安全有关的新问题；鼓励加大对粮食和农业产业的投资；利用营养信息为粮食安全和农业政策提供参考；确定东盟促进营养化提高营养水平的政策；制定和治理机制；制度、政策、制度和治理机制；制定和强化提高营养水平的政策/方案；建立实施、监测和评估体系	粮食安全
	《东盟与中日韩大米紧急储备协定》（APTERR）	2011 年 10 月	加强缔约方国家的水稻生产基础；预防水稻收获后的损失；通过有效的缔约国家大米储存政策，改进满足紧急大米供应需求的安排；促进大米价格的稳定，通过改进消费和营养的政策和方案；改善每一缔约方国家内脆弱群体的消费和营养；促进劳动机会、增加收入，特别是农村地区小稻农的收入	粮食安全、经济增长

续表

国别	政策	时间	要点	议题
东盟	《东盟关于在粮食和农业领域推广数字技术的指南》	2021年6月	整合有关数字技术利用状况的信息，这些信息有可能提高农业生产力和改善供应链的弹性，并制定一套关于粮食和农业领域利用数字技术的指导方针。该指南为地区农业的数字化转型提出了建议。更具体来说，该指南概述了利用数字技术改善农业和粮食系统所需的条件和行动，包括促进粮食和农业领域采用数字技术的干预措施	科技创新
	《东盟突发公共卫生事件战略框架》	2020年11月	加强东盟防范、发现、应对突发公共卫生事件的能力，加强东盟在保障区域公共卫生安全方面的合作	营养健康
	《东盟与中日韩教育行动计划（2018—2025）》	2018年9月	营造适应性和有利的环境，提供支持工具，在保证质量的前提下促进东盟与中日韩的国家间学生流动。重申《东盟与中日韩教育行动计划（2018—2025）》与《东盟教育工作计划（2021—2025）》保持实质性对接的重要性，以确保东盟各教育合作框架之间的效率和协同效应。重视奖学金对社会和经济发展的贡献，使学者、专业人士和政府高级官员受益。鼓励在线教育对公民教育的共享	教育水平
	《东盟经济共同体蓝图2025》	2015年11月	到2025年，将东盟建设成高度一体化、竞争力强、创新水平高、充满活力、互联互通和各领域合作进一步加强、韧性强、包容度高、以人为本以及融入全球经济的经济共同体	经济增长
	《东盟数字总体规划2025》	2021年1月	总体目标：将东盟建设成一个由安全和变革性的数字服务、技术和生态系统所驱动的领先数字社区和经济体	经济增长
	《东盟中小企业发展战略行动计划（2016—2025）》	2015年11月	促进中小微企业促进生产力、科技和创新，增加融资渠道，加强市场准入和国际化水平，加强政策及监管环境，促进创业和人力资本开发	经济增长

续表

国别	政策	时间	要点	议题
	《东盟能源合作行动计划》（APAEC）	2015 年 5 月	到 2025 年，将能源强度降低 32%，并使可再生资源占能源供应总量的 23%。目标是"加强能源连接和市场整合，实现能源安全、可及性，可负担以及可持续性"	气候变化
	《东盟灾害管理愿景 2025》	2021 年 1 月	该战略提出体制化和沟通、融资和资源动员，伙伴关系及创新，这些都是建设一个有韧性的东盟的关键要素，使能够在本地和整个区域内采取全面行动。这三个相互包容的战略要素，可以指导到 2025 年实施该战略的方向。首先，东盟需要利用和宣传其成就，使本地区成为灾害管理和应急响应方面的全球领导者。其次，2015 年后灾害管理和应急工作必须探索可持续和创新的方式，转变其为思灾害为思考形成害管理和应急需提供急资金和调动资源的非传统和新的伙伴关系更强的传统和应急的伙伴关系	气候变化
东盟	《东盟关于"同一个东盟，同一个响应：协力应对域内外灾害"的宣言》	2016 年 9 月	加强应对灾害的合作与协调机制，以实现更快速的反应，调动更多的资源，建立更强有力的协调，确保东盟集体应对灾害	气候变化
	《东盟联合应对灾害计划》	2017 年 9 月	目标是提供一个通用的框架，通过动员和联合响应所需的资产和能力。通过支持东盟成员国作出及时和明智的决定，提高东盟的反应速度；通过加强东盟备用安排，扩大应对规模；通过加强与协调的协调与协调之间的协调与合作，加强东盟国，东盟伙伴和其他人道主义行为体为行为体为行为体为实现该目标应对行动的团结，以最终实现该目标	气候变化
	《2025 年后灾害管理信息通信技术路线图》	2020 年 3 月	加强信息通信技术的发展和能力，以支持东盟灾害管理人道主义援助协调中心与东盟成员国的互操作性，以实现"一个东盟一个响应"该路线图原则上是全面适用的，可将各种活动合并为可实施的产出和确定的目标，并作为监测实施进展以便更好地进行灾害管理的工具	气候变化

续表

国别	政策	时间	要点	议题
澜湄五国	《澜沧江—湄公河合作五年行动计划（2018—2022）》	2018年1月	促进澜湄沿岸各国经济社会发展，增进各国人民福祉，缩小本区域发展差距，建设面向和平与繁荣的澜湄国家命运共同体。对接"一带一路"倡议，《东盟互联互通总体规划 2025》和《东盟愿景 2025》，致力于将澜湄合作机制打造成为独具其他湄公河次区域合作机制愿景，受南南合作激励的新型次区域合作机制，助力东盟共同体建设和地区一体化进程，促进落实《联合国 2030 年可持续发展议程》	经济增长
	《国家农业和渔业现代化计划（2021—2030）》	2022年6月	实现一个粮食和营养安全、有韧性、农民和渔民充分享有权利和繁荣的菲律宾	粮食安全
	2022年国情咨文	2022年7月	预计 2022 年菲律宾经济增长率将达到 6.5%~7%，2023~2028 年年均GDP 实际增长率将达到 6.5%~8%，到 2028 年，使贫困率降至 9% 或更低	经济增长
菲律宾	《菲律宾营养行动计划（2017—2022）》	2017年1月	遏制和解决菲律宾民众消瘦、发育迟缓和微量营养素缺乏以及超重和肥胖等问题	营养健康
	《菲律宾创新法案》	2019年7月	促进中小微型企业快速发展，推动企业创新，提升企业国际竞争力。主要关注粮食安全与可持续农业、"蓝色经济"（海洋资源）、教育、健康、安全、清洁和可靠能源、气候变化、数字基础设施、监管、经济与交通运输等多个领域	科技创新

续表

国别	政策	时间	要点	议题
老挝	《2016—2025年国家营养行动计划》	2015年12月	在个人层面解决直接原因，注重实现充足的食物消费和安全，强调生命的头1000天，减少由受污染的食物引起的疾病和损害人体吸收所消费食物能力的间接原因的流行；在家庭和社区层面解决根本原因，改善食品消费的安全性和多样性，以便人们能够随时增加地获得食物，此外，还需要注重改善孕产妇和儿童健康，清洁水和卫生，并提供健康的食物环境和求保保健服务	营养健康
	《国民健康计划（2017—2021）》	2016年12月	主要目标是，到2020年将基本公共卫生服务扩大到全部人口，同时增加财政保护	营养健康
	《国家教育战略计划（2016—2021）》	2016年1月	在五年内建立一个无障碍、公平和有效的国家教育体系。该计划最终目标是为当地青年和成年学生提供在21世纪取得成功所需的技能，并使他们能够实现自己的职业和终身学习愿望	教育水平
缅甸	《缅甸气候变化总体规划（2018—2030）》	2019年5月	该规划对标2030年联合国可持续发展目标，提出在2030年之前通过低碳实现气候发展成为应对气候变化的国家。规划共涉及六个优先领域：实现气候智能型农业、渔业及牧业，以保障粮食安全；对自然资源实施可持续管理，以实现可持续发展的能源，包括绿色可持续的能源；交通和工业系统，以实现可持续发展；建立有韧性，以保障人的健康及福祉；续发展的城市和乡镇；实施气候风险管理，以建立适应性强的社会发展教育及科学技术，以建立适应性强的社会	气候变化
越南	"2022—2030年阶段困难地区幼儿教育发展帮扶"计划	2022年12月	目标是力争到2030年实现25%的贫困地区幼儿班适龄儿童、95%的幼儿园适龄儿童能够上学，贫困地区100%的幼儿园适龄儿童获得照顾、教育，提出2030年新建设施齐全的学校，旨在保障教育公平，缩小区域发展差距，提高儿童获得幼儿教育的机会，同时保护和弘扬少数民族文化价值	教育水平

续表

国别	政策	时间	要点	议题
越南	《关于2021—2025年五年经济社会发展规划的决议》	2021年7月27日	经济方面：五年内GDP年平均增速达6.5%~7%；到2025年人均GDP达4700~5000美元；全要素生产率对经济增长的贡献率约达45%；社会劳动生产率年均增长6.5%以上；城镇化率达到45%；加工制造业占GDP比重达到25%以上；数字经济约占GDP的20% 社会方面：建设民主、和谐、公平和文明的社会。到2025年，农业劳动力占社会劳动力总量的比重达到25%左右；受训工人的比率达到70%；2025年城镇失业率低于4%；贫困率保持每年1%~1.5%的速度下降；每万人拥有10名医生和30张病床；健康保险参保率达到95%；平均寿命约达到74.5岁；新农村达标率达到80%以上	经济增长、营养健康
	《至2030年科技创新与发展战略》	2022年5月	发展与地区和世界紧密连接的国家创新生态系统，发展与国内和全球价值链、产业集群相关的工业、农业和服务领域的创新生态系统；其中，各大企业在引领各项创新活动中发挥核心作用，国家管理机关扮演创建便利体制和政策环境，以及推动企业、研究院、学校等之间连接的作用	科技创新
	《智慧城市发展规划》	2018年8月	这是2018~2025年越南发展可持续智慧城市总体规划以及2030年发展方向。该总体规划旨在发挥城市潜在优势，最大限度利用好人力资源及自然资源等，促进绿色增长和发展，提高生活质量及经济竞争力	科技创新
	《数字社会发展规划》	2020年6月	越南国家数字化转型计划将持续到2025年，其愿景将延续到2030年。这项规划的目标是在未来十年内将越南转变为一个稳定繁荣的数字化国家，通过一系列新技术和新模式，努力改变政府部门传统工作方式，创造一个安全、有保障和人性化的数字环境。为此，计划建设和发展越南宽带基础设施，升级4G移动网络，同时推出5G移动网络，以及在全国范围内普及智能手机	科技创新

续表

国别	政策	时间	要点	议题
越南	《2011—2020年越南绿色增长战略和2050年愿景》	2012年9月25日	一是减少温室气体排放并促进清洁和可再生能源的使用，具体目标为2011~2020年减少8%~10%的温室气体排放，至2050年每年减少1.5%~2%的温室气体排放；二是推进绿色产业发展，实施清洁工业化战略，经济有效地利用资源，鼓励发展绿色科技和绿色农业；三是推广绿色生活方式和鼓励消费可持续发展	气候变化
	《2019—2030年国家节能减排和有效利用能源规划》	2019年5月13日	2019~2025年，全国能源使用总量节约5%~7%，将能源损耗率降低至6.5%以下；2019~2030年，节能8%~10%	气候变化
	《投资促进战略（2023—2027）》	2022年12月	该战略提出三个对国家未来经济非常重要的核心概念，包括创新、技术和创造力；竞争力与快速适应能力。该战略侧重于通过鼓励创新和社会的可持续发展，向绿色和智能产业过渡，人才培养及创新中心的发展，加强泰国作为区域性商业、贸易和物流中心的地位，使泰国步入一个崭新的经济时代	经济增长
泰国	《泰国4.0战略》	2016年7月	泰国政府提出"泰国4.0"高附加值经济模式，推动更多高新技术和创新技术应用，企业创新真正成为推动泰国经济增长的主要动力。投资将在其中起到重要作用，国家投资政策向"核心技术、人才、基础设施"五大领域倾斜。汽车制造、智能电子、高端旅游与医疗旅游，农业与生物技术、食品深加工、航空与物流，生物能源与生物化工、数字经济、医疗中心十大目标产业将成为泰国经济发展的新引擎	科技创新、经济增长

续表

国别	政策	时间	要点	议题
泰国	《泰国数字发展路线图》	2020 年 10 月	推动泰国数字经济转化与快速发展的科技，消费习惯和商业环境相协调，帮助泰国在未来 20 年在数字经济方面取得成功。该数字经济路线图分为四大部分。一是建设数字科技人才，二是发展数字经济，三是推动社区数字能力建设，四是建设数字生态体系。泰国的目标是在 2022~2027 年成为全发展，建设数字创新发达国家，固定宽带发达国家，包括缩小数字鸿沟，特别是在农村地区，并为经济和社会可持续发展确立基础	科技创新
	《以 BCG 经济模式推动泰国发展的行动计划（2021—2027）》	2022 年 2 月	为推动疫后经济的可持续发展，泰国政府提出了 BCG 发展模式，该经济模式以发展生物经济、循环经济和绿色经济三大领域为基石，重点关注农业与粮食、健康与医疗、能源材料与生物化学、旅游和创意经济	气候变化
	《暹粒省旅游业发展总体规划（2021—2035）》	2021 年 3 月	通过实施诸多旅游项目，提升旅游质量和可持续性，以推动当地旅游业加快发展	经济增长
柬埔寨	《数字经济和数字社会政策框架（2021—2035）》	2021 年 3 月	该框架包含 139 项具体措施，计划在 2035 年完成柬埔寨的数字转型，使数字经济规模达到 GDP 的 5%～10%；到 2025 年，城市地区的高速互联网覆盖率将达到 100%，乡村地区则达到 70%；到 2030 年，实现主要公共服务数字化，私营企业数字技术普及应用率达到 70%，从事相关行业人员占就业人口比例达到 4%	科技创新
	《2030 年科技创新路线图》	2021 年 8 月	五项政策战略：加强科技创新的治理结构，发展国家科技创新劳动力，加强研究能力和质量，加强不同利益相关者之间的合作和创新联系，培育有利于创新的生态系统	科技创新

续表

国别	政策	时间	要点	议题
柬埔寨	《碳中和长期战略》(TS4CN)	2021年12月	该战略配合在2050年实现碳中和的承诺目标，促进绿色增长，减少温室气体排放，并发展可持续性的清洁能源。该战略确定了六个关键领域：农业、林业、交通、能源、工业产品、废弃物管理。计划到2050年使碳中和有关的经济措施对柬埔寨GDP增长的影响达到2.8%，创造44.9万个就业机会，并鼓励投资创新能源技术，如氢气发电、电能储存、能源互联网等	气候变化
印度尼西亚	《国家科技总体规划2017—2045》	2018年4月	通过科技创新，推动国家经济转型和发展	科技创新
	"太阳能群岛"计划	2022年4月	拟在4~5年内为数百万贫困家庭安装屋顶太阳能电池板	气候变化
	《2021—2024年数字印尼路线图》	2021年2月	涵盖数字基础设施、数字政府、数字经济和数字社会四个战略领域，六个战略方向，十大重点行业，数字化转型，以实现包容性数字化转型。重点行业包括数字化转型与旅游、数字贸易、数字金融服务、数字媒体和娱乐、数字农业和渔业、数字房地产和数字城市、数字教育、数字健康、行业数字化和政府机构数字化	科技创新

附录3

东盟各国减贫政治承诺

国家	政策文件或讲话	减贫目标	具体举措
老挝	《老挝第九个五年经济社会发展规划（2021—2025）》	持续推动可持续发展，帮助20多万个老挝家庭和3104个村落实现减贫	在农村发展和扶贫领域，颁布一系列法律法规和政策，如移民法、中央政治局第097号令，老挝政府关于扶贫和发展标准、确定战略、发展重点领域的第348号令等
	2022年12月，老挝总理宋赛·西潘敦在老挝第九届国会第四次会议上的发言	通过发展清洁、安全和可持续的农业，确保国家粮食安全，并按照工业化和现代化的目标，建设对国民经济有重大贡献的农业生产体系	发挥国内资源优势，改进农业生产系统，进一步夯实农业基础设施，用科技促进农业现代化。加快发展以中小企业为重点的农业综合企业，让企业更便利地获得低息贷款，开展贸易，打开产品销售市场
	2016年2月，老挝人民革命党第十次全国代表大会	提出争取在2020年摆脱欠发达状态，2025年成为中等收入发达国家，2030年成为中高收入的发展中国家	未提及
	《2023—2028年五年发展计划》	2023年将贫困率降低至16%~16.4%，到2028年逐步降至8.8%~9%	颁布扶贫大宪章，成立反贫困委员会，确保政府的基本部门在减贫计划当中有所作为
菲律宾	菲律宾发展计划（2017—2022）	到2022年将贫困率降低到14%	正式推出名为"大建特建"的大规模基础设施投资计划，投资8.4万亿比索（约合1660亿美元）；开展"菲律宾社会援助计划"；菲律宾社会福利和发展部牵头签署《"菲律宾社会援助计划"法案》

续表

国家	政策文件或讲话	减贫目标	具体举措
菲律宾	2022年国情咨文	到2028年，贫困率将降至9%或更低	抑制通货膨胀，延续并扩大基础设施建设方案，进一步推动经济增长和就业；实施可靠的财政管理，落实税收改革，增加税收，提高支出效率，以尽快解决疫情所带来的经济影响；全力支持引进高科技制造、医疗保健以及其他新兴战略性产业，促进马尼拉都会区以外地区的经济增长
	《2040年愿景》	到2040年，菲律宾成为富足的中产国家；人民充满智慧、富有创新精神、生活幸福、健康；多元化家庭充满活力；社会信任度高；抵御灾害能力强	未提及
柬埔寨	《2019—2023年国家发展战略计划》	2023年将全国贫困率降至10%以下	通过互联互通来改善农村的经济活动，通过技能发展促进社区发展，提供农村信贷进行创业，使农村经济活动多样化。启动一些综合计划，重点建设可持续和包容性的农村基础设施
	《2022—2030年农业发展政策》	实现农业领域3%的年增长率，提高农业领域劳动生产率，即将员工年工作产值从2019年的1986美元增至2030年的4625美元	总体目标是，通过提供高质量产品来增加具有高竞争力和包容性的农业增长，从而确保粮食安全和营养，并优先考虑土地、水资源、林业和渔业资源的可持续管理。为实现此目标，已确定了四个战略性政策目标：（1）增强农业价值链的竞争力；（2）增加对农业基础设施和农业务便利化的支持；（3）促进可持续的土地、林业和渔业资源管理；（4）加强机构管理和监管改革，促进人力资源发展，并解决新兴挑战

续表

国家	政策文件或讲话	减贫目标	具体举措
	越南共产党第十三次全国人民代表大会	到 2025 年，贫困发生率年均下降 1%~1.5%	出台有条件的扶持政策；强化对贫困人口的社会政策的信用，为无法工作的贫困用户提供社会保障；采取政策鼓励企业和合作社在生产经营产品消费等方面联合起来，发展贫困用户和准贫困用户参与的生产模式
越南	《国家可持续减贫目标规划（2021—2025）》	每年将全国贫困率降低 1%~1.5%，少数民族家庭贫困率降低 3% 以上，贫困地区贫困率降低 4%~4.5%。到 2025 年，贫困和接近贫困家庭的数量预计将减少一半。根据该计划，贫困家庭的适龄儿童入学比率将达到 90%	将投入至少 75 万亿越盾（约合 33 亿美元），重点关注全国范围内的贫困地区，改善当地社会经济基础设施，促进生产和贸易，提供基本社会服务，包括向符合条件的贫困家庭提供 4000 万越盾（约合 1700 美元）用于建造新房或 2000 万越盾（约合 810 美元）用于房屋维修
	《国家新型农村发展目标规划（2021—2025）》	到 2025 年，全国范围内建成新型农村的比例达到 80% 以上，达到先进标准的比例达到 40% 左右，达到示范区的比例达到 10% 以上	预计将在 2021~2025 年期间投入 2.45 万亿越盾（约合 1050 亿美元）。在新型农村建设和智慧农村发展中推进数字化转型，促进数字经济，更好地发展农村经济，创新农业经营模式等
印度尼西亚	2022 年 4 月 28 日，印尼国家发展规划部部长在雅加达举行的发展规划会议上的讲话	到 2023 年将贫困率从 8.5% 降低到 7.5%，到 2024 年消除极端贫困	社会各界共同努力消除极端贫困；加强对中央和地方社会保障工作的统筹协调；帮助极端贫困人口获得资金和市场，提高他们的生产力；整合社会保护和赋权项目，以提高极端贫困人口自力更生的能力

续表

国家	政策文件或讲话	减贫目标	具体举措
印度尼西亚	《2020—2024年中期发展计划》	2024年，贫困率控制在6.5%～7.5%，并消除所有极端贫困	为非正规部门、乡镇企业融资；向贫困家庭提供现金直接援助计划；强化农村经济发展；通过电子商务实现村庄数字化的战略
	2016年11月，印尼第一个国家自主贡献（NDC）；2022年9月，印尼加强国家自主贡献（Enhance NDC）	到2025年将贫困率降至4%以下	未提及
	《印尼愿景2045》和《国家中长期发展规划（2025—2045）》	到2045年消除极端贫困	未提及
泰国	《第十三个国民经济和社会发展5年计划（2023—2027）》	基于"不让任何人掉队"的原则，落实联合国可持续发展目标，解决长期贫困和代际贫困	成立贫困消除以及可持续性终身发展中心，学习中国精准扶贫经验。通过向贫困家庭的青少年提供优质教育和专业技能培训，同时发展全面包容的社会保障，并将其系统地结合起来，以确保所有人生活稳定，能够获得充分的社会保障，以可持续的方式摆脱贫困
	《国家20年发展战略规划（2018—2037）》	围绕"自足经济"，将泰国建设成为稳定、富裕、可持续发展的国家，力争到2037年跻身发达国家行列；创造社会公平，缩小收入差距，更公平地分配发展的利益，消除贫困	提高农业附加值，将农民增收的重点放在发展高质量农业和智慧农业上，提高农业生产力以及产品多样性、探索特色农业、生物农业、加工以及智慧农业

续表

国家	政策文件或讲话	减贫目标	具体举措
马来西亚	《第十二个马来西亚计划（2021—2025）》	到2025年，实现零极端贫困；确保所有人都能享有体面的生活；减少不平等	在联邦和地区层级设立专门的扶贫机构。制定基于数据驱动方法的扶贫政策；整合和集中贫困数据库；加强自下而上的项目；在基层层面，本地化扶贫解决方案；探索引入专项税作为扶贫项目资金来源的可能性；考虑使用Zakat, Waqf以及政府控股公司，私人实体和个人的捐款
	《2030年农村发展政策》（RDP2030）	实现繁荣、包容、可持续和全面的农村生活愿景	针对疫情后减贫问题，政府做了许多努力，如增加部分企业和住房租金的优惠力度并延长租金期限，实施农村企业在线外联计划，贫困家庭和土著居民的食品篮子计划，以及减免下属幼儿园费用等
缅甸	《缅甸可持续发展规划（2018—2030）》	在实现就业创造与私营部门主导增长的目标下，创造一个有利的环境，通过包括农业、工业和多元文化的实践来支持多样化和生产性的经济，作为减少农村地区贫穷的基础	改进和发展农业、水产养殖和粮食部门的教育和培训，以应对农民不断变化的需求；实施有针对性的农业计划，以应对特定的环境条件和消费需求

注：（1）《巴黎协定》要求每个国家制定并通报其2020年后的气候行动，即国家自主贡献（NDCs），并要求各国每五年更新一次。
（2）缅甸于2021年2月发生军事政变，《缅甸可持续发展规划（2018—2030）》为上一届政府制定。

附录 4
中国—东盟减贫合作大事记

年份	国家及地区	领域	事件
2012	东盟	科技创新	中国—东盟科技伙伴计划正式启动
2013	柬埔寨	基础设施	中国援建柬埔寨 6 号公路
	东盟	经济增长	中国提出共建"一带一路"倡议
	老挝	科技创新、粮食安全	中国—老挝合作农作物优良品种试验站在老挝成立
2014	老挝、柬埔寨、缅甸	减贫合作、粮食安全	中国提出"东亚减贫合作倡议",在老挝、柬埔寨、缅甸建立东亚减贫合作示范点
	东盟	科技创新	广西东盟技术转移中心获批成立
2015	老挝	基础设施	中老两国政府签署《中老两国间铁路基础设施合作开发和中老铁路项目合作协议》
2016	柬埔寨、老挝、缅甸、泰国、越南	科技创新、粮食安全	澜沧江—湄公河合作首次领导人会议召开,拟设立农业科技合作基金
	老挝、柬埔寨和缅甸	减贫合作、粮食安全	东亚减贫示范合作技术援助项目在老挝、柬埔寨和缅甸落地试点,首期项目金额 1 亿元人民币
2017	柬埔寨	基础设施、营养健康	中国援柬埔寨乡村供水项目首期工程开工建设
	东盟	科技创新	"一带一路"科技创新行动计划
	东盟	科技创新、粮食安全	云南省农业科学院倡议成立南亚东南亚农业科技辐射中心

续表

年份	国家及地区	领域	事件
2018	印尼	基础设施	"一带一路"建设和中印尼两国务实合作的标志性项目——雅万高铁全面开工建设
	老挝	营养健康	中国向老挝一中学捐赠一体化污水处理装置
	东盟	气候变化	中国—东盟减轻灾害风险管理研讨会召开
	东盟	科技创新	中国—东盟创新年启动仪式暨中国东盟创新论坛成功举办
	东盟	科技创新	第21次中国—东盟领导人会议发表《中国—东盟科技创新合作联合声明》
2019	越南	基础设施	中国电建承建的越南油汀500兆瓦光伏项目竣工
	柬埔寨	基础设施	金港高速正式开工
	泰国	减贫合作	泰国官员赴中国广西实地考察扶贫项目
	东盟	气候变化	中国—东盟减灾与应急管理高官论坛召开
	东盟	经济增长	国家发展改革委印发《关于支持云南省加快建设面向南亚东南亚辐射中心的政策措施》,鼓励中国(云南)与周边国家加强农业和经贸合作
2020	菲律宾	基础设施	中国援助菲律宾建设达沃河项目
	柬埔寨	营养健康	中国向柬埔寨派遣抗疫医疗队
	缅甸	营养健康	中国向缅甸派遣抗疫医疗专家组
	老挝	营养健康	中国向老挝派遣抗疫医疗专家组
2021	东盟		中国—东盟共同制定发布《中国—东盟全面战略伙伴关系行动计划(2022—2025)》

续表

年份	国家及地区	领域	事件
2021	东盟	营养健康	中国宣布将向东盟国家提供 1.5 亿剂新冠疫苗无偿援助，向东盟抗疫基金追加 500 万美元
	东盟	气候变化	中国—东盟设立灾害管理部长级会议机制
	东盟	气候变化	《中国—东盟灾害管理工作计划（2021—2025）》发布
	东盟	教育、科技创新	中国将启动科技创新提升计划，向东盟提供 1000 项先进适用技术，未来五年支持 300 名东盟青年科学家来华交流
	东盟	科技创新	《中国—东盟建设面向未来更加紧密的科技创新伙伴关系行动计划（2021—2025）》发布
2022	菲律宾	基础设施	中工国际签约菲律宾米沙鄢变电站改造项目
	菲律宾	基础设施	南网国际中标菲律宾电力项目
	菲律宾	基础设施	由中国政府出资、中工国际承建的菲律宾奇科河灌溉工程项目正式竣工
	东盟	经济增长	第 19 届中国—东盟博览会上，中国与东盟各国现场共签订投资合作项目 267 个，总投资 4130 亿元人民币，项目涉及高端金属新材料、绿色环保、轻工纺织、大健康和文旅体育、绿色化工新材料、机械装备制造等产业
	柬埔寨、老挝、缅甸、泰国、越南	减贫合作	澜湄合作减贫联合工作组第六次会议以线上形式召开，讨论并通过了《澜湄减贫合作指南（2023—2027）》
	东盟	经济增长	中国承诺在三年内向东盟提供 15 亿美元发展援助，支持东盟抗击疫情及经济复苏
	缅甸	基础设施	中国援助缅甸清甘周恩来凉亭修缮工程及其他水凉亭修复项目
2023	柬埔寨	基础设施	由中国路桥工程有限责任公司投资建设的柬埔寨第二条高速公路——金巴高速正式开工

中国国际减贫中心
IPRCC International Poverty Reduction Center in China

全球减贫与发展经验分享系列
The Sharing Series on Global Poverty
Reduction and Development Experience

2024 Annual Report on Poverty Reduction and Development in ASEAN

Edited by International Poverty Reduction Center in China

2024 Annual Report on Poverty Reduction and Development in ASEAN

Research Group

Leaders of the Research Group:

Wang Huaiyu, Li Xin

Members of the Research Group:

Chen Hongshu, Jia Xiaowei, Xu Liping, He Shengnian,

Liu Huanhuan, Yao Yuan, Wang Qiaoyu, Fan Honglin,

Su Zhiwen, Yang Shuangquan, Lin Lin, Wang Haoqian

Preface

Poverty is the biggest challenge facing the world today, and poverty eradication is the common responsibility of all mankind. ASEAN is one of the most densely populated regions in the world, and also one of the regions with the greatest differences in development levels. Promoting the poverty reduction process in ASEAN countries is of great significance to the eradication of poverty in the world. The COVID-19 pandemic has affected the development of ASEAN countries to varying degrees. After the outbreak of COVID-19, countries are actively seeking economic recovery, but the recovery is uneven within the region, while climate change, nutrition and health, education and other factors have brought uncertainty to sustainable growth and poverty eradication.

China and ASEAN are geological neighbors sharing close affinity and a longstanding friendship. In a speech, President of the People's Republic of China Xi Jinping stated that, the gains in China-ASEAN cooperation over the past 30 years are attributable to our unique geographical proximity and cultural affinity and, more importantly, to the fact that we have actively embraced the development trend of our times and made the right historic choice. Over the past 30 years and more, China and ASEAN have pressed ahead hand in hand with a more encompassing strategic partnership, and fruitful bilateral collaboration in political security, trade, and people-to-people exchange. China and ASEAN have become the largest trading partners with each other and foraged the most substantial and the most energetic strategic partnership.

In order to implement the Global Development Initiative (GDI), keep pushing forward collaboration in poverty reduction between China and ASEAN countries under the framework of China-ASEAN cooperation, and foster a closer China-ASEAN community with a shared future, the International Poverty

Reduction Center in China compiled the 2024 *Annual Report on Poverty Reduction and Development in ASEAN*. Its purpose is to review progress in poverty reduction across ASEAN countries before and after the COVID-19 pandemic from an all-around perspective. Using descriptive and comparative analysis, the report draws on data published by international agencies such as the World Bank, the Food and Agriculture Organization of the United Nations, the United Nations Development Programme and the ASEAN Secretariat, and discusses the achievements, practices, and future of poverty reduction in ASEAN from multiple dimensions and aspects.

The report holds that:

1. Before the pandemic, ASEAN countries achieved notable progress in poverty reduction. According to the extreme poverty line set by the World Bank and the poverty lines set by ASEAN countries, the poverty rate in ASEAN countries declined to varying degrees. The average Human Development Index (HDI) rose from 0.698 in 2012 to 0.733 in 2019. Multidimensional poverty was mitigated, and progress was made in multiple dimensions such as income, education, health, and living standards. However, there were still differences between countries in development and poverty reduction, as well as inequalities between urban and rural areas in terms of basic public services.

2. The pandemic delayed the progress of poverty reduction in ASEAN countries. The pandemic aggravated the vulnerability of low-income groups and less developed areas in ASEAN countries, and incurred an increase in the number of people returning to poverty and vulnerable groups in some countries. From 2020 to 2021, ASEAN countries experienced a negative annual average growth in the HDI, and some countries faced severe multidimensional poverty. Under the impact of income decrease and school closures, there was a higher risk of malnutrition and suspension of teaching activities, as well as a delay in poverty reduction in some countries. ASEAN and its member states revved up against the pandemic with multiple measures, while the international community also increased assistance to push poverty reduction forward.

3. Economic recovery after the pandemic boosted poverty reduction and development. According to some international agencies, ASEAN was forecast to see a robust recovery with an economic growth of 4.9-5.2 percent in 2023. ASEAN countries deepened trading partnerships with each other, scaled up trading activities, and facilitated free flow of goods, supply chain interconnection and service efficiency. Various measures were taken to encourage foreign investment and support the development of small, medium, and micro enterprises. With the rapid development of digital technology and internet infrastructure in ASEAN countries, governments unveiled policies and measures to boost the development of digital economy, ensure full employment, and lay a more solid foundation for poverty reduction and development.

4. New progress was made in addressing major issues of poverty reduction. ASEAN has presented strong resilience for food security, and an ongoing increase in the Global Food Security Index (GFSI) since 2021. The status of nutrition and health in ASEAN countries was improved, and the Global Hunger Index (GHI) dropped to the moderate level. There was also an ongoing fortification for the education system, and a higher level of inclusive education. All these countries revved up against climate change by moving forward to the energy transformation and emission reduction, which created the opportunities for employment and economic growth. There were also efforts to scale up technological innovation and human resource training and keep improving the effectiveness of poverty reduction.

5. There are broad prospects for poverty reduction and development across ASEAN countries. Economic recovery after the pandemic, trade and investment liberalization and facilitation, the rapid development of the digital economy, and solidified intra-regional collaboration have provided ASEAN with favorable opportunities for poverty reduction and better development. In the future, the cooperation between ASEAN countries and other developing countries including China should be facilitated through sharing of poverty reduction experience, collaboration in poverty reduction projects, and capacity building. This will help them jointly implement the Global Development Initiative, build a closer China-ASEAN community with a shared future, and act as a new driving force in maintaining regional and world peace, stability and prosperity.

This report has five chapters. Chapter 1, Poverty Reduction Progress in

ASEAN Countries under the Impact of the COVID-19 Pandemic; Chapter 2, Implementation of Major Poverty Reduction Issues in ASEAN; Chapter 3, International Development Assistance and Cooperation for Poverty Reduction in ASEAN Countries; Chapter 4, China-ASEAN Poverty Reduction Cooperation; Chapter 5, Outlook on Poverty Reduction in ASEAN Countries.

Chapter 1   Poverty Reduction Progress in ASEAN Countries Under the Impact of the COVID-19 Pandemic

1.1   Brief Information of ASEAN

The Association of Southeast Asian Nations (ASEAN) is an integrated political, economic and security cooperation organization based on economic cooperation. To establish a prosperous and stable community in the region, Indonesia, Thailand, Singapore, the Philippines and Malaysia issued the ASEAN Declaration (Bangkok Declaration) on 8 August 1967, officially announcing the establishment of the ASEAN. With the successive accession of Brunei (1984), Vietnam (1995), Laos (1997), Myanmar (1997) and Cambodia (1999), the ASEAN's membership has grown to ten. In November 2022, the ASEAN Leaders' Statement agreed in principle to admit Timor-Leste as the 11th member of ASEAN[1]. In accordance with the ASEAN Charter[2], the ASEAN Summit is the highest decision-making body of ASEAN, with the chairmanship rotating among member states. The ASEAN Secretariat, established in Jakarta, capital of Indonesia, is the administrative body serving the 10 ASEAN member states, and the Secretary-General of ASEAN is appointed by the member states on a rotational basis for a term of five years. The current ASEAN Secretary General is

---

1　Timor-Leste was not included in the analysis that used the ASEAN statistical data in 2022 and before. The analysis for Timor-Leste was provided separately to maintain the consistency.

2　In December 2008, the ASEAN Charter came into force, which is the first ASEAN document with universal legal significance and is binding on all member states.

Cambodian politician Kao Kim Hourn, who serves until 2028.

ASEAN[1] enjoys a strategic geographical position, and is rich in mineral resources. The ASEAN countries are all located in Southeast Asia, bordering China to the north and Japan across the sea, India and Bangladesh to the west, and the countries of Oceania to the east and south across the Pacific Ocean, they as a whole are located in the region where the Pacific Ocean meets the Indian Ocean, and Asia meets Oceania, making it a very important geopolitical location. Among them, Myanmar, Laos and Vietnam share land border with China, while the Philippines, Malaysia and Indonesia face China across the South China Sea. The ASEAN region is rich in oil and tin resources, and has the world's largest tin ore belt. Malaysia is the world's largest producer of tin sands. Indonesia is an important exporter of oil and natural gas. Thailand has the largest potash salt reserve in the world. Vietnam has a variety of mineral resources, with more than 50 kinds of mineral resources[2].

ASEAN is one of the regions in the world most affected by climate change[3]. In 2020, 14,768 out of every 100,000 people in Thailand were directly or indirectly affected by climate disasters, double the number in 2019. In Philippines, 8,723 out of every 100,000 people were directly or indirectly affected by climate disasters. In Indonesia and Myanmar, 2,388 and 2,494 out of every 100,000 people were directly or indirectly affected by climate disasters[4].

ASEAN is rich in agricultural products. Rice is the main food crop in ASEAN, and has a long history of cultivation. Thailand, Myanmar and Vietnam are important rice producers and exporters in the world. The region is also the

---

1 Brunei and Singapore are high-income countries. Since this report focuses on emerging economies and developing countries in the ASEAN region, Brunei and Singapore are not included in the subsequent analysis of poverty.

2 See: *Guide for Countries and Regions on Overseas Investment and Cooperation: ASEAN (2022)*, *Guide for Countries and Regions on Overseas Investment and Cooperation: Malaysia (2022)*, *Guide for Countries and Regions on Overseas Investment and Cooperation: Indonesia (2022)*, *Guide for Countries and Regions on Overseas Investment and Cooperation: Thailand (2022)*, and *Guide for Countries and Regions on Overseas Investment and Cooperation: Vietnam (2022)*.

3 See: *World Bank Annual Report 2023*.

4 Data from the ASEAN Secretariat.

world's largest producer of tropical cash crops such as rubber, palm oil, coconut and banana hemp. Thailand is the world's largest rubber producer, Malaysia leads the world in palm oil production and exports, and the Philippines is the world's largest coconut producer.

There is a large difference in land area among ASEAN member states. ASEAN covers a total area of about 4.5 million square kilometers[1]. With an area of 1.92 million square kilometers, Indonesia is the largest country in ASEAN in terms of land area. The total areas of Myanmar and Thailand are 680,000 square kilometers and 510,000 square kilometers respectively. The land areas of five countries, Malaysia, Vietnam, the Philippines, Laos and Cambodia are all between 180,000 and 330,000 square kilometers. Laos is the only landlocked country in the region.

There are differences in the development level and industrial structure among ASEAN member states. In 2022, ASEAN's GDP was US$3.6 trillion[2], accounting for about 3.6% of global GDP[3], and its population was about 670 million, accounting for 8.4% of the world's total population[4]. Malaysia and Thailand took the lead in economic development, with Malaysia's per capita GDP at US$12,448 and Thailand's per capita GDP at US$7,494.4[5]. GDP growth in both countries was quite modest, with Malaysia's GDP growing by 4.2%[6] and Thailand's 1.9%. The service sector accounted for more than 50% of GDP, and the agricultural sector accounted for less than 10% of GDP in both countries[7]. Both countries also led other countries in governance (see Table 1-1). The economic development level of Indonesia, the Philippines, Vietnam and Laos was in the middle of the ASEAN countries. The GDP growth rate of Indonesia was 4.3%, the Philippines 5%, Vietnam and Laos 6% from 2013 to 2022. The service sector accounted for 30%-40% of their GDP, while the agricultural sector

---

1   Based on *Guide for Countries and Regions on Overseas Investment and Cooperation: ASEAN (2022)* issued by Ministry of Commerce of the People's Republic of China.

2   Data from the *ASEAN Statistical Yearbook 2023*, excluding Timor-Leste.

3   According to the World Bank, global GDP in 2022 was US$100.88 trillion.

4   According to the World Bank, the world's total population in 2022 was 7.95 billion.

5   Data from the *ASEAN Statistical Yearbook 2023*.

6   The GDP growth rate is the average level from 2013 to 2022.

7   Data from the World Bank's public database (https://data.worldbank.org).

accounted for 10%-17% of their GDP[1]. The governance capacity of the four countries was in the middle of ASEAN. Cambodia and Myanmar had the lowest level of development, with per capita GDP of less than US$1,800. The GDP of Cambodia and Myanmar grew quite fast, at a rate of 5.7% and 5.4% respectively. The service sector accounted for 30%-40% of GDP, while the agricultural sector accounted for around 23% of GDP in both countries[2]. The governance capacity of both countries was relatively low (see Table 1-1).

Table 1-1   **Government governance capacity in ASEAN by country, 2017-2021**

Countries	2017	2018	2019	2020	2021
Singapore	89.03	89.22	88.82	88.82	89.22
Brunei	70.06	71.84	70.72	74.64	75.92
Malaysia	59.75	63.96	63.48	63.25	62.53
Indonesia	46.31	46.83	46.11	47.70	48.91
Thailand	43.00	41.46	43.84	43.85	43.76
Vietnam	40.18	39.75	39.76	42.25	42.25
Philippines	40.88	39.90	40.13	40.03	38.36
Timor-Leste	31.91	33.03	34.42	35.29	38.00
Laos	27.16	24.25	23.68	25.18	27.58
Cambodia	24.82	25.48	25.11	25.04	24.87
Myanmar	19.87	19.61	18.57	19.14	8.56

Sources: WGI database.

Agriculture is an important pillar in ASEAN. Agriculture is an important pillar of national economic development in most ASEAN member states. In 2022, the proportion of total agricultural production in GDP of ASEAN remained at 16.4%[3], which was still a large contribution to economic growth. Agriculture created large number of jobs in ASEAN countries. In 2022, Thailand's

---

1   Data from the World Bank's public database (https://data.worldbank.org).

2   Ibid.

3   Data from *ASEAN Key Figure 2023*.

agricultural output accounted for 8.8% of GDP, but accounted for 31.9% of the country's jobs. In Indonesia and Vietnam, the proportion of agricultural output in GDP was 12.4% and 11.9%, and accounted for 28.3% and 29.1% of the total number of new jobs respectively. In the Philippines, the agricultural sector accounted for one-tenth of the country's output and one-fourth of the country's jobs. In Cambodia and Myanmar, agricultural sector accouted for 22.2% and 22.6% of GDP, respectively[1]. Agricultural trade is an important source of foreign exchange for ASEAN. ASEAN agricultural products, especially tropical crops, have strong competitiveness in the international market, and the total trade has always been in a surplus, with a trade surplus of US$49.3 billion in 2022[2].

ASEAN is highly dependent on intra-regional trade. China and ASEAN are each other's largest trading partner. Intra-regional trade held the largest share of ASEAN trade between 2012 and 2022, with a share of 22% in 2022. Since 2020, China has become ASEAN's largest trading partner. The trade between China and ASEAN accounted for 18.8% of ASEAN's total, followed by the United States and the European Union, which accounted for 10.9% and 7.7% of ASEAN's total, respectively[3].

Infrastructure in ASEAN countries continues to improve. Indonesia, Malaysia, Thailand and Vietnam have extended electricity access to more than 99% of the population by 2022[4]. In Laos, the Philippines and Cambodia, 94%, 96% and 98% of the population had access to electricity respectively. Although Myanmar has made progress in electricity access, rising from 33% in 2016 to 62% in 2022, which is still far below that of other ASEAN member states. The annual growth rate of road length in ASEAN countries is 5.6%. The average annual growth rate of land-based social infrastructure development in Thailand is 12.7%. Malaysia, Vietnam and Myanmar all grew at over 7%. Cambodia and Laos grew at less than 4.5%. Road facilities in Indonesia and the Philippines have grown slowly, at around 1% over the past decade.

---

1   Data from the ASEAN Secretariat.
2   Data from *ASEAN Secretariat Yearbook 2023*.
3   Ibid.
4   Data from *ASEAN Key Figure 2023*.

The digital level has increased. Overall, internet coverage has improved significantly in all ASEAN countries. The internet coverage increased from 26.1% in 2013 to 72% in 2022[1]; the number of mobile phones per 100 people grew rapidly, from 88 in 2016 to 99.6 in 2022. Most ASEAN countries have basically achieved full coverage of 4G network. In 2020, the 4G network coverage in Singapore and Thailand reached over 98%, and that in other ASEAN countries also exceeded 80%[2]. The ASEAN countries have high enthusiasm for developing 5G network, even some of these countries have gradually promoted 5G application through small-scale commercial use and the establishment of experimental networks. The Philippines has become the first ASEAN country to realize 5G commercial use through the China-Philippines 4G/5G communication base station project[3]. Singapore, Vietnam, Indonesia, Laos, Malaysia and Cambodia have also successively deployed 5G networks in their territories.

ASEAN countries have a younger age structure and most of their population live in rural areas. In terms of population, most ASEAN countries have a younger age structure, only Thailand and Vietnam have entered ageing society. The majority of the population in most ASEAN countries live in rural areas. In Myanmar, the rural population accounts for nearly 70%. More than half of the population in Vietnam, Laos, Cambodia, the Philippines and Thailand live in rural areas[4]. In Cambodia ,the adult literacy rate and the net enrollment rate are less than 90%.[5]

The region is ethnically and culturally diverse. The spatial distribution of the population in ASEAN is uneven, and most of them are concentrated in the plains and estuary deltas. There are many ethnic groups in the region, with more than 100 ethnic groups in Indonesia and Myanmar, and more than 90 ethnic

---

1 Data from *ASEAN Statistical Yearbook 2023*.

2 See: China Mobile Research Institute, *Status and Trends of Information and Communication Infrastructure Development in Southeast and South Asia*, 2021.

3 See: "The Belt and Road Development Theory : Practical and Theoretical Exploration of Global Common Development", Xinhua News, October 19,2023.

4 Data from *ASEAN Statistical Yearbook 2023*.

5 Data from the ASEAN Secretariat, subject to the latest data published by each country.

groups in the Philippines[1]. The number of ethnic groups in other countries is between 20 and 50[2]. The official language of ASEAN is English, but the member states use a wide variety of languages. The member states have diverse religious beliefs. Thailand, Myanmar, Laos and Cambodia are Buddhist countries, Malaysia and Indonesia are Islamic countries, the Philippines is a Catholic country, and in Vietnam, people mainly believes in Confucianism[3]. Cultural diversity leads to differences in the values of member states, which increases the complexity of intra-regional integration.

In general, most ASEAN member states are developing countries, but there are great differences in development within the region. Malaysia has a relatively high level of development, with an industrial structure dominated by the service industry and a low proportion of rural population. Despite slow GDP growth, its internet coverage and government governance capacity are at the forefront of the region. Cambodia and Myanmar lag behind in development, but their economy grows at a fast speed. In the two countries, agriculture is the pillar of national development and most of the population live in rural areas. On the whole, there is still room for improvement in government governance capacity, education level and infrastructure. Laos is the only landlocked country, and its economy is witnessing rapid growth. Indonesia and the Philippines, both with a population of more than 100 million, are rich in resources but vulnerable to climate change. Vietnam and Thailand are also rich in resources and have booming trade in goods. With population growing at a slower rate, they have quite high ageing degree. Thailand is a country that affected the most by climate change in the region.

1　Zhou, J. X. (2018). Ethnic Division of Southeast Asian Countries and Thoughts on Related Issues. Guizhou Ethnic Studies, 39(2):1-7. (in Chinese)

2　Based on *Guide for Countries and Regions on Overseas Investment and Cooperation: Vietnam (2022)*, *Guide for Countries and Regions on Overseas Investment and Cooperation: Laos (2020)*, and *Guide for Countries and Regions on Overseas Investment and Cooperation: Cambodia (2020)* issued by Ministry of Commerce of the People's Republic of China.

3　Liu, J. G. (2014). The Characteristics of Religions in Southeast Asia and Their Role in China's Foreign Exchange: On the Characteristics of Chinese Religions in Southeast Asia. Journal of Overseas Chinese Historical Studies, (1):28-33. (in Chinese)

1.2   The Impact of the COVID-19 Pandemic on Economic and Social Development of ASEAN Countries

The ASEAN economy developed fast before the COVID-19 pandemic. From 2012 to 2019, ASEAN's GDP jumped from US$2.2 trillion to US$3.1 trillion, with an average annual growth rate of 5%; its per capita GDP rose from US$3,575 to US$4,641, with an average annual growth rate of 3.8%. Prior to the pandemic, ASEAN narrowed the gap with the global average with faster economic growth, and its extreme poverty rate reduced significantly. However, there were massive differences among countries. Thailand, Malaysia, and Indonesia were upper-middle income countries, whereas the Philippines, Myanmar, Vietnam, Cambodia, and Laos were lower-middle income countries.

The pandemic caused a negative economic growth to ASEAN countries until a gradual rebound in 2021[1]. The pandemic drove down ASEAN's GDP and per capita GDP in 2020, whose growth rates were -3.6% and -4.5%, both lower than the global average[2]. In 2021, the economies of ASEAN gradually recovered, with a GDP growth rate of 4.6% and per capita growth rate of 3.7% (see Figure 1-1). In 2020, Indonesia was listed as a lower-middle income country[3], while the growth rate on GDP per capita in the Philippines, Malaysia, and Thailand were -11%, -6.7%, and -6.4% respectively. From 2020 to 2022, except for Brunei and Myanmar, the per capita GDP of the remaining ASEAN countries returned to positive growth. The top three in terms of growth were Singapore, the Philippines and Malaysia with annual growth rate of per capita GDP being 6.7%, 5.1% and 4.8% respectively. Overall, the pandemic has caused significant economic fluctuations in some ASEAN countries, and the poverty reduction is facing a big challenge.

---

1   Brunei and Singapore are high-income countries. Since this report focuses on emerging economies and developing ASEAN countries, Brunei and Singapore are excluded in the follow-up analysis of poverty.

2   In 2020, the annual growth rate in global GDP and per capita GDP were -3.1% and -4.1%, respectively.

3   Based on the World Bank's country classifications by income level.

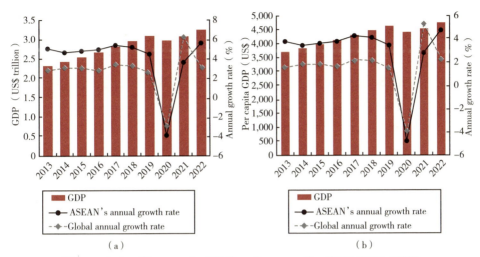

(a)　　　　　　　　　　　　　　　(b)

Figure 1-1　Changes in GDP and per capita GDP, 2013-2022

Sources: The World Bank (https://data.worldbank.org), at constant 2015 prices.

The impact of the COVID-19 pandemic on industries in ASEAN countries differed, with the countries with a higher proportion of GDP contributed by the service sector being hit the hardest. Overall, the agriculture sector held a large share in ASEAN's industrial structure, which is above the global average (see Figure 1-2). Compared with other ASEAN countries, Myanmar, Cambodia, and Laos have the highest proportion of GDP contributed by agriculture, all above 15%[1]. Manufacturing accounts for 62.7% of Brunei's economy, far above the proportion in other ASEAN countries. Indonesia and Vietnam also have a larger proportion of GDP contributed by manufacturing, accounting for 39.9% and 37.5%, respectively. The service sector in Singapore, the Philippines, Thailand, and Malaysia contributes more than 50% of their GDP. Due to the pandemic, the agriculture sector experienced negative growth in Singapore (-4.2%), Thailand (-3.5%), Malaysia (-2.4%), and the Philippines (-0.2%) in 2020. The manufacturing sector was hit hard in the Philippines (-13.1%), Malaysia (-6.1%), Thailand (-5.4%), Indonesia (-2.8%), and Cambodia (-1.4%) in 2020, while Laos, Myanmar, and Vietnam still witnessed 4% growth in the output value of the manufacturing sector. In 2021, except for Brunei (-4.2%),

---

1　Data from the World Bank's public database (https://data.worldbank.org).

the manufacturing sector recovered positive growth across ASEAN, especially in Singapore, Cambodia, the Philippines, and Laos, where the manufacturing sector grew by 13.3%, 9.4%, 8.5%, and 7.6%, respectively. Except for Myanmar and Vietnam, the service sector declined in other ASEAN countries due to the pandemic. Among them, the Philippines, Thailand, and Cambodia was hit the hardest by the pandemic, with annual growth rates of -9.1%, -7.0%, and -6.3% in 2020, respectively. In 2021, the service sector gradually recovered in all countries except Myanmar, Cambodia, and Laos.

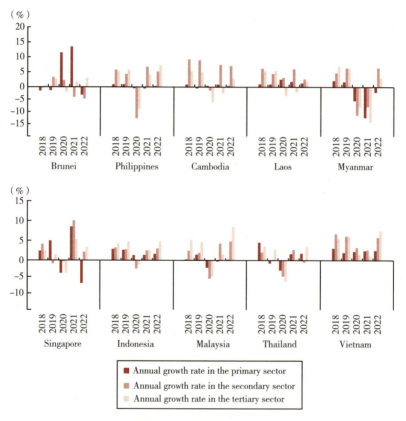

Figure 1-2 Annual growth rates of the three main sectors in ASEAN countries, 2018-2022

Note: In 2021, annual growth rates of the three main sectors in Myanmar were -12.5%, -20.6% and -18.4%, respectively.

Source: The World Bank's public database (https://data.worldbank.org).

The pandemic sped up the decline of annual growth rate in population. From 2012 to 2019, the average population growth rate in ASEAN was 1.1%, 0.06 percentage points lower than the global average (see Figure 1-3). Prior the pandemic, a year-on-year decline of 0.04 percentage points was witnessed in the annual population growth rate, which further went down by 0.06 percentage points in 2020 and 0.13 percentage points in 2021. The decline of growth in population sped up during the pandemic. In 2021, this trend of decline slowed down in all ASEAN countries except for Singapore. From the perspective of urbanization, most ASEAN countries have a higher proportion of rural population than the world average. In Cambodia, the rural residents accounted for at least 75% of its population. Vietnam, Laos, Myanmar, the Philippines, and Thailand also have more than half of their population living in rural areas. Brunei and Malaysia are the exceptions, with relatively low proportions of the rural population, both under 25%. As for the sheer number of rural population, Indonesia has over 100 million people living in rural areas due to its large population, followed by Vietnam, the Philippines, Myanmar, and Thailand, all of which have over 30 million people living in rural areas each. Malaysia and Laos have less than 10 million rural inhabitants each.

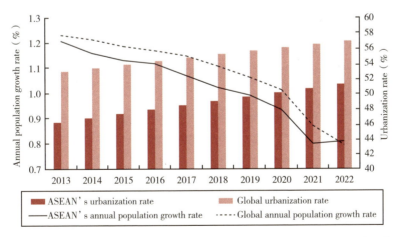

Figure 1-3   Changes in the annual population growth rate and urbanization rate of ASEAN, 2013-2022

Source: The World Bank's public database (https://data.worldbank.org).

The pandemic has changed the age structure of ASEAN countries, with some witnessing a decline in their working-age population. The working-age population is generally defined as those aged 15-64, the elderly population is aged 65 and above, and the underage population is aged 0-14. The proportion of the working-age population in most ASEAN countries remained relatively stable between 2017 and 2021, at around 60%-70% of the total population (see Figure 1-4). However, the proportion of underage and elderly populations varies significantly among ASEAN countries. According to the latest UN standards, a country is defined as ageing when the share of people aged 65 and above is above 7%. Thailand and Vietnam have surpassed this 7% threshold, with the proportion of the elderly population in Thailand exceeding 10%, indicating a high degree of ageing. The underage population will become the working-age population in the future, so a high proportion of this population can reflect a country's high potential of labor resources. The average proportion of the population aged 0-14 in Laos, Cambodia, and the Philippines is over 30%, higher than that in other ASEAN countries, representing a younger population structure. Compared to 2017-2019, the proportion of the population aged 0-14 in all ASEAN countries decreased between 2020 and 2022, with Timor-Leste experiencing the fastest decline, with a decrease of 2%, and Malaysia, the Philippines, and Laos experiencing the faster decline, with a decrease of approximately 1%. The proportion of the population aged 65 and above has increased in all countries in the region, with Singapore and Thailand recording the fastest increase, which experienced an increase of 2.9 percentage points and 1.9 percentage points, respectively. In addition, the pandemic has led to a decrease in the labor force in Singapore, Thailand, Vietnam, and Brunei. The labor force decreased by 2.5 percentage points, 1.1 percentage points, 0.5 percentage points, and 0.1 percentage points in these four countries, respectively, compared to the level before the pandemic.

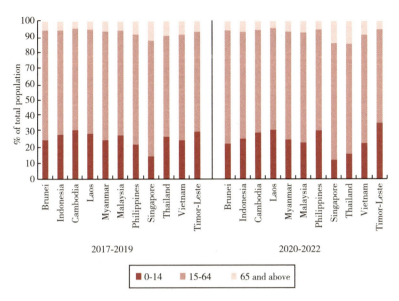

Figure 1-4   Average age structure of the population in ASEAN countries, 2017-2022

Source: Calculated on data from the World Bank's public database (https://data.worldbank.org).

The human development index[1] of ASEAN countries grew at a slower rate on the whole but continued to decline during the pandemic. From 2012 to 2019, the ASEAN countries witnessed continuous enhancement in the education and health conditions and income level of residents. The average Human Development Index (HDI) rose from 0.698 in 2012 to 0.733 in 2019. The level of human development in ASEAN maintained at the medium level[2], its gap with the global average was narrowed (see Figure 1-5). However, the HDI declined continuously during the pandemic. From 2020 to 2021, the average growth rate of ASEAN's HDI stood at -0.64%, below the global average (-0.41%). Except for Singapore, all ASEAN countries reported negative HDI growth. Among all ASEAN countries, the Philippines, Indonesia, and Malaysia suffered the greatest from the pandemic. In 2022, the average growth rate of ASEAN's HDI was 1.32%, 0.37 percentage points higher than the global average (0.95%).

---

1   Human development is measured by the UNDP in three key dimensions of human development: a long and healthy life, being knowledgeable and having a decent standard of living.

2   The UNDP's Human Development Index Classification.

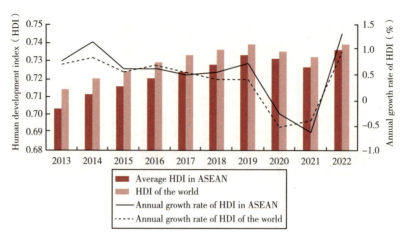

Figure 1-5   The value and annual average growth rate of Human Development Index of the world and in ASEAN, 2013-2022

Source: UNDP,*Human Development Report 2022/23.*

Health, education and income level have been adversely affected. In 2021, despite insignificant changes to the mean years of schooling in most ASEAN countries, there was a significant drop in life expectancy and expected years of schooling (see Figure 1-6). For the former, the largest decline occurred in Indonesia and the Philippines, with growth rates of -2.1% and -1.8% respectively; for the latter, the largest decline occurred in Laos and the Philippines, with growth rates of -1.6% and -1% respectively. During the pandemic, the per capita gross national income of Myanmar, the Philippines, Thailand, Malaysia and Cambodia showed negative growth. Myanmar, the Philippines and Thailand were most affected, with annual gross national income growth rates of -8.3%, -4.5% and -2.1% respectively. Life expectancy and years of schooling did not affect, while the average years of schooling increased, and the decline in per capita GNI slowed down. In short, the negative impacts of the pandemic on health, education and income have further increased the vulnerability of people in ASEAN countries and increased the likelihood of returning to poverty.

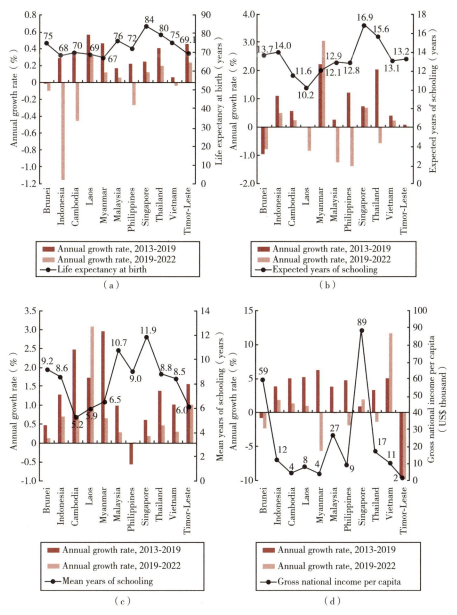

Figure 1-6   Changes in indicators of Human Development Index

Note: Gross national income per capita was calculated according to the PPP standard in 2017.

Source:UNDP, *Human Development Report 2023*.

The "digital divide" has led to greater inequality during the pandemic. From 2012 to 2019, there was an increasing number of fixed broadband and internet users and the number of mobile phones per 100 people (see Figure 1-7). In 2022, ASEAN's fixed broadband subscriptions and individuals using the internet accounted for 9.5% and 65% of the population[1]. There is a large difference in internet coverage among the ASEAN countries. In 2022, the internet coverage was the highest in Malaysia, Brunei and Singapore; Thailand and Vietnam was 88% and 79%, respectively, while in Timor-Leste, the internet coverage was the lowest (39.5%). Except for Singapore and Brunei, Vietnam experienced the highest fixed broadband coverage at 21.7% in 2022, followed by Thailand (18.5%), Malaysia (12.4%), the Philippines (7.6%), Indonesia (4.9%), and Cambodia, Laos, Myanmar and Timor-Leste experienced the lowest fixed broadband coverage below 3%. However, the pandemic throttled back digitalization. In 2020, the number of mobile cellular subscriptions per 100 people in ASEAN dropped by 3 percent from 2019, but slightly went upward in 2021. The digitization efforts in Thailand and the Philippines were considerably affected, with growth rate on mobile cellular subscriptions per 100 people of -12% and -11% in 2020, respectively. In 2021, Thailand experienced the highest number of mobile phones per 100 people at 169, Laos experienced the lowest number of mobile phones per 100 people at 65, respectively. The figure in the rest of the ASEAN countries was between 125 and 150[2]. While most countries have tried distance learning during the pandemic, it obviously failed to cover all families[3]. In 2020, 45.3% of primary schools in the ASEAN region were equipped with computers. Among them, all primary schools in Malaysia equipped with computers. The proportion in Vietnam, the Philippines, Indonesia and Myanmar was 84.6%, 70.5%, 40.4%, and 1.1%, respectively.[4] Students' limited participation in online education may reduce their future annual earnings by 3.8%[5], and digital divide is likely to further increase population inequality in the future.

---

1 Data from the World Bank's public database (https://data.worldbank.org).

2 Ibid.

3 Based on the UNESCO's "Startling Digital Divides in Distance Learning Emerge".

4 Data from *2022 ASEAN SDG Snapshot Report* issued by the ASEAN Secretariat.

5 Data from *World Bank East Asia and Pacific Economic Update* issued in October 2021.

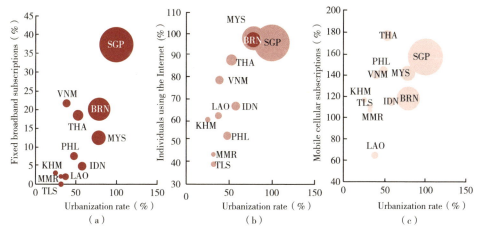

Figure 1-7 Digital development in ASEAN, 2022

Note: (1) The size of the dot is directly proportional to the country's per capita GDP.

(2) "Fixed broadband subscriptions (per 100 people)" data from 2021 for Laos, "Individuals using the Internet (% of population)" data from 2021 for Brunei, Cambodia, Laos, Myanmar, Philippines and Vietnam, Mobile cellular subscriptions (per 100 people) data from 2021 for Laos.

Source: The World Bank's public database (https://data.worldbank.org).

The pandemic has given rise to new forms and models of business. There were more opportunities for poverty alleviation as a result of digital economy[1]**.** Although the pandemic has led to negative economic growth in ASEAN countries, digitalization and informatization in those countries have begun to take shape before the pandemic, laying a foundation for the development of new business forms and models during the pandemic. The digital economy generated more opportunities for disadvantaged groups such as small and medium-sized enterprises (SMEs), women, and young adults to get rid of poverty. The size of the digital economy in ASEAN was US$102 billion in 2019 and reached US$116 billion in 2020, an year-on-year increase of 14%. In Southeast Asia. the annual growth rate of digital economy remained at 27% since 2021 and the return of the digital economy is expected to realize

---

1　The new business forms and models are embodied in the consumption patterns of e-commerce, mobile payment, online medical care, online education, online travel, takeout delivery, online car hailing and other online and offline integration.

US$100 billion in 2023[1]. Lockdown management during the pandemic has forced retailers to shift to online sales. The market size of the e-commerce retail sector in the ASEAN region grew to US$3 billion in 2019, which more than doubled to US$7 billion in 2020. The rapid growth of e-commerce has offered opportunities for women's empowerment, and led to a surge in demand for express delivery services. Ninja Van deliveries in Thailand increased by 300% in 2020, and the food delivery business in Southeast Asia increased by 183% in the same year[2]. Cold chain transport and IoT have provided technological support for SMEs to develop midstream food supply chains, while also boosting healthy dietary consumption and creating jobs for small-scale producers[3]. A large number of Internet "unicorns"[4] have been established, which have outstanding performance in ride-hailing, e-commerce, video games and online travel. Singapore, Indonesia, Thailand and Vietnam are the four largest markets of digital economy in the ASEAN region in terms of market size and development potential[5]. At present, the digital economy has created 160,000 jobs directly and 30 million jobs indirectly in Southeast Asia[6], which brings more possible opportunities for vulnerable groups to reduce poverty and get rich.

1.3 Poverty Reduction Progress in ASEAN

Extreme poverty[7] was effectively alleviated. Vietnam experienced the largest decline in the population living in extreme poverty among ASEAN countries with its extreme poverty rate dropping from 29.9% in 2002 to 0.7%

---

1   Data from *E-conomy SEA 2022* and *E-conomy SEA 2023*.

2   Data from Momentum Works and SIIA.

3   Based on *The State of Food Security and Nutrition in the World 2023* published by FAO in 2023.

4   Internet companies such as Garena, GOTO, Grab, Lazada, Shopee, Traveloka and VNG are considered to be the most influential "unicorns" in ASEAN.

5   Based on *Charting ASEAN's Digital Future: Emerging Policy Challenges* issued by the Singapore Institute of International Affairs (SIIA).

6   Indirect jobs refer to jobs created by the digital platform business, including transport driver partners, delivery riders, content creators, and personnel from third-party logistics companies that have e-commerce business.

7   The extreme poverty line is US$2.15 per person per day, according to the UN's *Sustainable Development Goals Report 2022*.

in 2020. Extreme poverty was also basically eliminated in Thailand and Malaysia (see Table 1-2). Although the extreme poverty rate in Indonesia dropped to 2.5% in 2022, more than 6.8 million people still lived in extreme poverty in 2022 due to its large population. The poverty rate in the Philippines showed no significant change in 2021 compared to that in 2018, but there was a slight increase in the number of people living in extreme poverty due to population growth. According to national poverty lines set by the each ASEAN countries, Thailand experienced the largest decline in the population living in extreme poverty among the ten ASEAN countries with its extreme poverty rate dropping from 42.3% in 2000 to 6.3% in 2021[1]. From 2012 to 2017, Myanmar and the Philippines experienced the largest decline in the poverty rate among ASEAN countries. The former experienced a plunge from 42.2% in 2015 to 24.8% in 2017, with around 3.5 million people being lifted out of poverty; the latter experienced a drop from 25.2% in 2012 to 16.7% in 2018, with around 6.6 million people getting rid of poverty. The poverty rate in Vietnam steadily went down from 28.9% in 2002 to 4.3% in 2022. Despite its small population, Timor-Leste has a high incidence of poverty and a prominent poverty problem.

Table 1-2　The proportion and number of people living in extreme poverty in the ASEAN countries

Countries	Extreme poverty rate (%)			People living in extreme poverty (million)		
	2002	2017	2022	2002	2017	2022
Vietnam	29.9	1.2[b]	1	24.1	1.1[b]	0.98
Indonesia	26.8	6.6	2.5	59.0	17.5	6.89
Laos	25.4	7.1[b]	–	1.4	0.5[b]	–
Philippines	13.6[a]	3[b]	3[c]	11.3[a]	3.3[b]	3.4[c]
Myanmar	6.2[d]	2	–	3.2[d]	1	–
Thailand	1.8	0	0[c]	1.2	0	0[c]

1　Data from the World Bank's PovcalNet (http://iresearch.worldbank.org/PovcalNet/) and ASEANstats database.

Continued

Countries	Extreme poverty rate (percent)			People living in extreme poverty (million)		
	2002	2017	2022	2002	2017	2022
Malaysia	1.6[a]	0	0[c]	0.4[a]	0	0[c]
Timor-Leste	40.9[e]	24.4[f]	–	0.37[e]	0.3[f]	–

Notes: (1) According to the international poverty line standards published by the World Bank in 2020, the poverty line is US$2.15 per person per day.

(2) Cambodia did not disclose relevant data on the poverty rate and the poor population.

(3) a, b, c, d,e and f represent data for 2003, 2018, 2021, 2015, 2001 and 2014, respectively.

Source: The World Bank's public database and *ASEAN Statistical Yearbook 2023*.

Before the pandemic, the income and consumption growth of the lower class in most ASEAN countries kept rising and benefited from the continuous trend of shared prosperity. In recent years, the average level of consumption or income of the bottom 40% increased significantly in ASEAN countries, outpacing their national averages except in Vietnam and Laos. Among these countries, the growth of Myanmar was the fastest in the terms of average consumption or income of the bottom 40%, with an average annual growth of 9.5% from 2015 to 2017, much higher than the national average of 1.3%. The average annual growth rate of consumption or income of the bottom 40% in Malaysia was 7% between 2011 and 2015, which was two percentage points higher than the national average. The average annual growth rate of consumption or income of the bottom 40% in the Philippines was 6.1% between 2015 and 2018, higher than the national average of 3.3%. In Thailand and Laos, the annual growth rates were the lowest, which were 2.2% and 1.9%, respectively. The average consumption and income growth rates for the bottom 40% in Vietnam and Laos were 0.7 and 1.2 percentage points lower than the national average, respectively.

Box 1-1 Poverty Line and Multidimensional Poverty

Poverty line. Poverty lines are international standards adopted by the World Bank to measure extreme poverty, typically reflecting the minimum amount of money in a country for the impoverished population to meet basic living needs such as nutrition, clothing, and housing. The World Bank announced that, from the autumn of 2022, the international poverty line was to be raised from US$1.90 per person per day to US$2.15 per person per day. It also updated the poverty line for lower-middle income countries and upper-middle income countries to US$3.65 per person per day and US$6.85 per person per day, respectively[a].

Multidimensional poverty. Multidimensional poverty is usually measured using the Multidimensional Poverty Index (MPI), which is an indicator system jointly proposed by the United Nations and the Oxford Poverty and Human Development Initiative. It includes three dimensions: health, education, and living standards, comprehensively reflecting the situation where individuals or families are deprived of multiple dimensions of welfare at the same time[b].

Shared prosperity. The World Bank measures a country's shared prosperity based on the consumption or annual income growth rate of the bottom 40% of the population in income distribution. The shared prosperity premium is the difference between the growth of the poorest 40% and the growth rate for the entire population[c].

Source: a. The World Bank (2022), Fact Sheet: An Adjustment to Global Poverty Lines.

b. 2022 Global Multidimensional Poverty Index (MPI) released by the United Nations Development Programme.

c. The World Bank, Poverty and Inequality Platform.

The pandemic delayed the progress of poverty reduction. According to national poverty lines set by each ASEAN countries, there was a modest increase in both the poverty rate and the number of people living in poverty in Cambodia, the Philippines, Indonesia, and Thailand after 2020. Among these four countries, Cambodia and the Philippines experienced a significant increase in the poverty rate. The poverty rate in Cambodia increased from 13.5% in 2017 to 17.8% in 2021, and that in the Philippines from 16.7% in 2017 to 18.1% in 2021, with 2.48 million people falling into poverty. In contrast, Indonesia and Thailand experienced a modest increase in the poverty rate. The poverty rate in Indonesia decreased from 10.6% in 2019 to 9.4% in 2021, with 2.31 million people falling into poverty, and Thailand experienced a rise from 6.2% in 2019 to 6.8% in 2020, with 500,000 people falling into poverty (see Figure 1-8). However, according to the international poverty line for upper-middle income countries (US$6.85 per person per day), Thailand experienced an increase in the poverty rate from 13.1% in 2019 to 13.2% in 2020, with more than 930,000 people falling into poverty.

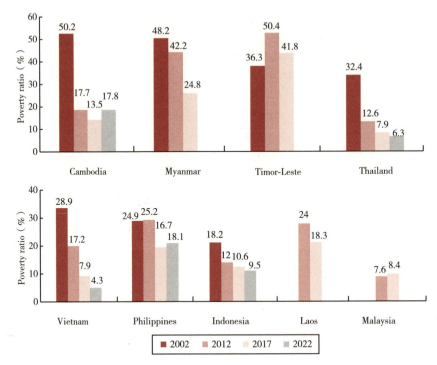

Figure 1-8   Proportion of the population below the national poverty line of some ASEAN countries

Notes: (1) Since Singapore and Brunei have completely got rid of poverty and both countries have stopped publishing data on the poor population, they are not included in the statistics.

(2) 2003, 2012, 2016, and 2020 data for Cambodia; 2016 and 2018 data for Laos; 2005, 2010, and 2017 data for Myanmar; 2022,2012,2017 and 2021 data for Thailand; 2015 and 2019 data for Malaysia; and 2003, 2012, 2018, and 2021 data for the Philippines;2001,2007 and 2014 data for Timor-Leste.

Source: The World Bank's Povcalnet and ASEANstats database.

Multidimensional poverty was mildly alleviated, but its severity differed across countries. The Global Multidimensional Poverty Index (MPI) of Timor-Leste is 0.222, while MPI in other ASEAN Countries stayed below 0.2 across ASEAN countries, but it was far higher in Myanmar, Cambodia, and Laos than in any other ASEAN countries[1]. The people living in multidimensional poverty accounted for over 37% of the poor population in Myanmar, and over 15% in

---

1 Data from *Multidimensional Poverty Index Report 2022*.

Laos and Cambodia [1]. The MPI of ASEAN countries declined as compared to previous years (see Table 1-3). Although Timor-Leste, Laos and Cambodia witnessed the greatest decline in MPI by 0.14, 0.101 and 0.1 respectively, they still have a high level of MPI and suffer severely from multidimensional poverty. In Myanmar, Thailand, Vietnam, and Laos, multidimensional poverty was mainly affected by the level of education, and people falling into poverty as a result of education deprivation accounted for 48%, 45%, 41%, and 40% of the multidimensional poor population respectively. However, in Cambodia, the Philippines, and Timor-Leste, multidimensional poverty was greatly affected by living standards, and people with poor living standards accounted for 45%-50% of the multidimensional poor population. Health exerted a greater impact on multidimensional poverty in Indonesia and Thailand than other countries, and people falling into poverty as a result of health problems accounted for 30% of the multidimensional poor population (see Figure 1-9).

Table 1-3   **Multidimensional Poverty Index and its changes in ASEAN countries**

Countries	MPI		Change of MPI	
	Year	Value	Period	Change
Cambodia	2022	0.070	2014-2022	-0.100
Indonesia	2017	0.014	2012-2017	-0.014
Laos	2017	0.108	2011-2017	-0.101
Philippines	2017	0.028	2013-2017	-0.009
Thailand	2019	0.002	2012-2019	-0.003
Vietnam	2020/2021	0.008	2013-2021	-0.012
Myanmar	2015/2016	0.176	–	–
Malaysia	2019	0.011	2016-2019	-0.004
Timor-Leste	2016	0.222	2010-2016	-0.140

Source: *Global Multidimensional Poverty Index 2023*, and the World Bank.

---

1   Calculated according to national poverty lines.

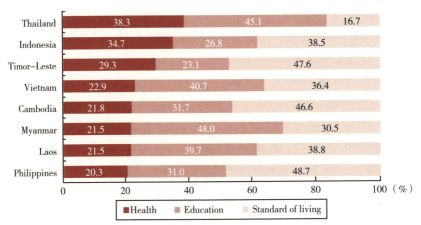

Figure 1-9   Contribution of deprivation in dimension to overall multidimensional poverty in some ASEAN countries

Source: *Global Multidimensional Poverty Index 2022.*

There were constantly improving living standards but inequalities in service provision between urban and rural areas. From 2012 to 2020, people's life in ASEAN countries has been getting notably better off[1] (see Figure 1-10). Brunei, Singapore, Malaysia, and Thailand basically achieved full coverage of electricity, basic drinking water, and basic sanitation services across urban and rural areas. However, the living standards in Myanmar and Cambodia were lower than other ASEAN countries, with the coverage of electricity, basic drinking water, and basic sanitation services below than global average. A large gap also existed in living standards between rural and urban areas in the two countries. In 2022, the proportion of the urban population with access to electricity in Myanmar was 31 percentage points higher than that of the rural population, and the availability of basic medical services in Cambodia's urban areas was 32 percentage points higher than that in rural areas. Laos featured a higher proportion of electricity users than many other ASEAN countries with no inequalities in electricity supply between urban and rural areas, but there was a large gap between urban and rural areas in the availability of water and basic medical services. The disparity in basic public services between urban and rural

---

1   Data from the World Bank's public database (https://data.worldbank.org).

areas means impoverished areas lag behind in infrastructure, education training, basic sanitation and other services, which may increase the pressure and difficulty of poverty reduction in these areas.

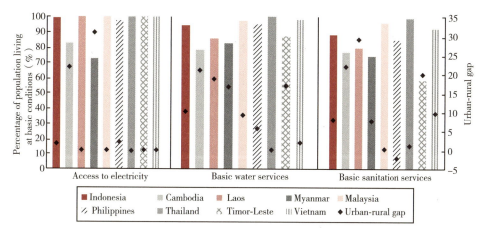

Figure 1-10   Living standards and urban-rural gap in some ASEAN countries in 2022

Note: 2021 data for "Access to electricity".

Source: The World Bank's public database (https://data.worldbank.org).

1.4   Progress in Poverty Reduction in ASEAN Countries

Among the ten ASEAN countries, Brunei and Singapore are high income countries, where poverty is not considered a major problem. Still, they track the living conditions of lower income groups. For example, the Social Support Group of Ministry of Social and Family Development of Singapore, through ComCare, supports low income families with basic living expenses, including tuition fees, and provides subsidies (COVID-19 Recovery Grant) to families unemployed due to the pandemic[1]. Except for Brunei and Singapore, other ASEAN countries still face varying degrees of poverty issues.

1.4.1   Malaysia

Malaysia has made great strides in eradicating poverty, but the rate of

---

1   Based on the data from the Ministry of Social and Family Development (MSF) of Singapore.

poverty reduction is slowing. Malaysia has basically eradicated extreme poverty. It falls in to the category of middle income countries, with the per capita gross national income of US$27,607 in 2019. Its poverty rate in 2018 was 3.4%[1]. In the same year, 5.6% of the households in Malaysia had a monthly income below the national poverty line. The COVID-19 pandemic hindered poverty reduction in the country. In 2020, the poverty rate in Malaysia increased to 8.4% based on the national poverty line. In addition, the country's income inequality, measured by the Gini coefficient, slightly increased from 40.7% in 2019 to 41.1% in 2020 (see Figure 1-11).

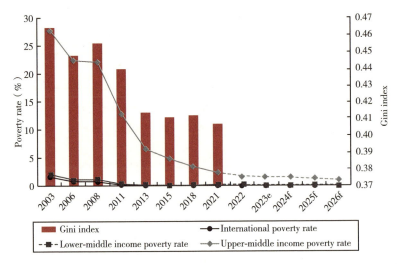

Figure 1-11   Poverty rate and changes of Gini coefficient in Malaysia

Notes: e=estimate, f=forecast. Dotted lines are the estimated or predicted value.

Source: The World Bank's Poverty and Inequality Platform.

Compared to urban areas, poverty and inequality are still severe in rural areas of Malaysia. According to the poverty line of upper-middle income countries, the proportion of people living in poverty is less than 10% in Malaysia. However, the poverty rate of its rural population, children under the age of 14, and uneducated population aged 16 and above are relatively high at 8%, 6%, and 7%, respectively (see Figure 1-12). The poverty rate in rural areas

---

1 The World Bank defines the poverty line of upper-middle income countries as US$6.85 per person per day.

is four times that in urban areas. The bottom 40% are mainly concentrated in rural, young, and uneducated populations. 63.4% of the rural population fall in the bottom 40%, nearly twice the proportion of the urban population. Among children and the uneducated population aged 16 and above, more than half are at the bottom in terms of income or consumption, who are hard to get rid of poverty and face higher risks of poverty. To prevent the further widening of the urban-rural disparity, the Malaysian government has taken a number of measures to promote inclusive rural development, such as improving healthcare, education, and other public infrastructure in rural areas, developing digital infrastructure, offering discounts and rent relief to some businesses and for selected housing, providing online outreach programs for rural entrepreneurs, launching food basket programs for impoverished families and indigenous people, and reducing kindergarten fees[1].

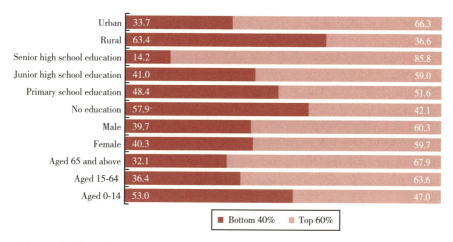

Figure 1-12   Distribution of consumption or income in different groups in Malaysia

Notes: (1) Educational attainment was surveyed over the age of 16.

(2) The bottom 40% and the top 60% refer to the proportion of people whose income or consumption level is in the bottom 40% and the top 60%, respectively.

Source: The World Bank's Poverty and Inequality Platform.

---

1   Based on "A Speech by Encik Abdul Kahar bin Abdullah, Secretary of the Strategic Planning Division of the Malaysian Ministry of Rural Development" released by the International Poverty Reduction Center in China in 2022.

Malaysia's economy has recovered strongly in the post-pandemic period, but went slowly with the poor population. Malaysia's real GDP reported negative growth in 2020 due to the pandemic, but the economy rebounded strongly in 2022, with a growth rate of 8.7%, 5.6 percentage points higher than that in 2021. According to World Bank's predictions, the poverty rate in Malaysia will decrease to 1.4%, 1.2%, and 11% from 2024 to 2026. However, risks to food safety are still a problem in Malaysia. The disease prevalence due to moderate or severe unsafe food between 2019 and 2021 was 15.4%, representing about 5 million people[1]. The pandemic has further worsened Malaysia's food safety issues. According to a survey report by the World Bank on the impact of COVID-19 on the poorest households[2], about 20% of households have run out of food in the past 30 days. In response, Malaysia proposed in its 12th Five-Year Plan to allocate MYR400 billion to revitalize the economy, enhance social welfare, safety, and inclusiveness, and promote environmental sustainability. In doing so, its ultimate goal is to build a "prosperous, inclusive, and sustainable Malaysia"[3].

1.4.2 Thailand

Thailand has basically eradicated extreme poverty, but the COVID-19 pandemic hindered the progress of poverty reduction and shared prosperity in the country. After 2012, the extreme poverty rate in Thailand remained below 0.1% and continued to decrease. The progress of poverty reduction in Thailand has slowed down since 2015, with increases in poverty rate and poor population in 2016, 2018, and 2020. The significant decrease in poverty rate in 2019 was attributed to the continuous increase in social assistance[4]. The poverty rate in Thailand slightly increased from 6.2% in 2019 to 6.8% in 2020 and then decreased to 6.3% in 2021. According to the poverty line for upper-middle income countries (US$6.85 per person per day), the poverty rate in Thailand was

---

1　Data from *Macro Poverty Outlook in Malaysia* released by the World Bank in 2023.

2　A monthly income of MYR2,000 or less.

3　Based on "Malaysia Launches New Plan Focusing on Post-COVID-19 Recovery", *People's Daily*, October 28,2021.

4　Data from *Poverty & Equity Brief in Thailand* released by the World Bank in 2023.

stable at 13.2% in both 2019 and 2020 and decreased to 11% in 2022. From 2014 to 2019, the annual growth in per capita income or consumption of the bottom 40% was 1.17 percentage points higher than the national average, indicating progress in shared prosperity. Affected by the COVID-19 pandemic, the Gini coefficient slightly increased from 0.348 in 2019 to 0.351 in 2021(see Figure 1-13).

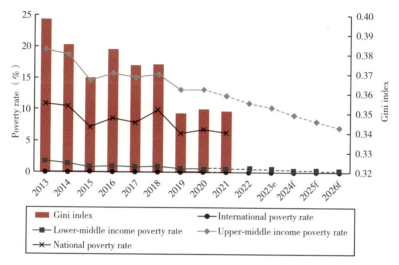

Figure 1-13　Poverty rate and changes of Gini coefficient in Thailand

Notes: (1) e=estimate, f=forecast. Dotted lines are the estimated or predicted value.
(2) Actual data for 2021. Nowcast for 2022-2023. Forecasts for 2024-2026.
(3) In 2020, the national poverty line in Thailand is 2,762 baht per person per month.
Source: The World Bank's Poverty and Inequality Platform.

Thailand's children and uneducated population have a higher incidence and a higher risk of poverty. In 2021, Thailand's highest poverty rate occurred among the uneducated population aged 16 and above, being 25%. 61.4% of them fell into the bottom 40% in terms of income or consumption level, indicating they were at higher risk of poverty. A higher level of education suggests lower poverty rate. The poverty rate among people aged 16 and above who had received primary, junior high, and senior high school education was 14%, 9%, and 1%, respectively. The proportion of people of these three groups falling in the bottom 40% in terms of income or consumption level were 48.6%, 31.6%, and 7.9%, respectively. Among different age groups, the poverty rate was higher among children and elderly people aged 65 and above, at 20% and 13%, respectively. The proportion of people in these two groups falling in the bottom 40% in terms of income or consumption level was 55.6% and 44.5%, respectively (see Figure 1-14).

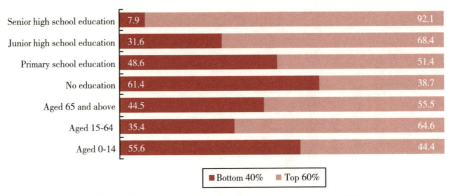

Figure 1-14 Distribution of consumption or income in different groups in Thailand

Notes: (1) Educational attainment was surveyed over the age of 16.

(2) The bottom 40% and the top 60% refer to the proportion of people whose income or consumption level is in the bottom 40% and the top 60%, respectively.

Source: The World Bank's Poverty and Inequality Platform.

The Thailand government has taken proactive measures to address the challenges of poverty reduction in the post-pandemic period. The World Bank expects that the extreme poverty rate in Thailand will decrease to 0 in the future. According to the poverty line for upper-middle income countries, the poverty rate will continue to decrease, being 9.1%, 8.1%, and 7.1% from 2024 to 2026, respectively. Despite the economic recovery, the discontinuance of some relief projects and rising commodity prices have placed greater burden on low income families. The income increase has failed to keep up with rising inflation[1]. The government of Thailand thus allocated THB60 billion to help 17 million people living below the poverty line across the country to get through difficulties. At the beginning of 2022, the government approved a budget of THB1.48 billion to fund selling low-priced goods in at least 3,000 sales points, including

---

1　Data from *Poverty & Equity Brief in Thailand* released by the World Bank in 2023.

convenience stores, shopping malls, markets, public areas, and gas stations, across 76 provinces as well as Bangkok and its surrounding areas[1]. In the 20-Year Agricultural Development Plan (2017-2036), Thailand emphasizes the need for "stability for farmers, prosperous agriculture, and sustainable development of agricultural resources". The plan also calls for cultivating smart farmers and applying inventions and modern technologies to agriculture. Learning from China's experience in poverty alleviation, Thailand has established a center for poverty eradication and sustainable lifelong development and a poverty reduction system that includes five levels: the national center, provincial centers, district level, sub-district level, and family level.

1.4.3 Indonesia

The COVID-19 pandemic slowed down poverty reduction in Indonesia. Indonesia became an upper-middle income country in 2019, with its per capita national income reaching US$11,498. The pandemic caused Indonesia's economy and its per capita income to shrink significantly in 2020, making the county fall back to the ranks of lower-middle income countries. This highlighted Indonesia's economic and social vulnerability. According to Indonesia's national poverty line, the poverty rate continued to rise in 2020 and 2021, reaching 9.8% and 10.1%, respectively. According to the international poverty line, the decrease of poverty rate in Indonesia slowed down significantly though the poverty rate did not rebound. In 2023, the poverty rate decreased by 0.6 percentage points compared to 2021, along with the economic recovery. The World Bank predicts that the poverty rate in Indonesia will continue to decline from 2024 to 2026. According to the poverty line for lower-middle income countries, Indonesia's poverty rate from 2024 to 2026 is expected to be 16.3%, 14.7%, and 13.2%, respectively (see Figure 1-15).

---

1   Collated based on *Guide for Countries and Regions on Overseas Investment and Cooperation: Thailand (2022)* released by Ministry of Commerce of the People's Republic of China.

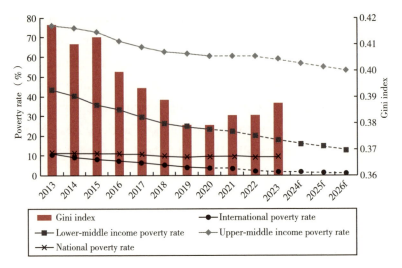

Figure 1-15　Poverty rate and changes of Gini coefficient in Indonesia

Notes: (1) e=estimate, f=forecast. Dotted lines are the estimated or predicted value.

(2) Actual data for 2023. Forecasts for 2024-2026.

(3) Indonesia's poverty line is defined by the National Bureau of Statistics (BPS) as the amount of money needed to get 2,100 calories a day, plus a small amount spent on other basic non-food items. Indonesia's national poverty line is calculated as a population-weighted average of 67 local poverty lines.

Source: The World Bank's Poverty and Inequality Platform.

Inequality in Indonesia has intensified, with a relatively large gap in consumption and income between urban and rural areas. In 2021 and 2022, Indonesia's Gini coefficient remained at 37.9 percentage points, an increase of 0.3 percentage points compared to 2018-2019. A high proportion of the population in rural areas, people with lower educational attainment, and children and the elderly were at the bottom of the consumption or income level. From 2017 to 2022, the annual growth rate of income or consumption for the bottom 40% of the population was 3.44%, 1.04 percentage points higher than the average annual growth rate of all residents. This indicates continuous progress of shared prosperity in Indonesia. The proportions of people falling in the bottom 40% population in rural and urban areas were 46.7% and 35%, respectively, with a gap of 11.7 percentage points, which is smaller compared to Malaysia. From the perspective of education level, the population aged 16 and above who have received primary education and those who have not received education have the highest proportions of people falling in the bottom 40% population, being 48.1% and 47%, respectively (see Figure 1-16). Faced with the high poverty rate in rural areas, the Indonesian government implemented a rural economic recovery strategy based on the poverty alleviation framework, which mainly included financing for the informal sector and township enterprises, providing cash and direct assistance to poor families, strengthening village enterprises to drive rural economic development, and reinforcing the strategy of boosting rural economy through village enterprises and digitizing villages through e-commerce. However, the intensification of inequality indicates that Indonesia still needs to expand the coverage of social assistance and improve the identification of target populations.

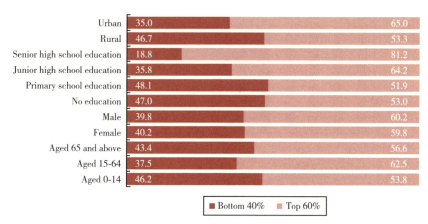

Figure 1-16   Distribution of consumption or income in different groups in Indonesia

Notes: (1) Educational attainment was surveyed over the age of 16.

(2) The bottom 40% and the top 60% refer to the proportion of people whose income or consumption level is in the bottom 40% and the top 60%, respectively.

Source: The World Bank's Poverty and Inequality Platform.

1.4.4   The Philippines

The COVID-19 pandemic hindered the poverty reduction process in the Philippines, and had a significant negative impact on economically developed regions. In 2020, due to the effect of the pandemic, the annual growth rate of the Philippines' per capita GDP declined by more than 10%. According to the Philippines' national poverty line[1], its poverty rate increased from 16.7% in 2018 to 18.1% in 2021, with an additional 2.3 million people falling into poverty (see Figure 1-17). During the pandemic, the poverty rate and the number of poor people in the Philippines increased significantly compared to other ASEAN countries.The poverty rate in the economically developed capital region, the central and southern regions of Luzon Island, and the central region of Visayas increased by 3 to 10 percentage points. In contrast, the poverty in Bangsamoro Autonomous Region in Muslim Mindanao (BARMM), the poorest area in the Philippines, decreased from 61.2% to 37.2%[2].

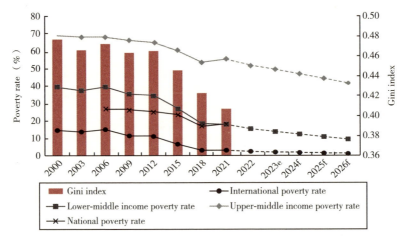

Figure 1-17   Poverty rate and changes of Gini coefficient in the Philippines
Notes: (1) e=estimate, f=forecast. Dotted lines are the estimated or predicted value.
(2) Actual data for 2021. Nowcast for 2022. Forecasts for 2024-2026.
Source: The World Bank's Poverty and Inequality Platform.

There is a significant gap in income and consumption levels among different groups in the Philippines. Since 2012, inequality in the Philippines has continued to improve, with the Gini coefficient decreasing from 46.5% to 40.7% in 2021. Nevertheless, the Philippines remained one of the countries with the highest Gini coefficient in ASEAN. Among the rural and urban populations in the Philippines, the proportion of the bottom 40% were 52.9% and 27.7%, respectively,

---

1   In 2018, the government of the Philippines adjusted the national poverty line to 25,815 Philippine pesos.

2   Data from *Poverty & Equity Brief in Philippines* released by the World Bank in 2023.

with an urban-rural gap of 25.2 percentage points. The proportion of rural poor population was 5%, while that of urban poor population was only 1%. In the Philippines, education has a significant positive impact on improving consumption or income level and reducing poverty. Among the population aged 16 and above who have not received education, the proportion of people living in poverty was up to 12%, far higher than that of other groups. Approximately 69.9% of this group were among the bottom 40% in terms of income or consumption. The proportion of people who have received primary, secondary, and high school education falling in the bottom 40% was 50.6%, 29.2%, and 11.2%, respectively (see Figure 1-18).

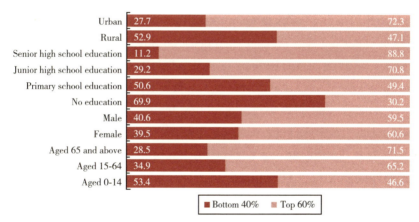

Figure 1-18   Distribution of consumption or income in different groups in the Philippines

Notes: (1) Educational attainment was surveyed over the age of 16.

(2) The bottom 40% and the top 60% refer to the proportion of people whose income or consumption level is in the bottom 40% and the top 60%, respectively.

Source: The World Bank's Poverty and Inequality Platform.

1.4.5 Myanmar

Myanmar has made significant progress in poverty reduction, however, the pandemic has worsened inequality. From 2002 to 2010, the average annual growth rate of GDP and per capita GDP in Myanmar remained above 8% and 10%, respectively. According to the national poverty line, Myanmar has successfully reduced the proportion of impoverished people from 48% in 2005 to 32% in 2015 and further reduced it to 25% in 2017. The extreme poverty rate decreased from

6.2% in 2015 to 2% in 2017. During this period, the rapid growth of the country's manufacturing and service industries contributed significantly to poverty reduction, resulting in a rapid decline in urban poverty. According to the World Bank's estimation, due to the impact of the pandemic, the GDP of Myanmar is expected to grow by 3% by September 2023, and its output is expected to be much lower than the level in 2019[1]. The inequality further worsened in the country, with some households unable to receive social assistance in a timely manner. The proportion of households with reduced consumption, increased borrowing, and reduced savings was increasing. The pandemic plunged the impoverished population into deeper poverty. The Myanmar government released the COVID-19 Economic Relief Plan (CERP) on April 27, 2020. The plan aims to improve the macroeconomic environment through monetary stimulus policies, mitigate the impact on private enterprises by improving investment, foreign trade, and banking services, alleviate the impact of COVID-19 on workers, reduce the impact of the pandemic on families, promote the development of innovative products and e-commerce platforms, improve the healthcare system, and increase funds for response to the pandemic and emergency funds[2].

There is a significant gap between urban and rural areas in Myanmar. 70% of Myanmar's population lives in rural areas, and one-third of the rural population live below the poverty line. According to the poverty line for lower-middle income countries, the poverty rate in rural areas is 24%, which is 2.7 times that in rural areas. From the perspective of consumption and income distribution, the proportion of the rural population falling in the bottom 40% is 47.3%, which is 2.2 times the proportion of the urban population during the same period. To promote rural development and poverty reduction, Myanmar is adopting a comprehensive and full-coverage rural transformation strategy by insisting on combining a people-centric strategy and a cross-sector rural development strategy to develop smart countryside and improve people's life and income while seeking green development. The initiative includes improving the living standards of rural people through rural infrastructure development, driving rural economic

---

1   Data from *Macro Poverty Outlook* released by the World Bank in 2023.

2   Based on *Guide for Countries and Regions on Overseas Investment and Cooperation: Myanmar (2022)* released by Ministry of Commerce of the People's Republic of China.

development through capital inputs, financial services, and technical assistance, promoting environmental protection, and enhancing the development capacity of rural people for achieving sustainable development[1].

The uneducated group, with relatively low income and consumption levels, faces severe problems of poverty. According to the poverty line for lower-middle income countries, the proportion of poor people is the smallest among aged 16 and above who have received high school education, which is only 2%. The poverty rate among the population aged 16 and above who have not received education reaches up to 32%, far higher than that of the educated population. From the perspective of consumption and income distribution, 55.4% and 40.5% of the population aged 16 and above who have not received education and those who have only received primary education fall into the bottom 40%, respectively. This means that more than half of the uneducated population's consumption or income level is the lowest (see Figure 1-19).

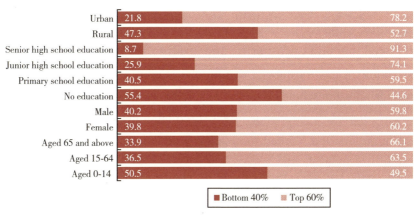

Figure 1-19   Distribution of consumption or income in different groups in Myanmar

Notes: (1) Educational attainment was surveyed over the age of 16.

(2) The bottom 40% and the top 60% refer to the proportion of people whose income or consumption level is in the bottom 40% and the top 60%, respectively.

Source: The World Bank's Poverty and Inequality Platform.

---

1   Based on "A Speech by Sai Myat Hein Soe, Assistant Head of the Department of Rural Development of the Myanmar Ministry of Cooperatives and Rural Development" released by the International Poverty Reduction Center in China in 2022.

1.4.6 Vietnam

Vietnam has made remarkable progress in poverty reduction, but the pace of reduction has slowed in recent years. Before the COVID-19 pandemic, Vietnam's economy grew rapidly, with its real GDP increasing from US$621 billion in 2012 to US$1,119 billion in 2022 and per capita income increasing from US$6,738 in 2012 to US$10,085 in 2021[1]. According to the poverty line for lower-middle income countries, the poverty rate in Vietnam decreased from 14% in 2010 to 3.8% in 2020, and the poor population decreased from 12.3 million in 2010 to 5 million in 2020. Vietnam's annual GDP growth rate recovered to 8% in 2022, and is expected to be within the range of 5.5%-6.5% in 2024-2026. Its poverty rate is expected to be 3.6%, 3.3%, and 2.9% from 2024 to 2026 (see Figure 1-20). Although Vietnam has lifted most households out of poverty, these people still face a great risk of falling back into poverty due to factors such as climate change, health problems, and labor market uncertainties. In response, the government announced to update, promote, and enhance the nationwide collaboration in poverty alleviation, ensuring no one fall behind, inspiring self-reliance, pursuing prosperity, and striving for a poverty-free Vietnam. The government has introduced conditional support policies to provide social security for poor households who are unable to work, issued specific policies to encourage enterprises and cooperatives to collaborate in production, operation, and consumption, and worked to develop production models that involve poor and low-income households[2].

Social inequality in Vietnam is worsening, and the process of shared prosperity is lagging behind. The Gini coefficient in Vietnam increased from 34.8% in 2014 to 36.1% in 2022, indicating that the gap between the rich and the poor was widening. From 2016 to 2020, the annual growth rate of income or consumption of the bottom 40% was 4.69%, 0.91 percentage points lower than the national average. The gap in social income and consumption keeps widening, and the process of shared prosperity is lagging behind.

---

1   Data from the World Bank's public database (https://data.worldbank.org). The indicators are expressed in current international dollars converted by purchasing power parity (PPP) conversion factor in 2017.

2   Based on the speech by Do Nam Trung, Consul General of Vietnam in Nanning at the 16th ASEAN-China Forum on Social Development and Poverty Reduction.

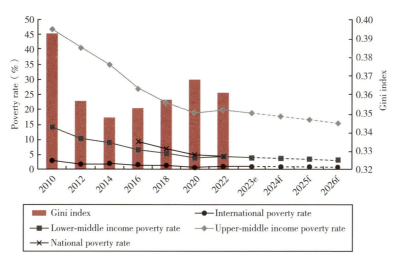

Figure 1-20   Poverty rate and changes of Gini coefficient in Vietnam

Notes: e=estimate, f=forecast. Dotted lines are the estimated or predicted value.

Source: The World Bank's Poverty and Inequality Platform.

The urban-rural gap in Vietnam is significant. People in rural areas and the uneducated may face greater economic and poverty risks. In rural areas, 52% of the population have the lowest income or consumption level in society, while only 19% of the urban population fall into the bottom 40%. The urban-rural gap in Vietnam is significantly greater than that in other ASEAN countries (see Figure 1-21). Among the uneducated population aged 16 and above, 20% live below the poverty line for lower-middle income countries, and 76% are the bottom 40%. This means that about half of the population in rural areas and those who have not received education are economically vulnerable and face a high risk of returning to poverty. The National Target Program on New-style Rural Development (2021-2025) aims to address these challenges by promoting rural economic development and creating "upgraded" new rural areas, model new rural areas, and village-level new rural areas[1]. The National Sustainable Poverty Reduction Goal Plan for 2021-2025 focuses on (1) implementing multidimensional, inclusive, and sustainable poverty reduction measures to

---

1　Based on "Draft Political Report Submitted to the 13th National Congress of the Communist Party of Vietnam Proposes Six Core Tasks for the New Term" on an electronic newspaper of the Communist Party of Vietnam, December 3, 2020.

prevent the recurrence and emergence of poverty; (2) helping impoverished individuals and households meet the minimum living standards, access basic social services, and improve their quality of life; (3) supporting poverty reduction efforts in coastal and island regions, targeting impoverished counties and particularly disadvantaged towns.

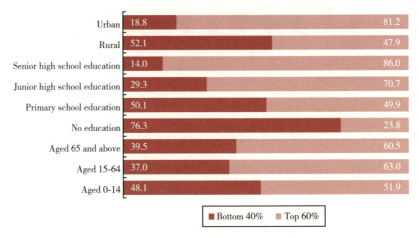

Figure 1-21   Distribution of consumption or income in different groups in Vietnam

Notes: (1) Educational attainment was surveyed over the age of 16.

(2) The bottom 40% and the top 60% refer to the proportion of people whose income or consumption level is in the bottom 40% and the top 60%, respectively.

Source: The World Bank's Poverty and Inequality Platform.

1.4.7 Cambodia

The COVID-19 pandemic has hindered Cambodia's economic development and increased the risk of returning to poverty. Before the pandemic, Cambodia made significant progress in poverty reduction, with the national poverty rate dropping from 50.2% in 2003 to 9.5% in 2019 (see Figure 1-22).In 2020, Cambodia's economy reported negative growth, with an annual GDP growth rate of -3.7%. The pandemic disrupted communication between Cambodia and other countries. In 2021, flights between China and Cambodia significantly decreased due to the pandemic, which severely affected Cambodia's tourism industry. However, the poverty rate in Cambodia increased by 8.3

percentage points in 2021 compared to 2019 due to the impact of the pandemic. The Cambodian government proposed to achieve inclusive development by addressing the employment and shared infrastructure issues in rural areas, especially those related to vulnerable groups, to improve the risk resilience of rural areas[1]. The National Social Protection Policy Framework 2016-2025 points out the need to further develop Cambodia's national social security system to benefit all its citizens, especially the poor and vulnerable groups[2]. At the same time, Cambodia is actively building the Farmer and Nature Net Association (FNN) to provide financial and technical support for small farmers in agricultural production and promote effective connections between small farmers and the market[3].

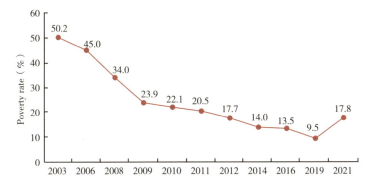

Figure 1-22   Poverty rate in Cambodia

Source: The World Bank's Poverty and Inequality Platform.

The Cambodian government has taken proactive measures to respond to the impact of the COVID-19 pandemic. One of the measures taken by the government is to actively encourage vaccination. As of 2022, the basic immunization coverage rate in Cambodia reached 87.3%, and the booster

1   Based on the speech by Sao Chivoan, Secretary of State of the Ministry of Rural Development of Cambodia, at the 17th ASEAN-China Forum on Social Development and Poverty Reduction.

2   Based on *Guide for Countries and Regions on Overseas Investment and Cooperation: Cambodia (2022)* released by Ministry of Commerce of the People's Republic of China.

3   Based on the speech by Kirth Chantharith, a village leader from Cambodia, on the 2023 ASEAN-China Village Leaders Exchange Day.

immunization coverage rate reached 62.2[1]. The government has also released the Strategic Framework and Programs for Economic Recovery in the Context of Living with COVID-19 in a New Normal 2021-2023. It aims to support Cambodia's economic growth to return to its potential speed by the end of 2023 and to strengthen the resilience of sustainable and inclusive social and economic development in the long run. It also pays attention to the development of socially vulnerable groups, aiming to reduce their economic vulnerability and risk of falling back into poverty. In 2021, the annual economic growth rate of Cambodia recovered to 2.4%, but it was still lower than the growth rate of 6.9%-7.5% between 2017 and 2019[2]. The industrial, service, and agriculture sectors grew by 5.7%, 0.3%, and 1.4%, respectively.

1.4.8 Laos

Before the COVID-19 pandemic, inequality worsened in Laos though it had made progress in poverty reduction. The national poverty rate in Laos decreased from 24.6% in 2012 to 18.3% in 2018, a decrease of 6.3 percentage points (see Figure 1-23). According to the poverty line of US$3.65 per person per day for lower-middle income countries, the international poverty rate in Laos decreased from 40.5% in 2012 to 31.9% in 2022, a decrease of 8.6%. However, the Gini coefficient increased from 36% in 2012 to 38.8% in 2018, indicating that the degree of inequality continued to deepen. From the perspective of consumption or income distribution, the annual growth in per capita consumption or income of the bottom 40% from 2012 to 2018 was only 1.9%, which was 1.17 percentage points lower than that of the country as a whole. The shared prosperity and shared prosperity premium[3] in Laos were at a relatively low level among the ten ASEAN countries, which suggests that the gap between the rich and the poor in Laos continued to widen. As of 2022, 6.9% of the population was still in extreme poverty.

---

1 Data from *Guide for Countries and Regions on Overseas Investment and Cooperation: Cambodia (2022)* released by Ministry of Commerce of the People's Republic of China.

2 Ibid.

3 The World Bank measures a country's shared prosperity based on the annual consumption/income growth rate of the bottom 40% of the population in income distribution. The shared prosperity premium is the difference between the growth of the poorest 40% and the growth rate for the entire population.

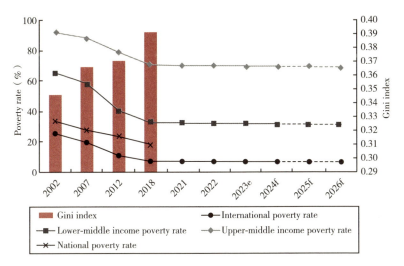

Figure 1-23　Poverty rate and changes of Gini coefficient in Laos

Notes: (1) e=estimate, f=forecast. Dotted lines are the estimated or predicted value.

(2) The national poverty line in Laos is based on the results of the Lao Expenditure and Consumption Survey (LECS), which reflects a minimum consumption threshold of 2,100 kcal per person per day. In 2019, Laos redefined the poverty calculation method. International poverty estimates for 2012 and 2018 have been revised according to the new poverty methodology.

Source: The World Bank's Poverty and Inequality Platform.

Significant gaps are observed in consumption and income between urban and rural populations and between groups with different levels of education. The poverty rate of the rural population is 10%, five times that of the urban population. Half of the rural population fall into the bottom 40% in terms of consumption and income levels, while the proportion of this group is only 19.3% in urban areas. A higher level of education indicates lower poverty rate and a higher level of consumption or income. Among the uneducated population aged 16 and above, up to 12% live below the international poverty line, but the proportions are only 6% and 2% for people that have received primary and junior high school education, respectively. From the perspective of consumption or income distribution, 56.4% of the uneducated population are the bottom 40%, compared to 38.6%, 19.7%, and 5% for people that have received primary, junior high school, and senior high school education falling in the bottom 40%, respectively (see Figure 1-24).

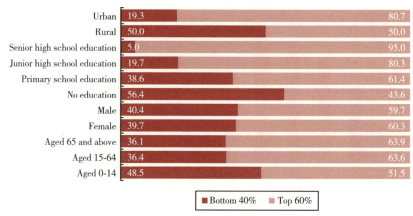

Figure 1-24   Distribution of consumption or income in different groups in Laos

Notes: (1) Educational attainment was surveyed over the age of 16.

(2) The bottom 40% and the top 60% refer to the proportion of people whose income or consumption level is in the bottom 40% and the top 60%, respectively.

Source: The World Bank's Poverty and Inequality Platform.

Laos has been facing significant challenges in poverty reduction since the COVID-19 pandemic. The economy of Laos has been gradually recovering in the post-pandemic period, and its GDP is expected to grow by 4% annually from 2023 to 2025. In May 2022, its employment basically returned to pre-COVID-19 levels. However, severe inflation in Laos is undermining the progress of poverty reduction. The country's inflation rate reached 40.3% in January 2023[1], which generated significant downward pressure and economic risks for people whose consumption or income was at the bottom of society[2]. More than half of households are choosing to reduce food consumption and education or medical expenses to cope with high inflation, especially in rural and impoverished areas[3]. In addition, the small coverage of social protection in Laos has made a limited contribution to poverty reduction, resulting in significant challenges for poverty reduction in Laos after the pandemic. The World Bank predicts that the proportion of people living below the international poverty line at US$3.65 per person per day in Laos will remain stable at around 31% from 2024 to 2026, suggesting slow

---

1   Data from the World Bank.

2   Data from *Poverty & Equity Briefs* released by the World Bank in 2023.

3   Ibid.

progress in poverty reduction (see Figure 1-23).

1.4.9　Timor-Leste

In Timor-Leste, the government has taken proactive measures to address the challenges of poverty reduction. Living standards have improved in the past decade. The proportion of people living below the national poverty line decreased from 50.4% in 2007 to 41.8% in 2014[1]. The government released the *National Action Plan for a Hunger and Malnutrition Free Timor-Leste* in 2014, which allocates US$176 million and aims to achieve *Zero Hunger* by 2025[2]. The prevalence of undernourishment in Timor-Leste decreased from 26.9% in 2014-2016 to 25% in 2017-2019[3]. The government made efforts to strengthen education system construction. There are now over 1,800 public and private schools. The net enrollment rate in primary school increased from 83% in 2008 to 92.3% in 2018. The net enrollment rate in secondary school increased from 35.5% in 2008 to 62.7% in 2018. In addition, child mortality decreased by 41% from 2013 to 2020[4]. Maternal deaths per 100,000 live births decreased form 694 in 2000 to 142 in 2017.

The COVID-19 pandemic hindered the poverty reduction process in Timor-Leste. The extreme poverty rate in Timor-Leste increased more than 5 percent in 2019. According to *Rapid Food Security Assessment* conducted in May 2020 in Timor-Leste, of a total of 1,200 households, 81% reported that the pandemic has affected their food and income sources, and 40% are choosing to reduce food consumption[5]. As of June 2020, the government allocated US$15 in electricity credits and US$100 per month for each household. The *Country Strategic Plan for 2022–2025* pays more attention to multi-sectoral approaches and actions to address malnutrition after the pandemic[6]. The World Bank expects that the extreme poverty rate in Timor-Leste will decrease from 29.3% in 2020 to

---

1　Data from the World Bank.

2　Based on "The National Action Plan for a Hunger and Malnutrition Free Timor-Leste", an article released by the Government of Timor-Leste on July 25, 2014.

3　Data from ADB Data Library.

4　Data from the World Bank.

5　Based on "Timor-Leste – Rapid Food Security Assessment 2020".

6　Based on Timor-Leste Country Strategic Plan (2023-2025).

24.4% in 2026, remaining higher than that before the pandemic (see Figure 1-25).

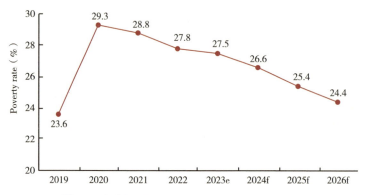

Figure 1-25   Poverty rate in Timor-Leste

Notes: (1) According to the international poverty line standards published by the World Bank in 2020, which is US$2.15 per person per day.

(2) The poverty rate of 2019 is measured according to the poverty line of US $1.90 per day (2011 PPP).

(3) e=estimate, f=forecast. Dotted lines are the estimated or predicted value.

Source: The World Bank's Poverty and Inequality Platform.

1.5 Summary

To sum up, the pandemic has intensified the pressure on the efforts of ASEAN countries to reduce poverty. Due to the impact of food insecurity on nutrition and health improvement, the poor people recover more slowly from health problems. Poverty among the uneducated over the age of 16 is a serious problem in Thailand, with a poverty rate of 25%. The pandemic has brought Indonesia back from an upper-middle income country to a lower-middle income country, highlighting its economic and social vulnerability. Several economically developed regions in the Philippines have been significantly affected by the pandemic, with their poverty rate increasing by 1%-10%. Education and poverty are closely related, and poverty is even more severe among those with low levels of education in the Philippines, which accounts for 12% of the population. There is a large gap between urban and rural areas in Myanmar, and the poverty rate in rural areas is 2.7 times that in urban areas. Among the uneducated groups in Myanmar, at least half of them have the lowest level of consumption or income, reflecting prominent poverty issues. The pandemic has reduced the contribution of manufacturing and services to Myanmar's GDP, and output is expected to be much lower than that in 2019. Vietnam is at greater risk of falling back into poverty in the face of climate change, health shocks, and labor market uncertainties. Cambodia is at increased risk of falling back into poverty due to the pandemic, and the poverty rate in 2021 increased by 8.3 percentage points compared to 2019. In Laos, income and consumption gaps exist between rural and urban areas and between people with different levels of education. The poverty issue is concentrated in rural areas, and the poverty rate in rural areas is five times that of urban poverty. 56.4% of the uneducated are at the bottom of the social consumption and income level. In addition, problems such as high inflation, food insecurity and inadequate social security system pose great challenges to poverty reduction in Laos. Although the distribution of the poverty population varies across ASEAN countries, the target population for poverty reduction is generally similar. The poverty reduction efforts should mainly focus on the lower class which is facing severe poverty problems and risks.

The digital economy brings development opportunities. Before the pandemic, ASEAN countries made progress in digitization, which laid the foundation for the emergence and expansion of new business forms and models during the pandemic. The digital economy can improve the productivity of small and medium-sized enterprises, increase job opportunities, and help vulnerable people escape poverty[1]. For example, the Malaysian government has taken a series of measures to narrow the gap between urban and rural areas and promote inclusive development in rural areas, including the development of digital infrastructure and the improvement of rural medical and education conditions. The Indonesian government is committed to boosting rural economic development through e-commerce and rural enterprises. In addition, ASEAN countries are actively deploying new digital infrastructure represented by 5G to promote digital development. All in all, digital economy has offered new opportunities for ASEAN countries to reduce poverty.

---

1   Data from *The State of Food Security and Nutrition in the World Report 2023* issued by FAO.

Chapter 2   Progress in the Implementation of Major Poverty Reduction Issues in ASEAN

In response to the impact of the COVID-19 pandemic on economic and social development and poverty reduction, the ASEAN countries sped up the fulfillment of the ASEAN Comprehensive Recovery Framework (ACRF) and its implementation plan. Importance was placed on the most affected industries and vulnerable groups for a more resilient, inclusive, and sustainable economic recovery to improve the risk coping capacity of vulnerable populations and mitigate the adverse impact of the pandemic on poverty reduction. After the pandemic, the ASEAN economy presented robust recovery. According to Asian Development Bank (ADB), ASEAN's average real GDP growth rate of 2024 is forecast to reach 5%.

2.1   Food Security

Food security and poverty reduction are interdependent. The Food and Agriculture Organization (FAO) of the United Nations, defines food security as a situation that exists when all people, at all times, have physical, social, and economic access to sufficient, safe, and nutritious food that meets their dietary needs and food preferences for an active and healthy life[1]. Poverty is the root cause of food insecurity, and the inability of the poor to access enough food to

---

1   FAO, An Introduction to the Basic Concepts of Food Security, 2009.

sustain their most basic survival needs is therefore a corollary of poverty[1]. Food insecurity and poverty are mutually reinforcing and cannot be separated[2]. On the one hand, poverty implies weak resilience to risks and shocks; on the other hand, food insecurity leads to malnutrition, deterioration of health, loss of capacity to work, increased mortality, and ultimately deeper poverty[3]. With the development of economic globalization, food security increasingly requires global and regional cooperation. To a certain extent, global food problems are more about circulation than production.

Guaranteeing regional food security requires full cooperation. Due to historical traditions and eating habits, there is a huge demand for rice in Southeast Asia[4]. Southeast Asia is one of the most densely populated regions in the world, where both major grain exporting countries (e.g., Thailand, Vietnam, Cambodia, Myanmar) and major grain importing countries (e.g., Indonesia, the Philippines, Malaysia) are located. Food security plays a crucial role in regional security. Studies have shown that the food supply chain in ASEAN is becoming problematic[5], and cooperation among member states is needed to address the challenges together.

A multitude of measures were taken to ensure food security. Ensuring food security and improving the resilience of the food supply chain can reduce the risk of falling into poverty due to starvation, increase the production capacity of sustainable agriculture, and help those who depend on agriculture to get rid of poverty. The ASEAN and its member states have released an array of policies to enhance intra-regional cooperation and ensure food security. Important policies include the ASEAN Integrated Food Security (AIFS) Framework and the Strategic Plan of Action on Food Security in the ASEAN Region (SPA-FS) 2021-2025,which were rolled out to ensure long-term food security and improve

---

1   Rose, D., Basiotis, P.P., and Klein, B.W. (1995). Improving Federal Efforts to Assess Hunger and Food Insecurity.

2   Barrett, C.B. (2006). Food Aid as Part of a Coherent Strategy to Advance Food Security Objectives.

3   Walingo, M.K. (2006). The Role of Education in Agricultural Projects for Food Security and Poverty Reduction in Kenya. International Review of Education, 52: 287-304.

4   Yao, Y. C. and Li, B. (2021). Production, Trade and Reserves: Food Security in Southeast Asia and China-ASEAN Food Cooperation. Southeast Asian Studies, 251(2):38-56,154-155. (in Chinese)

5   ASEAN Prosperity Initiative, *ASEAN Integration Report 2022*.

farmers' livelihoods in ASEAN countries. Besides, the ASEAN Plus Three Emergency Rice Reserve (APTERR), the ASEAN Food Security Information System (AFSIS), and the ASEAN Guidelines on the Utilization of Digital Technologies for ASEAN Food and Agriculture Sector were designed and implemented to improve the resilience of the food supply chain.

The government of Thailand granted minimum price subsidies for major agricultural products such as rice, cassava, and corn, and rolled out the Thai Rice Strategies (2020-2024) to ensure food supply. It proposed to develop 12 new rice varieties including soft rice, hard rice, fragrant rice and high nutrition rice in 5 years, which shall fit the characteristics of "short, low, large and excellent". The Ministry of Agriculture, Forestry and Fisheries of Cambodia officially launched a quality certification system for rice seeds to identify the quality of rice seeds through a labeling system for certification to improve rice yield and quality. Improving and ensuring the quality of grain is an important initiative of the Cambodian government to promote agricultural modernization, which aims to increase the contribution of agriculture to the national economy, increase farmers' income and reduce the poverty rate. The Philippines formulated the National Agriculture and Fisheries Modernization and Industrialization Plan 2021-2030 and launched an agricultural commodity system roadmap and a comprehensive land use plan to achieve sustainable poverty alleviation by diversifying employment channels for farmers and fishermen and continuously increasing their income. From 2019 to 2021, ASEAN countries witnessed a downturn for rice export but a notable upturn for import. The import value in 2021 reached US$3,101 million, increased by US$952 million from 2019 with an increase rate of 44.3% (see Figure 2-1). Increase in rice import by ASEAN countries ensured food supply and reduced the risk of falling into poverty due to starvation during the pandemic.

Food security in ASEAN countries gradually recovered after the pandemic. The Global Food Security Index (GFSI) generally showed an upward trend across ASEAN countries from 2012 to 2018, but it dropped to 60.3 in 2019. The spread of the COVID-19 pandemic severely impacted the agricultural supply chain of ASEAN, disrupting the food supply chain and causing fluctuations in food and agricultural product prices. This has affected the improvement of the nutritional and health status of the impoverished population. In 2020, the annual growth rate of ASEAN's GFSI was -1%. This downturn was notably mitigated with countermeasures taken by each country. The GFSI showed an upward trend from 2020 to 2022 and returned to positive growth in 2021. Its growth stood at 1.2% in 2022, demonstrating the resilience of ASEAN's food supply chain (see Figure 2-2).

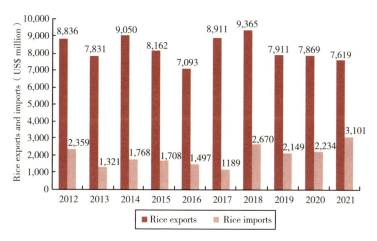

Figure 2-1   Rice exports and imports of ASEAN countries, 2012-2021

Source: *ASEAN Statistical Yearbook 2022.*

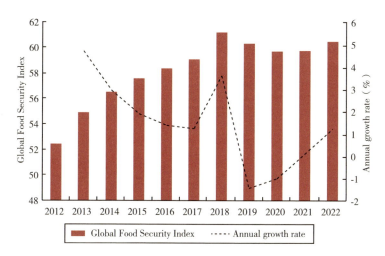

Figure 2-2   Global Food Security Index across ASEAN, 2012-2022

Source: *Global Food Security Index Report.*

Box 2-1   Global Food Security Index

The Global Food Security Index (GFSI) is derived from the *Global Food Security Index Report* published by the Economist Intelligent unit (EIU) based in Britain. It is based on official data from institutions such as the World Health Organization, the Food and Agriculture Organization of the United Nations, and the World Bank. With a dynamic benchmark model, it comprehensively evaluates the food security status of 113 countries worldwide, including food price tolerance, food supply capacity, quality and safety assurance capacity, sustainability, and adaptability.

Sources: *Global Food Security Index Report*.

Significant differences in food security are observed among ASEAN member states. Rice is the main food crop in ASEAN and plays a crucial role in ensuring food security in ASEAN countries. The per capita rice production of ASEAN countries can be divided into two distinct groups. The per capita rice production is over 400 kilograms in countries such as Cambodia, Myanmar, Laos, Vietnam, and Thailand, except for a few years, while the per capita rice production is below 300 kilograms in countries such as Indonesia, the Philippines, Malaysia, and Brunei (see Figure 2-3). Cambodia's per capita rice production increased steadily from 2013 to 2022, with a growth rate far exceeding that in other ASEAN member countries from 2017 to 2021. The per capita rice production of the Philippines, Malaysia, Brunei, and Vietnam is more stable compared to other countries.

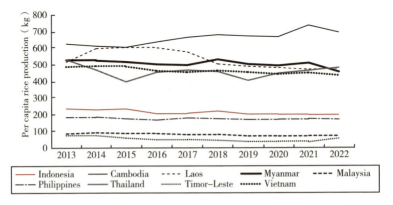

Figure 2-3   Per capita rice production in some ASEAN countries, 2013-2022

Source: World Bank, https://data.worldbank.org; *ASEAN Statistical Yearbook 2022*.

2.2 Economic Growth

Economic growth is the main driver of large-scale poverty reduction[1]. The poverty-reducing effects of economic growth are manifested in two main ways. First, economic development provides employment and income-generating opportunities for poor groups. Second, economic growth makes the government more capable of helping poor groups. As the process of economic globalization advances, trade and investment have become more liberalized and facilitated. Trade liberalization can promote economic growth, and value chains are one of the innovative mechanisms for poverty reduction in developing countries, enabling the connection of poor groups to world markets. The digital economy is booming and has a positive effect on job creation and optimizing the structure of labor demand, and has become an important driving force leading the growth of the national economy.

Efforts were stepped up in deepening inter-regional trading partnerships to restore trade growth. ASEAN formulated the ASEAN Digital Masterplan 2025 to facilitate trade across ASEAN countries through digital services. The governments of ASEAN countries introduced specific measures to step up the free flow of goods and increase supply chain interconnection and service efficiency. Malaysia, Thailand, and the European Union (EU) signed a partnership agreement to facilitate trade with each other. Laos continued to tap its trade potential through the China-Laos Railway and actively scaled up its participation in the global value chain. In 2020, there was a decrease in trade value across ASEAN countries. In 2021 and 2022, the trade presented a return to positive growth and a higher share of trade in GDP (see Figure 2-4). Trade recovery help poor people benefit from the dividends of trade policies and trade activities.

---

1   Wang, S. G. (2008). Overcoming Poverty in Development: Summarizing and Evaluating China's 30-Year Experience in Large-Scale Poverty Reduction. Journal of Management World, (11):78-88. (in Chinese)

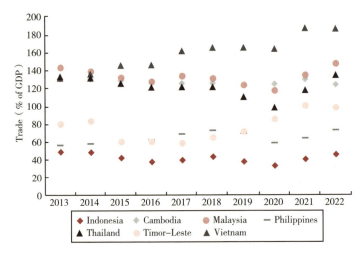

Figure 2-4   Trade-to-GDP ratio in some ASEAN countries, 2013-2022

Source: The World Bank's public database (https://data.worldbank.org).

Box 2-2   Thai-Chinese Rayong Industrial Zone Promotes Neighborhood Prosperity and Local Employment

The Thai-Chinese Rayong Industrial Zone, formally open in 2006, is located in Rayong Province, an important industrial base in Thailand. As one of the first overseas economic and trade cooperation zones of China, the industries of the zone are mainly focused on automotive and motorcycle parts, machinery, new energy, new materials, electronic appliances, building materials, and hardware, which are traditionally advantageous industries of China. After 16 years of development, the Thai-Chinese Rayong Industrial Zone has become an industrial cluster and a manufacturing and export base in Thailand. As of 2022, the industrial park has attracted 180 Chinese manufacturing enterprises and more than 30 supporting enterprises to invest in Thailand, providing over 45,000 jobs for the local area.

Sources: a. Based on "Thailand Lost 550,000 Tourism Jobs in the Second Quarter of 2021", released by Ministry of Commerce on June 30, 2021.

b. Based on "Thai-Chinese Rayong Industrial Zone, Promoting Neighborhood Prosperity and Local Employment", released by the Xinhua News Agency on November 20, 2022.

Persistent efforts were made to optimize the environment for foreign investment, contributing to growth in foreign investment against the economy downtrend in the pandemic. From 2012 to 2018, ASEAN countries presented an upward trend for FDI net inflows. Although FDI climbed to US$176.3 billion in 2019, there was a slump by 28.3% to US$126.4 billion in 2020 due to the impact of the pandemic (see Figure 2-5). In order to encourage foreign investment, ASEAN countries adopted an array of measures. For example,Vietnam promulgated an Amendment to Investment Law to provide higher incentives for special investment projects; Thailand rolled out the New Investment Promotion Strategy (2023-2027) to ensure a stable business environment with rule-based support; Indonesia unveiled a subsidy program for electric vehicles (EVs) to encourage international investors to establish an EV value chain. Malaysia strengthened its trade with China, and the value of trade between the two countries reached US$203.6 billion in 2022, up by 15.3% from the previous year[1]. Except for Myanmar and the Philippines, there was a higher average annual growth rate of foreign investment in Indonesia, Cambodia, Malaysia, Thailand, and Vietnam after than before the pandemic. China and ASEAN were each other's largest trading partner, and as of July 2023, the cumulative investment between them amounted to US$380 billion[2].

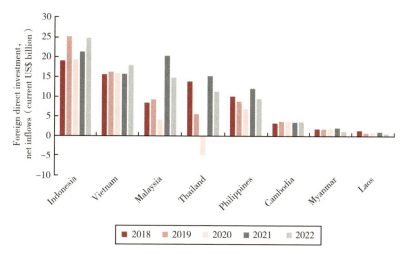

Figure 2-5   Foreign direct investment in some ASEAN countries, 2018-2022

Source: The World Bank's public database (https://data.worldbank.org).

---

1   "Relations between China and Malaysia", released on the official website of Ministry of Foreign Affairs of the People's Republic of China.

2   See: "China-ASEAN economic and trade cooperation upgraded and upgraded".

Vigorous support was offered to boost the development of micro, small, and medium enterprises and promote full employment. From 2019 to 2022, ASEAN countries saw an inverted-V trend in the unemployment rate (see Figure 2-6). Since 2021, most ASEAN countries have experienced a decline in the unemployment rate in varying degrees. Micro, small and medium-sized enterprises employed 85%-97% of the working-age population in ASEAN countries, playing a leading role in creating employment. ASEAN supported the implementation of the ASEAN Strategic Action Plan for SME Development 2016-2025, encouraging micro, small and medium enterprises to participate in the digital economy, enhance digital skills and market access, and achieve sustainable, inclusive, and resilient growth. The ASEAN Business Advisory Council presented the Digital STARS program in 2020 for the main aim of promoting entrepreneurship and the digital transformation of micro, small and medium enterprises. In 2021, the Council unveiled another project entitled Harnessing Impact with Resilient Employability to empower the working-age population in ASEAN.

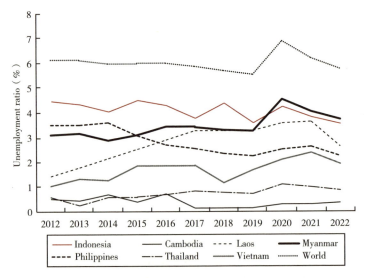

Figure 2-6　Unemployment rates in some ASEAN countries, 2012-2022

Source: The World Bank's public database (https://data.worldbank.org).

Box 2-3   COVID-19 Impact on Thailand's Tourism

Tourism is a pillar of the tertiary sector in Thailand, accounting for almost one-fifth of the country's GDP. The COVID-19 pandemic has had a devastating impact on Thailand's tourism industry, with the number of foreign tourists arriving in the country plummeting to 6.70 million from January to December 2020, dropping by 83.2% over the previous year. The total revenue of the tourism industry was THB332,013 million, a year-on-year decrease of 82.6%. For example, the tourism industry in Chiang Mai, a major tourist destination in Thailand, has also been hit hard by the pandemic. In 2019, the province received over 11 million tourists, an increase of 4% compared to the previous year, with 60% of the tourists being foreign tourists (The Nation, 2019). Tourism contributed THB67,393 million in revenues to Chiang Mai, ranking 6th in the country (Chillpainai, 2019). However, the pandemic has brought a huge impact on the country's tourism industry.

The Thai Tourism Commission stated that 550,000 people in the country's tourism industry lost their jobs in the second quarter of 2021. Starting from April 2021, few foreign tourists visited the country, which has severely impacted its tourism industry. Compared to the first quarter, the proportion of temporary closures of almost all types of tourism activities increased, with 59% of hotels, 27% of spas, health preservation, and massage establishments, and only 3% of entertainment venues open for business. Most sites only retain 51% of employees, who receive an average salary of only 65% compared to the past.

Source: Based on "Situation of Thailand's Tourism is Grim due to COVID-19", released by Ministry of Commerce on July 7, 2021.

2.3 Nutrition and Health

Nutrition and health are prerequisites for lifting individuals and families out of poverty. Human capital theory recognizes that health is an important human capital, and that good health is a prerequisite for individuals to participate in economic and social activities, especially productive activities that generate income[1]. Health affects labor productivity and thus individual and family poverty. Specifically, health reduces poverty through both effective labor inputs and output levels. Higher levels of health in the labor force are associated with a

---

1   Zhang, Z. F. (2017). Research on Medical Insurance Against Poverty in the Context of Precise Poverty Alleviation Policy. Probe, (2):81-85. (in Chinese)

lower probability of illness, less downtime, longer life expectancy and working life, and an increase in the amount of effective labor time invested. At the same time, a healthier workforce has more energy and greater cognitive ability, and can take on more intensive work and improve the efficiency of labor output or the effectiveness of business projects, thus contributing to poverty reduction.

Box 2-4　Global Hunger Index

The Global Hunger Index (GHI) is a comprehensive index released by the International Food Policy Research Institute (IFPRI), that reflects the rates of malnutrition relative to the total population and the low birth weight and mortality among children under five years old in developing countries.

Sources: Global Hunger Index Database, https://www.globalhungerindex.org/.

Of all the factors contributing to poverty, illness is the first factor and has a far greater impact on poor families than any other factor contributing to poverty[1]. When a family member is ill, the most immediate impact is on the family's financial situation. On the one hand, going to the doctor will increase household expenditure. On the other hand, the patient's ability to work is reduced or lost, which reduces the income of their families. And the reduction in labor hours of the patient's family members for caring the patient can also reduce the family's income. When families are unable to pay medical bills, it affects all aspects of the family's investments. Typically, poor households reduce their food and nutrition expenditures and their investment in the health of other family members. In the long run, this increases the health vulnerability of other family members, affecting the long-term development of the household and having a negative impact on household income[2].

The ASEAN countries took active measures to alleviate the negative impact of the pandemic on people's health and medical conditions. In order to alleviate the economic and social impact of the pandemic, ASEAN rolled out the 2020 ASEAN Strategic Framework for Public Health Emergencies, and

---

1　Wang, S. G, and Liu, M. Y. (2019). Role Mechanism, Implementation Dilemma and Policy Choice of Health Poverty Alleviation. Journal of Xinjiang Normal University (Edition of Philosophy and Social Sciences), 40(3):82-91,92. (in Chinese)

2　Hong, Q. M. and Chang, X. Y. (2010). Analysis of the Interaction Between Disease and Poverty Among Rural Residents in China. Issues in Agricultural Economy, 31(4):85-94,112. (in Chinese)

established the ASEAN Center for Public Health Emergencies and Emerging Diseases (ACPHEED), the ASEAN Anti-epidemic Fund, and the ASEAN Regional Reserve of Medical Supplies (RRMS) for Public Health Emergencies. Laos launched the National Nutrition Strategy (NNS) 2016-2025 and National Plan of Action on Nutrition (NPAN) 2021-2025. It shows that the government is highly supportive and concerned about national nutrition. The National Plan of Action on Nutrition (NPAN) 2021-2025 pays more attention to multi-sectoral approaches and actions to solve malnutrition. The Philippines formulated the Philippine Plan of Action for Nutrition (PPAN) 2017-2022. On October 11, 2022, the Department of Education and the Department of Health of the Philippine jointly launched the Healthy Learning Institute in the basic Education to strengthen school health and nutrition programs. Brunei adopted the National Dietary Guidelines for Healthy Eating as a guide for school canteen and school feeding programs, offering guidance on adult and infant diets, and food hygiene, safety and labelling. Vietnam unveiled the Education Support and Feeding Program for Poor Children to provide nutritious meals for more than 30,000 poor children across the country. In terms of health, the ASEAN countries made efforts on improving medical and health facilities, and formulated medical security systems for disadvantaged groups. Malaysia emphatically catered its basic medical and health services to special groups including the poor population. Myanmar launched the Myanmar National Health Plan (2017-2021), which was designed to provide basic sanitation facilities and services for the poor.

On the whole, ASEAN has witnessed great improvement in nutrition and health status. From 2012 to 2021, most ASEAN countries presented a downward trend in the Global Hunger Index, prevalence of undernourishment, maternal mortality ratio, maternal deaths per 100,000 live births, and the under-five mortality rate (see Figure 2-7 and Figure 2-8). People's nutrition and health in Cambodia, Laos, and Myanmar have been effectively improved. The share of undernourished people plunged from 37.6% (2000-2002) to 3.1% (2019-2021) in Myanmar, and from 31.2% to 5.1% in Laos.[1] Malnutrition is an important

---

[1]   Data from FAOSTAT (https://www.fao.org/faostat/en/), and the World Bank's public database (https://data.worldbank.org).

factor affecting poor people's health, and the improvement of nutrition and health showed the effectiveness of poverty reduction measures by ASEAN countries.

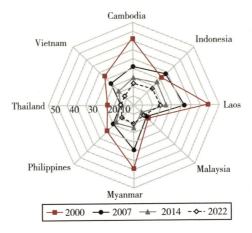

Figure 2-7   Changes of ASEAN's Global Hungry Index in 2000, 2007, 2014 and 2022

Note: GHI classification: ≤ 9.9, Low; 10.0-19.9, Moderate; 20.0-34.9, Serious; 35.0-49.9, Alarming; ≥ 50.0, Extremely alarming.

Source: Database of Global Hungry Index (GHI).

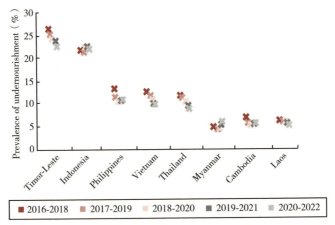

Figure 2-8   Changes of the prevalence of undernourishment (3-year average) in some ASEAN countries

Source: FAOSTAT, https://www.fao.org/faostat/en/.

The pandemic prevented the improvement in the nutrition and health of some low-income countries. Compared with the period from 2017 to 2019, the share of undernourished people in Indonesia and Laos increased by 5.1 percentage points and 1.9 percentage points respectively from 2018 to 2020. Both the number and share of undernourished people in Cambodia and Myanmar also increased from 2019 to 2020 (see Figure 2-8). The rate of reduction in undernourishment has been slowed down in Timor-Leste. The pandemic led to decreased household income, and thus the food expenditure of some households[1]. In 2020, there was at least one adult member who ate less than usual in 30 days in 11% of households in Myanmar, and there were also 7% of the households facing the risk of food shortage[2]. The number of people who were unable to afford a healthy diet in ASEAN countries as a whole decreased from 2017 to 2019, but this figure increased significantly in 2020 (see Figure 2-9). The continuous spread of the COVID-19 pandemic severely impacted the agricultural supply chain of ASEAN, disrupting the food supply chain and causing fluctuations in food and agricultural product prices. This has affected the improvement of the nutritional and health status of the impoverished population.

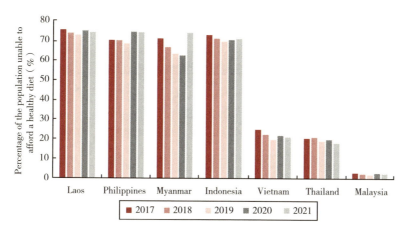

Figure 2-9   People unable to afford a healthy diet in some ASEAN countries, 2017-2021

Source: FAOSTAT, http://www.fao.org/faostat/en/.

---

1   Data from *How Hard are Families Hit by the COVID-19 Crisis? Six Insights from Our Household Surveys in East Asia and Pacific* by the World Bank.

2   Data from *Monitoring COVID-19 Impacts on Households in Vietnam* by the World Bank.

The pandemic worsened medical and sanitation conditions. From 2015 to 2020, there was an upward trend for the average life expectancy in ASEAN. However, the impact of the pandemic resulted in a dip in life expectancy from 74 years old in 2020 to 73 years old in 2021. Life expectancy in all ASEAN countries declined to varying degrees in 2021 (see Figure 2-10). The pandemic also affected the provision of medical services, placing children at greater risk of development delay and emaciation at an early stage[1], while aggravating their nutrition and health. This in turn negatively affected life expectancy, particularly for the impoverished population in low-income countries.

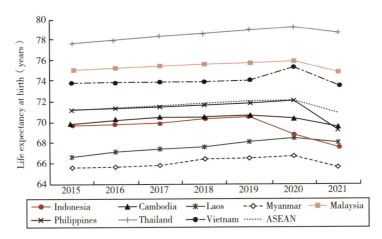

Figure 2-10   Changes of life expectancy in some ASEAN countries, 2015-2021

Source: World Bank, https://data.worldbank.org.

2.4 Education Level

Education is a fundamental human right that makes an important contribution to human development and poverty reduction[2]. In ASEAN countries, educational equity issues are prominent and children's education is advancing slowly. Cai Fang (2020) argued that the accumulation of human capital

---

1 Bill & Melina Gates Foundation, *Goalkeepers Report (2020)*.

2 Data from *ASEAN Statistical Yearbook 2022*.

is an endogenous driving force for preventing people from falling into and returning to poverty due to illness, interrupting the intergenerational transmission of poverty, and alleviating relative poverty. [1] At the same time, human capital is an important source for a country or region to achieve long-term economic growth. Heckman and Corbin (2016) found that human capital formation has critical and sensitive periods, that childhood is early investment in children produces the greatest returns in human capital, and that sustained and accurate investment in children's human capital is an important initiative to support long-term national development[2].

Efforts were made to strengthen education system construction in poor areas and improve the inclusiveness of education. *Under The ASEAN plus Three Cooperation Work Plan (2023-2027)*, The ASEAN Plus Three Plan of Action on Education 2018-2025, a plan jointly launched by ASEAN and China, Japan, and the Republic of Korea, supported inclusive education through inclusive schools, alternative learning systems, special education, distance learning, among other forms of education. In 2020, ASEAN countries garnered a surge in the preschool participation rate from 74.4% in 2016 to 76.2%. In the same year, 45.3% of primary schools in ASEAN countries were equipped with computers, and 90.8% of primary school teachers met the minimum teaching requirements[3].

Among ASEAN countries, Vietnam implemented the program Supporting the Preschool Education Development in Disadvantaged Areas for 2022-2030, aiming to ensure access to education for 25% of nursery-age children and 95% of kindergarten-age children in poor areas, and care and education for 100% of the children enrolled in kindergartens in poor areas by 2030. Myanmar formulated and launched the Education for All National Action, aiming to promote the coverage of children, residents in border areas, ethnic minorities, and adults in its education system. Before the pandemic, the overall literacy rate, school enrollment rate, and education completion rate of the youth of ASEAN increased on the whole. Malaysia, Indonesia, Thailand, and Vietnam

---

1   Cai, F. (2020). How to Unlock the Second Demographic Dividend?. International Economic Review, (2):9-24,4. (in Chinese)

2   Heckman, J.J., & Corbin, C.O. (2016). Capabilities and Skills. Journal of Human Development and Capabilities, 17: 342 - 359.

3   Data from *The 2022 ASEAN SDG Snapshot Report* by ASEANstats.

had high rates of completing primary, junior high school, and senior high school education. Education in Myanmar, Cambodia, and Laos developed rapidly, but the completion rate of education was still relatively low compared to other countries. The gender ratio in primary and junior high schools in ASEAN countries was basically 1 : 1 in 2021. Cambodia and Laos have made significant progress in addressing gender inequality in education. From 2017 to 2019, Malaysia's average number of years of schooling reached 10.27. The Philippines and Brunei also have a great number of years of schooling, both above 9. The average number of years of schooling in these three countries was higher than the then-world average (8.43). In Indonesia, Thailand, and Vietnam, the average number of years of schooling was between seven and nine, while those in Laos, Myanmar, and Cambodia were less than six (see Figure 2-11).

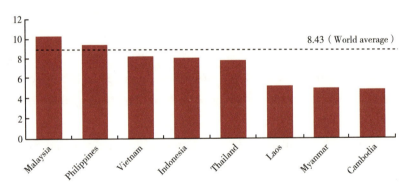

Figure 2-11   The average numbers of years of schooling in some ASEAN countries, 2017-2019

Note: According to the *Human Development Report*, the indicator calculates the average number of years of schooling for people aged 25 and over, which is converted from the official length of each stage of education.

Source: *Human Development Report* by UNDP. The figures are calculated based on the report and the item "world average" in this figure is corresponding to the item "world" in the database.

The spending on education reduced across ASEAN countries due to the COVID-19 pandemic, which negatively affected the vulnerable and poor people in remote areas. The spending on education in other ASEAN countries accounted for a smaller share of government expenditure in 2021 than in 2017, except for Indonesian and Vietnam (see Figure 2-12). In response to the pandemic, the governments allocated funds to enact public health emergency response measures and reinforce the security system, while reducing their spending on education. Although ASEAN countries employed a wide range of measures to ensure the running of educational activities, economic underdevelopment and substandard networks affected the completion rate of education in some countries. Among the families with schooling children before the pandemic in Cambodia and Myanmar, less than 30% completed education during the pandemic[1].

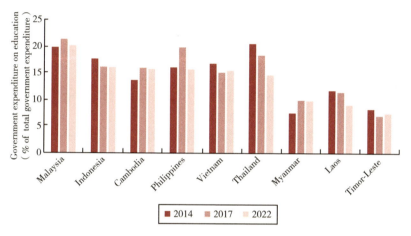

Figure 2-12   General government expenditure on education in some ASEAN member states in 2014, 2017 and 2022

Note: (1) The general government expenditure on education is expressed as its proportion to the government expenditure on all sectors.

(2) Data from 2021 for Indonesia, Cambodia and Timor-Leste, and data from 2019 for Myanmar.

Source: The World Bank's public database (https://data.worldbank.org).

The pandemic had a significant impact on the education of girls, children in remote areas, and ethnic minorities. Children in most countries participated in learning or educational activities via television, classroom assignments, and the internet during school closures due to the pandemic. The ratio of girls to boys in high school in Cambodia decreased significantly during the pandemic, from 1.25 : 1 in 2019 to 1.03 : 1 in 2021. The closure of schools

---

1   Date from the Household Monitoring Systems to Track the Impacts of the COVID-19 Pandemic on the COVID-19 Household Monitoring Dashboard.

affected approximately 26% of families with children in Myanmar. Less than 40% of the children from families in Thailand and Laos were still able to participate in learning or educational activities during school closures. The probability of students from ethnic minority families in Laos continuing to participate in learning activities during school closures was only 19.4%, and online learning was more common for students in urban areas. Indonesia suspended classes for a total of 666 days from February 16, 2020 to April 30, 2022, the longest school closures among 206 countries with available data. Despite the longest school closure days, over 90% of children from families in Indonesia were still able to participate in learning or educational activities during school closures. The Philippines suspended classes for a total of 562 days, including six days of partial closures (see Figure 2-13).

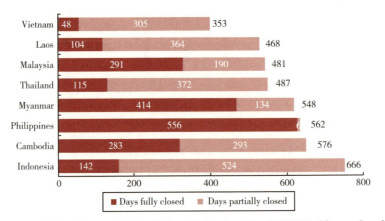

Figure 2-13   Days of school closed during the COVID-19 pandemic
Source: The global map of school closures in different countries released by UNESCO.

2.5 Technological Innovation

Technological innovation has reduced hunger and poverty. In their studies, scholars have tried various methods to deal with poverty, one of which is technological innovation. You et al. (2020) emphasized in his paper that closing the technological gap between developing and developed economies helps reduce poverty in less-developed countries. [1] Poverty in developing Asia,

---

1   You, K., Dal Bianco, S., and Amankwah-Amoah, J. (2020). Closing Technological Gaps to Alleviate Poverty: Evidence from 17 Sub-Saharan African Countries. Technological Forecasting and Social Change, 157: 120055.

including ASEAN countries, is concentrated in rural areas, and agricultural growth is considered crucial for poverty reduction. Technological innovation provides technical support for agricultural production in impoverished areas. By optimizing the allocation of factors in family agriculture and improving the efficiency of agricultural production, it reduces the transaction costs of agricultural production and operation, and promotes the improvement of the efficiency of family agriculture and the reduction of production costs in impoverished areas, thus contributing to poverty reduction and income growth of poor families.

The pandemic exerted a negative impact on technological innovation. The lockdown put a halt to research projects in laboratories, restricted travel of R&D personnel and discontinued human capital training. These exerted a negative impact on technological innovation. Across ASEAN countries, there were fewer patent applications in 2020 than in 2019, and the largest decrease occurred in Indonesia (see Figure 2-14).

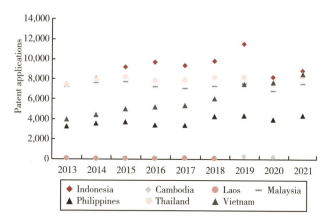

Figure 2-14 Number of patent applications in some ASEAN countries, 2013-2021

Note: (1) The number of patent applications is the sum of the number of non-resident patent applications and resident patent applications.

(2) Patent applications are worldwide patent applications filed through the Patent Cooperation Treaty procedure or with a national patent office for exclusive rights for an invention - a product or process that provides a new way of doing something or offers a new technical solution to a problem. Patents protect the inventions of the patent owner for a limited period, normally 20 years.

Source: The World Bank's public database (https://data.worldbank.org).

Box 2-5   Transforming Technological Innovation into Realistic Productivity Supporting Poverty Reduction

Philippine-Sino Center for Agricultural Technology: The Philippine-Sino Center for Agricultural Technology was established in Nueva Ecija province, the Philippines in 2001, mainly for the research and promotion of hybrid rice varieties. Hybrid rice experts from China are stationed in the Philippines to provide technical guidance. After 21 years of development, the center has promoted 514,400 hectares of commercial hybrid rice in the Philippines. The projects of rice cultivation and seed production technology demonstration sites cover 29 provinces in the Philippines, benefiting more than 300,000 households and increasing local grain production by 4,821 million kilograms. In March 2022, at the completion ceremony of the third phase of the center's technical cooperation project, then-Philippine Agriculture Secretary William Dar noted that China's hybrid rice planting techniques had helped the Philippines steadily increase rice yield, playing an important role in ensuring food security and improving farmers' lives.

Sources: Based on "Filipino Farmers: We Believe in Chinese Hybrid Rice Technology", released on the official website of China's Belt and Road Initiative, August 29, 2022.

Efforts were intensified in technological innovation and human resource training to promote poverty reduction through science and technology. Through effective intellectual property protection, among other measures, ASEAN countries created an open and fair environment for technological innovation. These countries also promoted and participated in technological innovation activities, including the 10+3 Center for the Gifted in Science (AGGS), the ASEAN Plus Three Young Scientist Innovation Forum, and the Youth Innovation Camp and its awards ceremony. An array of strategic plans was also implemented to promote technological innovation.

Vietnam launched the Strategy for Science, Technology and Innovation Development until 2030, a strategy that laid down a systematic plan for its technological innovation and development system. According to the strategy, science, technology and innovation will play an important role in the development of spearhead industries, and the proportion of the value of high-tech industrial products in the processing and manufacturing industries will reach at least 45% by 2030. Cambodia launched the Cambodia's Science, Technology &

Innovation Roadmap 2030, which is expected to become the key for the country to achieve sustainable development goals. It is aimed at enhancing national technological innovation capabilities, fostering a vibrant innovation ecosystem, and facilitating effective recovery from the pandemic in an inclusive, resilient and sustainable manner. The roadmap is built on five strategies, namely enhancing the governance of the science, technology and innovation (STI) system, building human capital in STI, improving scientific research capacity and quality, strengthening collaboration and networking between key stakeholders, and fostering an enabling ecosystem for innovation. Indonesia unveiled the Master Plan of National Research (RIRN) 2017-2045, a plan committed to promoting economic transformation and development through technological innovation. Notable achievements have been made in the fields of agricultural technology, marine science, clean energy, medicine and health so far. The Philippines promulgated the Philippines Innovation Act to boost the rapid development of micro, small, medium enterprises, encourage innovation among domestic companies, and enhance their international competitiveness. The innovation act mainly focuses on fields such as food security, sustainable agriculture, blue economy (marine resources), education, health, safety, clean and reliable energy, climate change, governance, infrastructure, digital economy, and transportation. Generally speaking, ASEAN countries have actively enhanced their scientific and technological innovation capabilities, and accelerated the transformation of advanced and applicable technologies into real productivity to support poverty reduction in ASEAN.

2.6 Climate Change

Climate change is widely recognized as a key factor affecting poverty. Leichenko et al. (2014) reviewed the literature on climate change, vulnerability, and poverty and observed that climate variability and change can exacerbate poverty, especially in underdeveloped countries and regions, through many direct and indirect channels which had been identified in relevant studies, though climate change has not been deemed the sole cause of poverty.[1] The direct channels are rooted in a long-standing impact assessment framework, which assumes a direct connection between biophysical changes, market reactions, and poverty results. The indirect channels assume that the causal chain between climate exposure and poverty is complex and influenced by individual and family characteristics, as well as other factors such as decision-making processes, socio-economic conditions, institutions, and governance quality. He also emphasized that climate change is related to poor health and political conflicts, which are important factors affecting poverty[2]. However, the impact of climate change varies with different groups of people. By examining reports from various international institutions, Hallegatte et al. (2017) found that while climate change has limited impacts on the non-poor population, the poor population may be severely affected by climate change. [3] This is because the poor are more susceptible to environmental impacts and receive less support from friends and family, financial systems, and social safety nets after being impacted. The geographical location of ASEAN countries makes them more susceptible to the impact of climate change. Bayudan-Dacuycuy et al. (2019) analyzed the relationship between heavy rainfall and long-term and short-term poverty in the Philippines and found that rainfall is one of the factors affecting household wages and income, whether in agriculture or non-agriculture sectors.[4] In addition, the impact of rainfall on corporate revenues is also significant, especially in the service and industrial sectors. The research results of McElwee et al. (2017) indicate that the income of impoverished households in Vietnam is more sensitive to the impact of floods.[5] However, compared to the poverty

1   Leichenko, R., and Silva, J. A. (2014). Climate Change and Poverty: Vulnerability, Impacts, and Alleviation Strategies. Wiley Interdisciplinary Reviews: Climate Change, 5(4): 539-556.

2   Leichenko R, O'Brien K. Environmental Change and Globalization: Double Exposures. New York: Oxford University Press, 2008: 167.

3   Hallegatte, S., Rozenberg, J. (2017). Climate Change Through a Poverty Lens. Nature Climate Change, 7:250-256.

4   Bayudan-Dacuycuy, C., and Baje, L. K. (2019). When It Rains, It Pours? Analyzing the Rainfall Shocks-poverty Nexus in the Philippines. Social Indicators Research, 145(1): 67-93.

5   McElwee, P., Nghiem, T., Le, H., and Vu, H. (2017). Flood Vulnerability Among Rural Households in the Red River Delta of Vietnam: Implications for Future Climate Change Risk and Adaptation. Nat Hazards, 86:465-492.

situation of households, the relationship between the family age structure and participation by livelihood institutions is more closely related to the impact of floods.

Climate change placed ASEAN countries at greater risk of falling into poverty due to natural disasters. Climate change increases the uncertainties of agricultural production and may lead to severe natural disasters. Due to their susceptibility to climate change, poor or vulnerable people are at greater risk of falling into or returning to poverty due to natural disasters, which has hindered the progress of poverty reduction in ASEAN countries. From 2016 to 2021, the number of people affected by climate change in ASEAN countries accounted for 20%-30% of the total population. In some areas, the affected people even struggled with the shortages of water, food and medicine. ASEAN countries have kept strengthening policy support in order to cope with the adverse impact of climate change on the progress of poverty reduction. In terms of agricultural production, ASEAN countries channeled tremendous efforts to develop climate-smart agriculture in rural areas and lay down a food standard that can cater to sustainable development in the future. These efforts aimed to effectively promote agri-food system transformation and mitigate and adapt to climate change. In terms of disaster risks, the Southeast Asia Disaster Risk Insurance Facility (SEADRIF) provides services such as risk identification, risk control and insurance to fortify the financial system against disasters and climate shocks. Indonesia unveiled a disaster risk financing and insurance strategy in 2018, and the Philippines issued a catastrophe bond for earthquakes and typhoons. In 2021, when Typhoon Rey breached the parametric trigger for wind, the catastrophe bond paid out US$52.5 million to the Philippine government.

Box 2-6   Economic Losses Caused by Natural Disasters in ASEAN Countries

In May 2022, natural disasters resulted in 35 deaths and disappearances and 15 injuries in Vietnam. 24 houses collapsed, 738 houses were damaged to varying degrees, and 3,078 houses were flooded. The flooded area of rice and crops reached 55,725 hectares, and 2,375 hectares of other crops were damaged.

49,434 heads of livestock and poultry died or were swept away by floods, and 1,210 hectares of aquaculture farms were damaged. Natural disasters also caused damage to embankments, channels, riverbanks, and coasts, resulting in economic losses of approximately US$21 million.

Affected by the super cyclonic storm Mocha, heavy rainstorms successively hit western and northern Myanmar, southern Bangladesh, and eastern India, with severe or extremely severe rainstorms occurring in some areas. According to Agence France-Presse, as of May 19, 2023, Cyclone Mocha had caused 145 deaths in Myanmar, and many affected people in the country were facing shortages of drinking water, food, and medicine.

Sources: a. "Severe, Complex, and Unpredictable Situation of Natural Disasters in 2022", released by Vietnam News Agency on June 2, 2022.

b. "Cyclone Mocha Attacked Myanmar, Killing 145; Super Typhoon Mawar Landed on Guam, Causing Serious Damage", released on hyqqw.com on May 26, 2023.

The imperative climate action offers new ways to reduce poverty in ASEAN. Scientific energy transformation and emission reduction help stimulate technological innovation and create opportunities for employment and economic growth, thus contributing to poverty reduction and greater equality[1]. ASEAN countries have actively participated in the climate action. In terms of energy transformation and emission reduction, ASEAN unveiled the ASEAN Plan of Action for Energy Cooperation (APAEC) 2016-2025 Phase II : 2021-2025 to reduce energy intensity by 32% and achieve the target of 23% share of renewable energy in total energy supply by 2025. Most ASEAN countries upgraded their commitments of Nationally Determined Contribution (NDC) under the Paris Agreement. In terms of renewable energy, Indonesia promulgated a simplified electricity pricing model and electricity subsidies for specific power plants at the end of 2020 to prompt solar and hydropower generation. The Philippine government planned to unveil new energy power generation policies that allow 100% foreign ownership to encourage foreign investment in new energy infrastructure. However, from 2012 to 2019, ASEAN countries presented an upward trend in per capita CO_2 emissions. Among these countries, Malaysia

---

1 Development Research Center of the State Council of China, World Bank, "Forty Years of Poverty Reduction in China: Drivers, Lessons, and Future Policy Directions", September 2022.

ranked at the top for per capita CO_2 emissions, while Myanmar and Timor-Leste ranked at the bottom (see Figure 2-15). Responding to climate change is not an overnight process, but it is closely associated with each country's development stage and industrial structure. With a great many coal-fired power plants, ASEAN now stands at a crossroads of shifting from fossil fuel to renewable energy, ready to create tremendous jobs for the poor. ASEAN is expected to cut 75% of their energy-related CO_2 emissions by 2050[1].

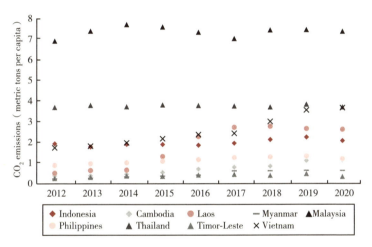

Figure 2-15   Changes of per capita CO_2 emissions in some ASEAN countries, 2012-2020

Note: This indicator is up to 2020.

Source: The World Bank's public database (https://data.worldbank.org).

Box 2-7   Malaysia Actively Promoting Energy Transformation and Pressing Ahead with Poverty Reduction

In response to global energy shortages and environmental crises, over 100 countries, including Malaysia, pledged to reach net zero emissions by 2050 at the 26th UN Climate Change Conference of the Parties (COP26). Malaysia's effective renewable energy initiatives have helped develop the renewable energy industries, which may create new jobs and help reduce poverty. For example, the 12th Malaysia Plan (12MP) includes a carbon tax credit scheme

1   International Renewable Energy Agency (IREA), "Renewable Energy Outlook for ASEAN: Towards A Regional Energy Transition (2nd Edition)", October 2022.

that taxes companies that use fossil fuels based on their carbon emissions. Other effective policies include Net Energy Measurement (NEM) 3.0, Smart Automation Grants (SAG), and Green Investment Tax Allowance (GITA) have contributed to the booming of Malaysia's clean energy industries. In specific, NEM allows homeowners to obtain electricity compensation by installing photovoltaic systems. SAG helps adopters install intelligent AIoT energy solutions. GITA provides up to 48% tax credits for eligible enterprises.

Affordable household photovoltaics can help reduce poverty. The cost of photovoltaic systems has fallen by 85% in the past decade, while their power generation efficiency has increased from 2% in 1955 to over 20% today. Malaysian photovoltaic manufacturers are now offering rent-to-own schemes that allow homeowners to install photovoltaic systems with reduced upfront payment. This can save up to 90% of monthly electricity bills for homeowners. Surveys show Malaysia has the potential to deploy 3.2 million sets of household photovoltaic systems. By offsetting the cost of purchasing photovoltaic systems with savings on electricity bills, this initiative helps reduce energy bills and contributes to poverty reduction in Malaysia.

Source: "Accelerating Carbon Neutrality! Malaysia's 'Package' of Policies Promotes Energy Transformation" https://news.solarbe.com/202201/18/350105.html.

2.7 Summary

ASEAN countries have made good progress in implementing the UN Millennium Development Goals and promoting the process of poverty reduction. The pandemic has intensified the risks and uncertainties of poverty reduction and development in ASEAN countries.

First, ASEAN countries are facing a severe test of food security. They have introduced a series of policies to ensure the stability and smooth flow of regional food supply chains and enhance the resilience of regional food supply chains. Second, the nutrition and health problems of poor groups in low-income countries remain prominent. It is thus necessary to accurately identify those who have become poor or returned to poverty due to illness, improve the social security system, and improve the utilization efficiency of limited medical resources. Third, the pandemic has exacerbated inequality in access to education, disrupting the development of education for women, remote areas or ethnic minorities. Fourth, although ASEAN countries face challenges in economic growth and full employment, the development of the digital economy and micro, small and medium-sized enterprises has brought opportunities to promote full employment. Fifth, extreme weather conditions have increased the risk of falling into poverty due to natural disasters in ASEAN countries. Sixth, the potential of scientific and technological innovation to reduce hunger and poverty remains to be strengthened, and scientific and technological cooperation and poverty reduction will become an important part of ASEAN's external cooperation in the future.

Poverty is a comprehensive and difficult life situation with diverse causes and manifestations. Poverty reduction and poverty alleviation also require the joint action of multiple measures. Food security, nutrition and health, education, economic growth, climate change and scientific and technological innovation do not exist in isolation and affect poverty alone. In fact, they are closely related to each other. For poor people, food security is the primary goal of their survival, based on which they need to have access to safe and nutritious food to improve their nutrition and health conditions and lower the probability of illness. Providing better access to education for children helps reduce the risk of intergenerational poverty transmission. Adults may take on more intensive work to increase the efficiency of labor output and generate more income. With the intensification of climate change, agriculture is the first to be affected. In response, countries are actively promoting the development of climate adaptability and smart agriculture, which puts new and higher requirements for agricultural scientific and technological innovation. At the same time, the pandemic has accelerated the development of the digital economy, with e-commerce, fintech and mobile games creating new opportunities for the development of small and medium-sized enterprises and promoting full employment.

Chapter 3　International Development Assistance and Cooperation for Poverty Reduction in ASEAN Countries

As a regional multilateral organization, ASEAN has received assistance and support in social development and poverty reduction from dialog and development partners like China, the United States, Japan, and the Republic of Korea. This includes grants from China, the ASEAN-China Cooperation Fund, the ASEAN-Japan Cooperation Fund, and the ASEAN-USAID Inclusive Growth in ASEAN through Innovation, Trade and E-Commerce project. International organizations and financial institutions like the United Nations, World Bank, and ADB also assist in the development of ASEAN and its member states. To cope with the impact of COVID-19, ASEAN established the COVID-19 Response Fund, while dialog partners, cooperation partners, and international institutions also provided assistance to ASEAN and its member States through various channels[1].

3.1　Overall Change in International Aid

ASEAN received ongoing aid from the international community. From 2013 to 2022, ASEAN received US$119.77 billion worth of official development assistance from the international community, accounting for 6% of total amount

---

[1] Based on *Guide for Countries and Regions on Overseas Investment and Cooperation: ASEAN (2022)* released by Ministry of Commerce of the People's Republic of China.

of global international aid. The amount received from 2020 to 2022 equaled US$36.44 billion, accounting for 30% in the total amount. The amount for 2020 and 2021 each was far higher than that in 2019.

Vietnam, Indonesia, and Myanmar were the main aid recipients. Vietnam has established development partnerships with 28 countries/regions and 23 multilateral organizations, mainly including Japan, the European Union, and the Republic of Korea, as well as international financial institutions such as the World Bank and the Asian Development Bank. Since 1992, over US$95.6 billion of aid has been committed to Vietnam, averaging US$3.4 billion every year[1]. From 2011 to 2021, Myanmar benefited from 1,822 official development assistance (ODA) projects funded by 88 foreign governments or institutions. The committed value of these projects amounted to US$16.78 billion, of which US$8.42 billion had been made available. The value of completed projects reached US$5 billion, and projects worth US$9.5 billion are under implementation. Projects worth US$1.5 billion have been proposed or are pending approval[2]. Since 1960, Cambodia has received ODA commitments totaling US$29.19 billion and actual aid of US$18.16 billion. Japan, the United States, France, Germany, and the European Union as well as the Asian Development Bank, United Nations agencies are among the main aid providers. The ODA received by Cambodia has been increasing at an average annual rate of 10% since 2001, accounting for approximately half of Cambodia's national development budget[3]. Thailand has gradually transformed from a recipient country of development assistance to a donor country with its economic and social development, though it still receives assistance from China, developed countries, and international organizations in areas such as talent, facilities, and technology (see Figure 3-1).

1　Based on *Guide for Countries and Regions on Overseas Investment and Cooperation: Vietnam (2022)* released by Ministry of Commerce of the People's Republic of China.

2　Based on *Guide for Countries and Regions on Overseas Investment and Cooperation: Myanmar (2022)* released by Ministry of Commerce of the People's Republic of China.

3　Based on *Guide for Countries and Regions on Overseas Investment and Cooperation: Cambodia (2022)* released by Ministry of Commerce of the People's Republic of China.

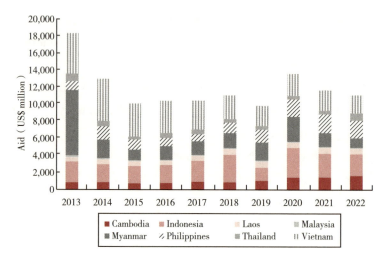

Figure 3-1   Official development assistance received by some ASEAN countries, 2013-2022

Source: Database of OECD, at current prices.

The pandemic led to a surge in bilateral, multilateral, and private aid[1]. During the COVID-19 pandemic, the international community increased its assistance to some ASEAN countries, especially Vietnam, Myanmar, and the Philippines, which still received high levels of aid. The aid received by the Philippines increased considerably in 2020-2022, with an increase of 35.7% , 45.2% and 37.3%, respectively, compared to 2019. In 2020, Cambodia received ODA commitments totaling US$7.71 billion and actual aid of over US$2 billion, of which 58% was spent on infrastructure projects, 26% on agriculture, 9% on public management, and 7% on talent development. In the same year, the Philippines received overseas ODA of US$30.7 billion, including US$29 billion in the form of preferential loans (accounting for 94%) and US$1.7 billion as grants (accounting for 6%) [2]. The amount of bilateral aid in 2020-2022 was more than 1.1 times that in 2019, and the amount of multilateral aid increased

---

1   According to the OECD Database, official development aid is divided into multilateral aid and bilateral aid, with bilateral aid including development assistance (DAC) and non-DAC. Private aid is counted separately and is not included in official aid.

2   Based on *Guide for Countries and Regions on Overseas Investment and Cooperation: The Philippines (2022)* released by Ministry of Commerce of the People's Republic of China.

by 40.1% in 2020, 15.5% in 2021, and 2.9% in 2022 from 2019. Private aid also increased during the pandemic though the amount was small. In 2020-2022, the private sector presented an increase of international aid worth US$368 million from 2019 (see Figure 3-2).

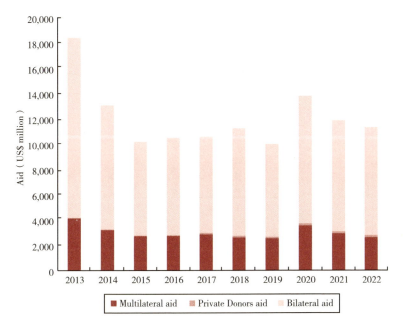

Figure 3-2   Multilateral, bilateral and private aid received by some ASEAN countries, 2013-2022

Source: Database of OECD (OECD.Stat), at current prices.

Bilateral aid was the main source of aid during the pandemic. With a share in excess of 75% in the total, the bilateral aid to ASEAN countries was mainly offered by the United States, Japan, and the Republic of Korea. From 2013 to 2022, the bilateral aid from the United States, Japan, and the Republic of Korea to ASEAN accounted for 62% of the total. Japan contributed US$42.32 billion, accounting for 47% of the total. The aid from the United States and the Republic of Korea amounted to US$8.68 billion and US$5.04 billion, accounting for 9.6% and 5.6% of the total respectively. The multilateral aid presented an upward trend during the pandemic. The amount of multilateral aid in 2021 and in 2022 equaled US$2.9 billion and US$2.6 billion, up by 15.5% and 2.9% from

2019, respectively. The private aid maintained steady growth though the amount was small. Its total amount in 2021 and in 2022 equaled US$150 million and US$170 million, up by 30.7% and 46.7% from 2019, respectively (see Figure 3-3).

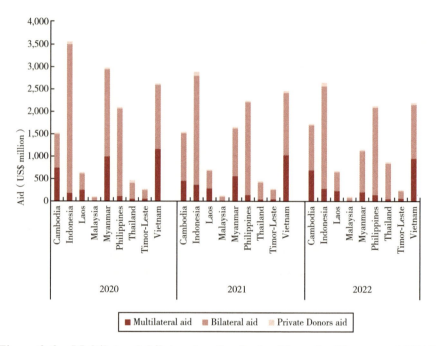

Figure 3-3   Multilateral, bilateral and private aid received by some ASEAN countries, 2020-2022

Source: Database of OECD (OECD.Stat), at current prices.

During the pandemic, ASEAN mainly received assistance in infrastructure construction[1]. There are similarities and differences in the areas in which ASEAN countries received assistance. Cambodia received assistance mainly in the construction of social infrastructure such as education, water supply

---

1   According to the definition in the database of the Organization for Economic Cooperation and Development (OECD), aid can be subdivided into the following categories by sector: (1) Social infrastructure and services: education, water supply and sanitation, etc; (2) Economic infrastructure and services: education, energy, transportation, communication infrastructure and services, etc; (3) Production sectors: Agriculture, forestry and fishery, industry, mining, and construction, and trade and tourism, etc; (4) Multi-sector/cross-Cutting: Environmental protection, etc; (5) General Programme Assistance: Food assistance, etc; (6) Debt relief; (7) Humanitarian aid; (8) Others.

and sanitation. The total amount of ODA aid received by Cambodia increased after the pandemic, from US$710 million in 2019 to US$1.24 billion in 2020. Although the amount in 2021 decreased compared to 2020, it was still 17% higher than that in 2019. The Philippines received assistance mainly in economic infrastructure and production, involving transportation, communication, and agricultural infrastructure. Malaysia received aid mainly in social infrastructure and education services. Laos received assistance mainly in the construction of education, energy, and agricultural infrastructure. The total amount of ODA aid received by Laos has fluctuated between US$300 million and US$500 million a year, with the highest amount received in 2014. Thailand mainly received aid for transportation and communication infrastructure. The total amount of aid received by the country experienced explosive growth in 2016, especially in the fields of transportation and communication as part of economic infrastructure and services, increasing 4-5 times compared to 2015. In addition, compared to the level in 2019, the aid received by Thailand increased by 60.1% and 30% in 2020 and 2021, respectively. The aid received by Indonesia has mainly gone to the fields of transportation and communication as part of economic infrastructure and services. The total amount of aid received by it presented a trend of first increasing and then decreasing, with the highest of US$3.7 billion received in 2017. The aid received by Indonesia increased by US$12.2 billion in 2021, and US$9.9 billion in 2022, respectively, compared to the level in 2019. In these two years, the aid received increased to nearly the level in 2017. Vietnam mainly received assistance in the construction of transportation and communication infrastructure. The total amount of aid received by Vietnam remained above US$2.5 billion before 2016 but gradually decreased after 2016. It reached the lowest level of US$580 million in 2018 and slowly increased to US$1.2 billion in 2021. Myanmar mainly received assistance in project construction and debt relief. The total amount of aid received by Myanmar reached the highest level of US$6.2 billion. The two major fields of aid accounted for 33.1% and 42.4% of the total, respectively (see Figure 3-4).

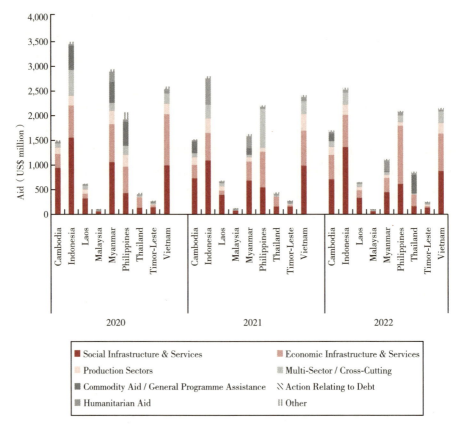

Figure 3-4   Total aid received by some ASEAN countries in different areas, 2020-2022

Source: Database of OECD (OECD.Stat), at current prices.

3.2   Aid from International Agencies to ASEAN Countries

The World Bank provided low-cost loans to ease the financial burden on ASEAN countries in poverty reduction. From 2012 to 2021, the average annual amount of assistance offered by World Bank to ASEAN countries equaled US$1.24 billion, accounting for 40% of assistance from multilateral institutions to ASEAN. From 2012 to 2022, the World Bank launched 313 financial assistance projects for ASEAN, with an investment of US$111.5 billion, including US$107.5 billion in loans and US$4 billion in grants from the International Development Association (IDA) and the International Bank for Reconstruction and Development (IBRD)[1]. During the pandemic from 2020 to 2022, the World Bank provided US$46.3 billion in financial support to ASEAN, accounting for 41.5% of the total. The International Development Association shortened the disbursement period from three years to two years and pledged US$75 billion for emergent needs across ASEAN countries. The World Bank approved a US$50 million loan for Myanmar's COVID-19 emergency response project for expanding intensive care units (ICUs) in selected hospitals, strengthening the capacity building of health workers and officials, and carrying out community participation activities throughout the country. The project covered eight central-level hospitals, 43 regional-level and provincial/state-level hospitals in Myanmar (see Figure 3-5).

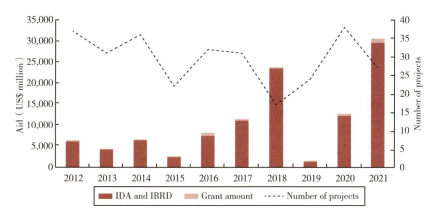

Figure 3-5   Total ODA and projects received by ASEAN from the World Bank, 2012-2021

Source: The World Bank's public assistance projects (https://projects.worldbank.org/en/projects-operations/projects-list).

International agencies offered development assistance through a variety of means. The Food and Agriculture Organization of the United Nations (FAO)

---

1 As the largest development bank in the world, the International Bank for Reconstruction and Development (IBRD) supports the World Bank Group's mission by providing loans, guarantees, risk management products, and advisory services to middle-income and creditworthy low-income countries, as well as by coordinating responses to regional and global challenges. Despite the eligibility to borrow from the International Development Association (IDA) based on their per capita income, Cambodia, Laos, and Myanmar can borrow and receive assistance from the IBRD as they are creditworthy for some of its loans.

and United Nations Development Programme (UNDP) provided US$4 million and US$16 million in assistance funds respectively to ASEAN mainly for agricultural infrastructure in 2021. In 2023, the FAO and the Green Climate Fund jointly assisted the Philippines in developing smart agriculture. From 2012 to 2021, the Asian Development Bank and the European Union (EU) maintained a high level of aid to ASEAN, accounting for 23.2% and 12.2% of the total amount of multilateral aid. During the pandemic, they further scaled up assistance to the region (see Figure 3-6). In 2022, the EU supported energy transition in Vietnam with private and public funding worth US$18 billion.

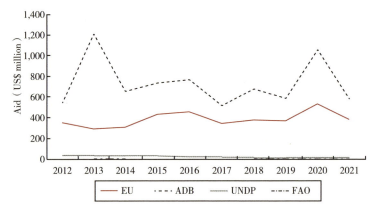

Figure 3-6 Aid received by ASEAN from international organizations, 2012-2021

Source: Database of OECD (OECD.Stat), at current prices.

Regional multilateral organizations provided assistance to ASEAN countries in different fields of development through loans and other means. Asian Development Bank (ADB) provided assistance to ASEAN countries through loans and other means to support their development in different fields and response to the impact of COVID-19. ADB and World Bank are the largest multilateral organizations providing assistance to the Philippines, accounting for 28.52% and 20.97% of the aid received by the Philippines, respectively[1]. In

---

1 Data from *Guide for Countries and Regions on Overseas Investment and Cooperation: The Philippines (2022)* released by Ministry of Commerce of the People's Republic of China.

2019, ADB approved a US$50 million loan for the Employment Training and Education Project to help Laos improve enrollment and secondary education levels. ADB also approved three loans worth US$140 million to help Laos develop its agriculture, education, and public finance management[1]. To support sustainable economic growth in Indonesia, ADB has pledged to provide financing support for green energy power plants, geothermal and solar projects in the country[2]. During the COVID-19 pandemic, ADB provided US$6.6 million under the framework of the Greater Mekong Subregion (GMS) Health Security Project to help Myanmar strengthen its early response to the pandemic. ADB also provided US$30 million in loans to Myanmar to help the Myanmar government make immediate investments in township hospitals in 31 regions to better respond to COVID-19 and other future public health threats[3]. In addition to ADB, Asian Infrastructure Investment Bank (AIIB) approved a US$1 billion loan in 2020 to assist Indonesia in COVID-19 prevention and control. In 2021, AIIB provided full financing support worth IDR 1.7 trillion (approximately US$120 million) for the Mandalika Urban and Tourism Infrastructure Project (MUTIP) in Lombok Island, Indonesia. This was the first time that AIIB had provided independent financing in Indonesia and financing in the tourism infrastructure development field[4].

Box 3-1   Assistance from International Organizations Drives Social Development and Poverty Reduction in ASEAN

1. World Bank Assists in Indonesia's Post-COVID-19 Economic Recovery[a]

Indonesia suffered its first economic recession in nearly 20 years due to the COVID-19 pandemic. The country is now facing significant challenges in investment and trade, which are hindering its ability to attract foreign direct

---

1   Based on *Guide for Countries and Regions on Overseas Investment and Cooperation: Laos (2022)* released by Ministry of Commerce of the People's Republic of China.

2   Based on *Guide for Countries and Regions on Overseas Investment and Cooperation: Indonesia (2022)* released by Ministry of Commerce of the People's Republic of China.

3   Based on *Guide for Countries and Regions on Overseas Investment and Cooperation: Myanmar (2022)* released by Ministry of Commerce of the People's Republic of China.

4   Based on *Guide for Countries and Regions on Overseas Investment and Cooperation: Indonesia (2022)* released by Ministry of Commerce of the People's Republic of China.

investment, limiting its integration into the global value chain, and driving up domestic food prices. In 2021, the World Bank's Executive Board approved US$800 million in funding to support Indonesia's investment and trade policy reforms and to help accelerate the country's economic transformation and post-COVID-19 economic recovery. This assistance was in line with the Country Partnership Framework (CPF), which aims to support the Indonesian government's plan to attract investment and improve economic competitiveness. The funding will be used to attract foreign direct investment, increase the number of skilled professionals in the labor market, and promote private investment in the renewable energy industry.

2. FAO and GCF Provide Assistance to Help the Philippines Develop Smart Agriculture[b]

Green Climate Fund (GCF) announced on March 13,2023 that it will allocate US$145.3 million to support three new projects with the Food and Agriculture Organization (FAO) of the United Nations in Bolivia, Cambodia, and the Philippines. These projects will help small farmers and rural communities in these countries adapt to climate change and build climate resilience. In the Philippines, the US$39.2 million investment will help the country's agricultural system adapt to climate change and will directly benefit over 1.25 million people within seven years. In Cambodia, the US$42.8 million project will help small farmers in the northern part of the Tonle Sap Basin improve their disaster preparedness capabilities. Maria Helena Semedo, Deputy Director-General of FAO, said that innovative climate financing could help transform the agricultural food system and strengthen the adaptability and resilience of rural areas to climate change.

3. Asian Development Bank Will Support Indonesia's Fiscal and Investment Reforms[c]

Asian Development Bank (ADB) approved a US$1 billion policy loan in 2018 to support Indonesia's public expenditure reform and improve the country's investment environment. The fiscal and public expenditure management plan in the second phase will be funded by a loan of US$500 million, and the growth acceleration investment plan in the final phase will receive another loan of US$500 million. The first loan will help the Indonesian government complete the budget cycle and expand social assistance projects. It is in line with the goal of ADB to improve budget management and transparency in the country. This plan enables the government to increase target expenditures and improve the quality of expenditures in key areas such as healthcare and education. This plan will help the government improve the efficiency of public and private investment while also addressing investment restrictions at the local levels. In May 2018, Indonesia obtained an investment grade rating from the world's "three major" credit rating agencies (Fitch, Standard & Poor's, and Moody's).

Sources: a. Based on "World Bank Approvals US$800 mln Development Financing for Indonesia", released by the Indonesian news agency ANTARA on June 16, 2021.

b. Based on "2023 Rural Development Information Summary in China and Other Countries (11th Issue)", released by the International Poverty Reduction Center in China on May 19, 2023.

c. Based on "US$1 Billion Loan from the Asian Development Bank to Support Indonesia's Fiscal and Investment Reforms", released by the China-Indonesia Cultural Exchange Center of Central China Normal University on June 9, 2018.

3.3   Developed Countries' Assistance to ASEAN Countries

The United States, Japan, and the Republic of Korea are the main developed countries providing assistance to ASEAN. From 2013 to 2022, the total aid provided by the three countries to ASEAN accounted for 62% of the total bilateral aid received by the region. Japan provided the most aid, at US$42.23 billion, accounting for 47%. The United States and the Republic of Korea provided US$8.7 billion and US$5.04 billion in assistance to the region, respectively, accounting for 9.6% and 5.6%, respectively.

The assistance from the United States to the ASEAN region has remained stable and has mainly gone to Indonesia, the Philippines, Vietnam, and Myanmar. The United States provided US$8.7 billion in ODA to ASEAN from 2013 to 2022. Of it, US$2.6 billion was provided from 2020 to 2022, accounting for 30% of the total, and the amount of aid received in each of the two years increased more than 14% compared to the US$800 million in 2019. Among the recipient countries, Indonesia and the Philippines received the most aid from the United States, at US$2.2 billion and US$1.9 billion, respectively, far more than that received by other countries. The amount of aid received by ASEAN countries from the United States increased to various extents considering the impact of COVID-19 (see Figure 3-7).

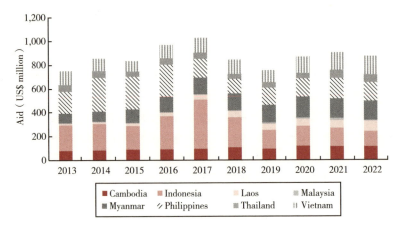

Figure 3-7   Aid received by some ASEAN countries from the United States, 2013-2022

Source: Database of OECD (OECD.Stat), at current prices.

Japan has offered considerable assistance to Southeast Asia. From 2013 to 2022, ASEAN received a total of US$42.3 billion in ODA from Japan. About 30% was received during the pandemic. Japan's aid to ASEAN increased by 33% in 2020, 5.1% in 2021 and 9.1% in 2022, compared to the average level in 2019. Among the recipient countries, Vietnam and Myanmar received the most aid from Japan, at US$10.7 billion and US$9.9 billion, respectively, far more than that received by other countries. During the pandemic, Indonesia, the Philippines, and Myanmar were the main recipients of aid from Japan, each accounting for over 20% (see Figure 3-8).

Japan's assistance to Indonesia, the Philippines, and Myanmar was mainly reflected in infrastructure construction. In 2020, the Philippines received a total of US$1.1 billion in aid from Japan, with the fields of transportation and communication as part of economic infrastructure accounting for over 40%. Compared to 2019, the aid received by the Philippines for transportation and communication decreased by 46% in 2020. Indonesia received a total of US$1.3 billion in aid from Japan in 2020, more than that received in 2019 and most being economic infrastructure assistance, accounting for over 20% of the aid. Compared to 2019, Indonesia received more aid in project assistance and multi-sectoral assistance in 2020. Japan's total aid to Indonesia decreased to

US$1.03billion in 2021, most of which was used for economic infrastructure development. Myanmar received a total of US$1.05 billion in aid from Japan in 2020, mainly in the fields of transportation and communication, accounting for 31%. Compared to 2019, Myanmar received more aid in the fields of social and economic infrastructure and multi-sector cooperation in 2020. The total amount of aid received for infrastructure construction reached US$0.6 billion, and the aid in the economic fields was twice that in 2019, respectively. Japan's aid to Myanmar decreased to US$0.4 billion in 2021.

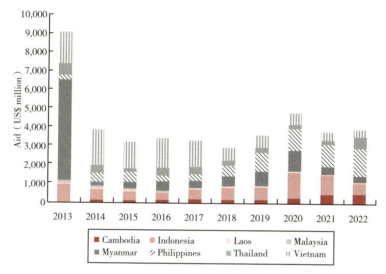

Figure 3-8   Aid received by some ASEAN countries from Japan, 2013-2022

Source: Database of OECD (OECD.Stat), at current prices.

The Republic of Korea continued to increase its aid to ASEAN. Between 2013 and 2022, ASEAN received a total of US$5 billion in ODA from the Republic of Korea, 35.8% of which was provided during the pandemic. The Republic of Korea also increased its investment in the ASEAN region in 2020-2021, with an annual increase of US$120 million, compared to 2019 (see Figure 3-9).

Among the recipient countries, Vietnam received the largest share of aid from the Republic of Korea, with a total of US$1,661 million, far more than that received by other countries. Vietnam was one of the major recipient of aid from

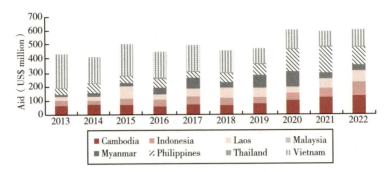

Figure 3-9   Aid received by some ASEAN countries from the Republic of Korea, 2013-2022

Source: Database of OECD (OECD.Stat), at current prices.

the Republic of Korea. In 2020, the Republic of Korea's ODA to ASEAN amounted to US$140 million, an increase of 26% from the previous year. The Republic of Korea provided more than US$200 million in aid to Vietnam only before 2015, with a focus on assisting in road construction and communication infrastructure. Its aid to Vietnam rapidly decreased thereafter and started to present a slight increase in 2019 in the field of agricultural infrastructure. Compared to 2019, the Republic of Korea increased its aid to Vietnam in the health and humanitarian fields in 2020 and increased its aid in education in 2021 (see Figure 3-10).

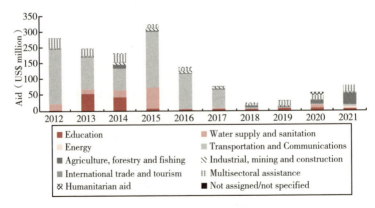

Figure 3-10   Sectoral assistance received by Vietnam from the Republic of Korea, 2012-2021

Source: Database of OECD (OECD.Stat), at current prices.

3.4   Cooperation Among ASEAN Countries

In 2015, ASEAN formulated the *ASEAN Economic Community Blueprint 2025,* which aims to achieve five key milestones by 2025, including: (1) a highly integrated and cohesive economy; (2) a competitive, innovative, and dynamic ASEAN; (3) enhanced connectivity and sectoral cooperation; (4) a resilient, inclusive people-oriented, and people-centered ASEAN; and (5) a global ASEAN. To this end, Lancang-Mekong Countries joint released *Five-Year Plan of Action on Lancang-Mekong Cooperation (2018-2022)* in 2018. This Plan of Action aims at contributing to the economic and social development of sub-regional countries, enhancing well-being of the people, narrowing the development gap within the region.

ASEAN countries expanded areas of cooperation to jointly response to the pandemic and other challenges. In response to the impact of the COVID-19 pandemic on economic and social development, and poverty reduction, the ASEAN countries sped up the fulfillment of the *ASEAN Comprehensive Recovery Framework (ACRF)* and its implementation plan. *ACRF* includes improving health services, social protection, economic integration, inclusive digital transformation, and sustainable development in agriculture, energy, etc. To ensure long-term food security and improve rural residents' livelihoods in ASEAN countries, ASEAN released the *ASEAN Integrated Food Security (AIFS) Framework* and the *Strategic Plan of Action on Food Security in the ASEAN Region (SPA-FS) 2021-2025* in 2020. To response to the negative effect of natural disasters of poverty reduction, ASEAN countries joint released the *ASEAN Strategic Framework for Public Health Emergencies* and *ASEAN Vision 2025 on Disaster Management.* In addition, to enhance the diffusion and application of digital technologies, ASEAN formulated the ASEAN Digital Masterplan 2025 to facilitate trade across ASEAN countries through digital services.

Chapter 4 China-ASEAN Poverty Reduction Cooperation

It is important to adhere to building a community with a shared future for China and ASEAN. China and ASEAN are geographically contiguous and consanguineously related and have maintained a long-standing friendly relationship. Since 1991, when China and ASEAN started the dialog process, they have worked together to enrich their strategic partnership and yielded fruitful results in the three major fields of cooperation, namely political security, economic trade, and social and cultural cooperation. China and ASEAN are now each other's largest trading partner, most meaningful cooperative partner, and most dynamic strategic partner. In 2021, China and ASEAN joint released the Plan of Action to Implement the ASEAN-China Strategic Partnership for Peace and Prosperity (2022-2025), and announced a comprehensive strategic partnership between the two sides at the ASEAN-China Special Summit to Commemorate the 30th Anniversary of ASEAN-China Dialog Relations. The plan notes the vision to build a peaceful, safe and secure, prosperous, beautiful, and amicable home in the region and serves as a blueprint and guide to the construction of a closer China-ASEAN community with a shared future.

4.1 Summary of China's Poverty Reduction Experience

Since the 18th National Congress of the Communist Party of China (CPC) in 2012, the CPC Central with Xi Jinping at its core has placed a high priority on poverty elimination in state governance. The CPC Central Committee has implemented targeted poverty reduction and alleviation strategies, mobilizing the energies of the whole Party, the whole country, and the whole of society to win the battle against poverty. As a result, all of the 98.99 million rural residents, 832 counties and 128,000 villages that fell below the current poverty line have been lifted out of poverty. In addition, regional poverty has been eliminated on the whole[1]. Currently, China is solidly consolidating and expanding the achievements in the fight against poverty while comprehensively promoting rural revitalization.

4.1.1   Experience from the fight against poverty

China's poverty reduction strategy has gone through four periods: relief-based poverty alleviation, development-driven poverty alleviation, comprehensive poverty alleviation, and targeted poverty alleviation. The characteristics of poverty and the driving forces, measures, and means of poverty reduction vary with different periods.

Relief-based poverty alleviation (1978-1985). In the early stages of reform and opening up, the poverty rate in rural areas in China exceeded 80%. The main driving force for China to eradicate extreme poverty during this period was to promote agricultural income growth and improve agricultural productivity. During this period, China enhanced relief-based poverty alleviation in rural areas, actively promoted the reform of the rural land system, and established a dual-level management system based on a household contracted responsibility system and a combination of unified and decentralized operations[2]. This stimulated farmers' enthusiasm, unleashed productivity, and provided strong support for grain yield increase, multi-source income growth for farmers, and national economic development. During this period, the rural population living in extreme poverty decreased from 250 million to 125 million, and the poverty rate in rural areas decreased from 30.7% to 14.8%[3].

---

1   Xi Jinping.(2021). Speech at the National Conference to Review the Fight Against Poverty and Commend Individuals and Groups Involved，Beijing: Central Compilation and Translation Press.

2   Based on "Reform of China's Rural Land System"，published by Han Changfu, Director of the Central Rural Work Leading Group Office and Minister of Agriculture and Rural Affairs in 2018.

3   Fan, X. J. (2007). Basic Experience of Poverty Alleviation and Development with Chinese Characteristics. Qiushi, 200，468(23): 48-49. (in Chinese)

Development-driven poverty alleviation (1986-2006). Development-driven poverty alleviation emphasized the reliance on the local resources and economic development of impoverished areas to address poverty problems. With the continuous deepening of rural reform, China's poverty alleviation targets were gradually shifting to poor areas at the county and village levels. In 1986, the State Council Leading Group Office of Poverty Alleviation and Development (LGOP) was established. The Circular on Strengthening Economic Development in Poor Areas released in 1987 formalized the guiding conception of development-driven poverty alleviation. The 8-7 National Plan for Poverty Reduction Program released in 1994 promoted poverty reduction through subsidized loans, work-relief programs, universal compulsory education, and improvement of the medical security system. At the same time, China put forth strategies for developing the western region and the rise of the central region and reduced regional disparities through policies such as large-scale infrastructure investment, fiscal transfer payments, and subsidies. During this period, the proportion of people living in extreme poverty in China decreased from 81.2% in 1984 to 22.1% in 2005, and approximately 5.53 million people were lifted out of extreme poverty[1].

Comprehensive poverty alleviation (2007-2012). Comprehensive poverty alleviation was mainly realized through the combination of development-driven poverty alleviation driven by industrial development and trade with the social security system. In 2007, the rural minimum living guarantee system was rapidly promoted nationwide, which marked the formation of a governance system that combines development-driven poverty alleviation with securing basic needs for poverty alleviation in China. During this period, the government mainly provided cash transfers to impoverished populations who were unable to participate in economic activities through social assistance, transfer payments, and other means. China also formulated a series of social security policies aimed at reducing rural poverty, including the new rural cooperative medical insurance, rural pension insurance system, and rural living security system. During this period, the proportion of people living in extreme poverty in China decreased from 18% in 2008 to 8.5% in 2012, and approximately 123 million people were lifted out of

---

1   Data from the World Bank's PovcalNet (http://iresearch.worldbank.org/PovcalNet/).

extreme poverty[1].

Targeted poverty alleviation (2013-2020). According to the 2010 national poverty line, the proportion of rural poor population dropped to below 10% in 2013, mainly concentrated in remote areas in the central and western regions. The release of the Outline of Development-driven Poverty Alleviation in Rural Areas (2011-2020) in 2011 marked the transition from poverty alleviation focusing on regions to targeted poverty alleviation focusing on households. The 18th National Congress of the Communist Party of China proposed the fundamental strategy of targeted poverty alleviation, which included "Six Precisions" and "Five Key Measures", and made arrangements on who to provide assistance, who to receive assistance, how to provide assistance, how to quit assistance, and how to prevent falling back into poverty. The "Six Precisions" require that the entire poverty alleviation process be precise in terms of identifying target groups, planning carefully projects, making good use of funds, following through with measures on a household-by-household basis, assigning first secretaries in consideration of local needs, and setting clear objectives. The "Five Key Measures" refer to poverty alleviation policy measures adapted to the causes of poverty, mainly related to employment and industrial development, relocation, ecological compensation, education, and social assistance for basic needs. In addition, the Targeted Poverty Alleviation during the 13th Five-Year Plan specifies measures supporting the battle against poverty, including innovative systems, increased policy guidance, and strengthened organizational implementation to ensure the smooth implementation of targeted poverty alleviation. As of the end of 2020, China completely eradicated extreme poverty, and targeted poverty alleviation had effectively solved the "last mile problem" in China's battle against poverty.

4.1.2   Progress in the connection of consolidating and expanding the achievements of poverty alleviation and rural revitalization in China

Holding the bottom line to prevent people from returning to poverty on a large scale. Resolutely holding the bottom line to prevent people from

---

1   Data from the World Bank's PovcalNet (http://iresearch.worldbank.org/PovcalNet/).

returning to poverty on a large scale is an essential prerequisite for effective connection of consolidating and expanding the achievements of poverty alleviation and rural revitalization. In the speech at the National Conference to Review the Fight Against Poverty and Commend Individuals and Groups Involved held on February 25, 2021, President Xi Jinping emphasized that China's complete victory in the fight against poverty signified that a substantial step forward had been made in the CPC's efforts to unite and lead the people in the pursuit of better lives and common prosperity. Xi also stressed that the country must take concrete steps to consolidate and expand upon the outcomes of the fight against poverty as part of their efforts to promote rural revitalization, so that the foundations of poverty eradication would be more solid and the effects would be more sustainable. The fight against poverty and rural revitalization strategies has a consistent logic, representing the transition from the eradication of extreme poverty to the governance of relative poverty. Poverty alleviation aims to achieve "Two Assurances and Three Guarantees" for the rural poor people and focuses on the eradication of extreme poverty by guaranteeing food and clothing. Rural revitalization focuses on the governance of relative poverty by building a long-term mechanism to solve relative poverty, resolving the imbalance between urban and rural development and insufficient rural development, and fundamentally narrowing the gap in living standards and quality between urban and rural areas. Compared to extreme poverty, relative poverty is an issue involving more dimensions and deeper problems. Without addressing extreme poverty, the issues relating to agriculture, rural areas and farmers will not be fundamentally resolved, and comprehensive rural revitalization will not be possible. The Chinese government has leveraged digital technology to continuously strengthen dynamic monitoring to prevent poverty-returning and implemented targeted assistance measures to eliminate the risk of falling into and returning to poverty.

Enhancing the intrinsic development capacity of regions and people lifted out of poverty. A long-term mechanism based on endogenous growth must be established to consolidate the achievements of poverty alleviation. High priority has always been given to industrial development, from poverty alleviation through creating new economic activity to industrial prosperity in rural revitalization. Industrial development is the primary intersection of consolidating the achievements of poverty alleviation and rural revitalization. Industrial prosperity is a prerequisite for solving all rural problems and should be incorporated into the entire process of poverty alleviation and rural revitalization. The revitalization of industries is fundamental to rural revitalization and serves as a key strategy to ensure stable poverty alleviation of poor people and enhance the intrinsic development capacity of regions and people liberated from poverty. In 2022, the proportion of proportion of the central government subsidies for rural revitalization for industrial development exceeded 55%. Each county that has shaken off poverty has cultivated 2-3 characteristic leading industries. Nearly 3/4 of the population that have got rid of poverty have established a close interest linkage relationship with new business entities[1]. Poverty alleviation through creating new economic activity is an endogenous and fundamental path to poverty alleviation. Integrating the development of primary, secondary, and tertiary sectors can extend the agricultural product industry chain, improving the self-development ability of impoverished groups, enhancing their capacity of independent development, and injecting an inexhaustible source of driving force into rural revitalization. For example, in Rongjiang County, Qiandongnan Prefecture, Guizhou Province, the small fragrant chicken industry has benefited 2,136 people from 505 poor households through "contract farming". The average income of poor households has increased by over RMB3,000, representing notable poverty alleviation effect of the small fragrant chicken industry. In Meishu Township, Zhaohua District, Guangyuan City, Sichuan Province, 300 farmers in five villages kept 40,000 laying hens and have realized sales revenues of RMB900,000 on a cumulative basis. The Yade Fine Brown Wool Fabric Cooperative in Kangxiong Township, Renbu County, Tibet Autonomous Region achieves an annual sales revenue of over RMB5 million, providing jobs to more than 100 people and helping them increase their income by RMB3,500 per person. The employment of laborers that have got rid of poverty has remained stable, with the scale of workforce employment reaching

---

1   See: http://www.moa.gov.cn/hd/zbft_news/2022nyncjjyxqk/.

32.8 million in 2022, an increase of 1.329 million compared with the end of 2021, exceeding the annual target task by 2.6 million[1]. Rural employment and entrepreneurship have gained momentum, with the local and nearby employment rate exceeding 90%. Driven by industries and employment, the per capita disposable income of rural residents nationwide reached RMB20,133 in 2022, an increase of 4.2% in real terms, and the ratio of per capita income between urban and rural residents was 2.5, a decrease of 0.05 compared with 2021[2].

Continuously reducing regional development disparities. Stable assistance policies are important measures to ensure the stability of poverty alleviation in impoverished areas and reduce regional disparities. The central government has introduced relevant policy measures to ensure smooth transition and coordination. At the national level, 160 key counties have been identified for targeted assistance in rural revitalization. Adjustments and improvements have been made to the pairing assistance between eastern and western areas. The Ten Thousand Enterprises Prospering Ten Thousand Villages initiative has been implemented to maintain overall stability in targeted assistance efforts by central departments. First Party secretaries and resident working teams are continuously deployed to facilitate the flow of resources such as funds and talents to the central and western regions, and ensure the effective implementation of various assistance measures. Efforts are being made to effectively utilize the "command baton" of assessment, that is, conducting assessment on effective connection of consolidating and expanding the achievements of poverty alleviation and rural revitalization, in order to promote the implementation of policies, responsibilities, and work tasks.

Building a beautiful and harmonious countryside that is desirable to live and work in. Building a beautiful and harmonious countryside that is desirable to live and work in is a major strategic task for comprehensively promoting rural revitalization and moving faster to build up China's strength in agriculture. In

---

1 See: http://www.moa.gov.cn/hd/zbft_news/qmtjxczx/ wzzb_29371/.

2 See: http://www.moa.gov.cn/hd/zbft_news/2022nyncjjyxqk/.

accordance with the arrangements made at the 20th CPC National Congress, China is embarking on a new journey of comprehensively promoting the great rejuvenation of the Chinese nation through a uniquely Chinese modernization process. The country will comprehensively promote rural revitalization, move faster to build up China's strength in agriculture, and steadily promote the revitalization of businesses, talent, culture, ecosystems, and organizations in the countryside. The goal is to build a beautiful and harmonious countryside that is desirable to live and work in. The country has worked to build a modern rural industrial system to promote the integrated development of primary, secondary and tertiary industries in rural areas. Based on county-level coordinated planning for industrial development, efforts are made to retain more value-added stages of industries in rural areas and increase the proportion of farmers' share in value-added revenue. Rural construction initiatives are implemented to coordinate the development of rural infrastructure and public service systems, persistently improve the rural living environment, and promote the toilet revolution in rural areas based on local conditions. Efforts are also made to enhance the village landscape and appearance based on local characteristics, regional features, and ethnic characteristics. Rural management is strengthened and improved by innovating rural management methods and approaches, promoting the use of scoring systems, listing systems, digitization, and other governance methods. China also works to update outmoded and undesirable habits and customs by cultivating social civility in rural areas, fostering desirable family customs, and nurturing simple folk customs.

4.1.3 Comprehensively promoting rural vitalization

The smooth transition from poverty alleviation to comprehensively promote rural vitalization is a historic shift in the focus of tasks addressing the issues relating to agriculture, rural areas and rural people. In the context of profound changes unseen in a century around the world, the Fifth Plenary Session of the 19th CPC Central Committee required accelerating the development of a new development pattern with domestic circulation as the main body and dual domestic and international circulations complementing each other[1]. The issues relating to agriculture, rural areas and rural people are the fundamental pillars of China's development and the "ballast stones" for achieving a soft landing in crisis and ensuring economic stability and progress. The No. 1 central document for 2023 pointed out that, it must persist in taking the solution of the issues relating to agriculture, rural areas and rural people as the top priority of the whole Party's work, mobilize the efforts of the whole Party and the whole society to promote rural revitalization, and accelerate the modernization of agriculture and rural areas. The aim of accelerating the creation of a dual circulation pattern as mentioned above is to drive the integration of resource factors and regional interconnection, foster a new type of urban-rural relationship, and consolidate the achievements of poverty alleviation.

Utilizing the digital economy to open up new spaces for employment and income generation. Digital technologies such as artificial intelligence, blockchain, cloud computing, big data, and 5G are accelerating their penetration into agriculture and rural areas, providing great development opportunities for promoting rural revitalization. The coverage of the internet in rural areas in China has increased significantly. As of June 2022, the rural internet penetration rate was 58.8%, and the number of rural internet users reached 293 million according to the *50th Statistical Report on the Development of the Internet in China* released by the China Internet Network Information Center. In recent years, the Chinese government has released a number of policies to support the digital economy to empower rural revitalization, including the Development Plan for Digital Agriculture and Rural Areas (2019-2025) (released in December 2019), the 14th Five-Year Plan for National Informatization (December 2021), the Digital Rural Development Action Plan (2022-2025) (January 2022), and the Key Points for Development of Digital County side in 2022 (April 2022). With the increasing applications and popularity of mobile internet in rural areas, a great many digital technology products, digital platforms, and software services targeting the issues relating to agriculture, rural areas and rural people

---

1   The Recommendations of the CPC Central Committee for Formulating the 14th Five-Year Plan for Economic and Social Development and Long-Range Objectives Through the Year 2035, released by the official website of the State Council of the People's Republic of China in 2020.

have empowered farmers to engage more efficiently in rural production and operation, providing more opportunities for rural employment and high-quality industrial development. The No. 1 central document for 2023 requires promoting high-quality rural development by mainly expanding and strengthening the agricultural product processing and circulation industry, accelerating the development of modern rural service industry, cultivating new rural industries and new business forms, and cultivating and strengthening people-enriching industries in counties. The Digital Rural Development Action Plan (2022-2025) released in 2022 clearly points out the need to focus on developing the rural digital economy and adhere to overall coordination and urban-rural integration. Local governments in China have encouraged efforts to launch the developing agriculture with digital business campaign and implement the "internet Plus" project for agricultural products going out from villages into cities. They have utilized e-commerce and strong domestic logistics networks to integrate rural areas into the urban supply chain, broaden the sales channels of agricultural products, and help farmers increase their income through multiple channels.

Accelerating the development of green and low-carbon agriculture and promoting the transformation of agriculture. China has pledged to "reach a peak in its carbon dioxide (CO_2) emissions before 2030 and achieve carbon neutrality by 2060". This "carbon peaking and carbon neutrality" commitment has driven the green transformation of agricultural production practices and the entire agricultural product value chain, stimulated technological innovation, created employment and economic growth opportunities, and promoted agricultural green transformation through agricultural technology promotion, becoming the main driving force of improving agricultural productivity.

Integrating rural economic activities with the ecological environment to activate the value of rural ecological resources. In 2005, Xi Jinping, who was then the Secretary of the Zhejiang Provincial Committee, for the first time put forward the concept of "Lucid waters and lush mountains are invaluable assets" during a survey of Yucun in Anji County, Zhejiang. The report of the 19th National Congress of the Communist Party of China emphasized the need to "maintain harmonious coexistence between humans and nature" and to "develop green development methods and lifestyles". For China's future ecological civilization construction and green development, it is essential to establish and practice the concept of "Lucid waters and lush mountains are invaluable assets". Under this concept, eco-environmental activities for poverty alleviation and ecological revitalization are inherently consistent with each other. Rural society has the spatial ecological resource value of integrating resources, assets, and capital. It has the potential to become a new driving force and growth pole, naturally becoming the foundation of ecological transformation. For example, Anji County, in Zhejiang Province, adheres to the development strategy of "building an ecological county" by promoting the construction of demonstration villages of beautiful countryside and the improvement of boutique tourism belts, exploring a path of eco-prosperity for getting better off and maintaining a beautiful environment, and enhancing rural residents' income and living standards while improving the eco-environment[1].

Continuously improving the effectiveness of social security governance, and promoting common prosperity through high-quality social security. It is necessary to consider institutionalized social security policies integrating targeted poverty alleviation to address the future changes in the characteristics of China's low-income population. China has effectively utilized the professional knowledge of international organizations to improve poverty alleviation policies and data. A large number of human resources have been allocated to targeted poverty alleviation. In addition, the country has used comprehensive survey data to identify poor areas and households, determined government intervention policies as needed, and achieved policy goals through the goal responsibility system of officials at all levels. The sound social security system had also helped better protect families in urban and rural areas from adverse impact. During the COVID-19 pandemic, China provided income support to migrant workers living and working in cities and low-income groups, to compensate for wage losses

---

1 Based on "Continuously 'Advancing' the Construction of Beautiful Countryside in Anji, Zhejiang", published *People's Daily* in 2020.

and prevent them from being unable to access medical and health services due to insufficient income.

4.2   Implications of China's Experience for Poverty Reduction in ASEAN

Strengthening top-level design and promoting poverty reduction according to local conditions. Poverty reduction is a complex task that requires policy departments to take a holistic approach, grasp the linkages between food security, nutrition and health, education, economic growth, climate change and scientific and technological innovation, and give full play to the strengths of national institutions. ASEAN countries experience different progress in poverty reduction, as well as different historical background, resource endowment and practical challenges. With due consideration of local realities, ASEAN countries can better advance the poverty reduction process. Malaysia and Thailand, which have a high level of development, have entered a critical period of poverty reduction. They should accurately identify the causes of poverty, consolidate the achievements of poverty reduction, and prevent poverty-returning on a large scale. With regard to economic and social fragility, the Indonesian government may seek to establish a long-term mechanism to stabilize poverty reduction. In addressing the unequal development opportunities of the poor, the government of the Philippines and the government of Vietnam may accelerate the cause of poverty reduction by building a governance system that combines development-driven poverty alleviation with securing basic needs for poverty alleviation. Cambodia, Laos and Myanmar are still in the stage of large-scale poverty reduction. They may advance the process of poverty reduction through universal education, improved health care systems and subsidized loans. At the same time, they may introduce relevant policies to narrow the urban-rural gap and realize that the fruits of development are shared by the people. In addition, the complexity and systemic nature of poverty reduction requires policy coherence, precision and stability.

Improving the quality and efficiency of agriculture through scientific and technological innovation. Developing agriculture is of great significance for the rural poor to get rid of poverty. In terms of production, Myanmar and Laos may strengthen the construction of farmland infrastructure through international cooperation, actively carry out farmland protection and ecological environment protection, and upgrade the level of farmland infrastructure such as power transmission and distribution. In terms of agricultural technology, the countries vulnerable to climate change, such as Vietnam, Indonesia and Thailand, may promote the application of water-saving agricultural technologies and improve agricultural water use efficiency to adapt to climate change. They need also to guide water-scarce regions to jointly carry out research on water-saving technologies, and promote the construction of bases for the demonstration and dissemination of water-saving agricultural technologies. In terms of scientific and technological cooperation, Vietnam has taken the lead in cooperating with China on germplasm resources, building experimental stations for good crop varieties, and upgrading the development of the seed industry through the introduction of high-yield and high-quality varieties. Other member states may seize the development opportunities of the Belt and Road Initiative and Regional Comprehensive Economic Partnership (RCEP) to continue to conduct practical and effective exploration in the field of agricultural science and technology cooperation, so as to enhance the region's food production capacity. In terms of regional food security, ASEAN should enhance its productive capacity for food security, strengthen cooperation on emergency rice reserves and releases, and improve the management of and response to food emergencies. Besides, it should encourage transnational cooperation among research institutions and strengthen cooperation in the areas of research capacity, green agriculture, digital agriculture and sustainable development.

Improving education and nutrition to provide equal opportunities of development. Development is the key to solving all problems. While economic growth can alleviate poverty through the "trickle-down effect", neglecting the issue of creating equal opportunities of development will mitigate the effectiveness of poverty reduction. While developing comprehensive and inclusive social security, the ASEAN countries may promote urbanization, formulate more inclusive development policies, narrow the urban-rural income gap, and provide equal development opportunities for people living in rural and urban areas. In terms of education, ASEAN countries, especially those with faster economic growth rates, such as Thailand and Vietnam, may increase their focus on vocational and technical education, especially in the area of the digital economy, and promote the training of digital talents under a digital literacy framework to strengthen the talent reserve for the digital era. At the same time, more efforts should be devoted to enhancing education for school-age children in poor areas. In particular, more attention should be paid to the nutrition of poor children in low-income countries and regions. The government may provide nutritious meals to eliminate malnutrition and enhance the ability of the poor to afford a healthy diet. With regard to healthcare, ASEAN countries have widely differing levels of economic development. They may further promote intra-regional cooperation in healthcare, especially cooperation and mutual support among regions with different levels of development, in order to promote the reduction of disparities in the levels of healthcare and education within ASEAN countries based on the principle of inclusiveness and strengthen the resilience of the region's development.

Developing the digital economy to improve economic resilience. Developing is the foundation and guarantee for poverty eradication. Some ASEAN countries were currently experiencing a return to poverty. High-quality and resilient development should be pursued to increase resilience to risks. At present, COVID-19 pandemic has changed the way people live, and the digital economy is growing rapidly. Digital transformation may facilitate the creation and accumulation of social wealth. The development of the digital economy is now a rightful place for ASEAN to enhance its economic resilience and achieve high-quality development. In order to accelerate poverty reduction in ASEAN, it shall promote digital development and cooperation among ASEAN members, becoming a leading digital community and economy powered by secure and transformative digital services, technology and ecosystems. It shall upgrade the quality and expand the coverage of fixed and mobile broadband infrastructure in ASEAN members and provide trusted digital services to create a competitive market for digital services. It shall also improve the quality and expand the use of e-government services. While providing digital services that connect businesses and facilitate cross-border trade. This will help strengthen the ability of businesses and people to participate in the digital economy and build an inclusive digital society. Furthermore, it shall provide data tools and digital skills training to micro, small and medium-sized enterprises, underemployed youth, and youth in rural and remote areas to allow development opportunities to reach more people.

Strengthening cooperation with neighboring countries to jointly address climate challenges. Combating climate change requires the joint efforts of all countries in the ASEAN region. Strengthening cooperation with neighboring countries, especially emerging economies, would help ASEAN member states to learn from successful experiences, enhance their capacity to respond to climate change, reduce the risks and uncertainties posed by climate extremes to food security and economic development, and explore the establishment of a market mechanism for the realization of ecological values. For climate-vulnerable low-income countries such as Cambodia and Myanmar, development assistance such as the Green Climate Fund and the Global Environment Facility (GEF) may be offered to enhance their capacity to respond to climate change.

4.3 Overview of China-ASEAN Poverty Reduction Cooperation

Presently, the global economic recover is losing steam, while issues such as currency inflation, food, and energy security have become austere. The world is confronted with a multitude of challenges. In the face of an intricate international landscape, China and ASEAN countries respect and help each other, and the comprehensive strategic partnership between them now enjoys a sound momentum, establishing an example of regional collaboration for mutual benefit.

ASEAN is one of China's important international political and economic partners. In 2020, China and ASEAN became the largest trading partner of each other. In 2021, the bilateral relationship between China and ASEAN was further upgraded to a comprehensive strategic cooperative partnership. The establishment of the China-ASEAN Free Trade Area has led to frequent exchanges and rapid growth of bilateral trade of agricultural products and enhanced the interdependence of economic development between the two sides. Promoting regional economic cooperation is an important part of developing global partnerships and building new international relations[1]. In the loose international organization, three of its members are China's land neighbors, and four of them face China across the sea. The countries in the region have different development levels and enjoy diverse resource conditions and institutional environments. This has made China's promotion of cooperation with ASEAN under the Belt and Road Initiative through targeted and differentiated consultation and agreements with ASEAN countries[2].

China continued to increase assistance to ASEAN. Since the beginning of the 21st century, China's international assistance to ASEAN countries has been steadily increasing on the whole. Notable progress has been made, particularly in fields such as infrastructure development, poverty reduction, disaster relief, and human resources development cooperation. In 2016, China's overall assistance to the ASEAN region increased significantly to US$11.6 billion, representing an increase of more than eight times compared to the previous year[3]. In 2017, the East Asia Poverty Reduction Demonstration Cooperation Technical Assistance Project was launched as a pilot program in Laos, Cambodia, and Myanmar. The initial phase of the project had a funding amount of RMB100 million[4]. In the past six years, the value of new contract signed between China and the Philippines for construction projects in the Philippines has nearly tripled, with an annual scale surpassing US$10 billion[5]. Chinese companies have actively participated

---

1   Liu, Z.W. (2014). East Asian Production Networks, Global Value Chain Consolidation and Trends in East Asian Regional Cooperation. Journal of Contemporary Asia-Pacific Studies, (4):126,156, 160 (in Chinese); Zhong, F. T. (2020). Covid-19 Pandemic and U-shaped Economic Recovery in Southeast Asia: An International Political Economy Analysis. Southeast Asian Studies, (5): 1-23,154 (in Chinese); Sun, Y. R., He, Y., and Li, B. (2021). China's View of Economic Security in the Past 20 Years after Its Entry into WTO. World Economy Studies, (12):42-53,132-133. (in Chinese)

2   Deng, Q. M., Liu, Y. N., and Wu, X. L. (2018). Study on Deepening China-ASEAN Cooperation in the Context of "Belt and Road" : Problems and Paths to Realization. Fujian Tribune, (12):195-200. (in Chinese)

3   Data from AidData database.

4   See: https://www.gov.cn/xinwen/2016-10/18/content_5120623.htm.

5   Data from the Regional Comprehensive Economic Partnership (RCEP).

in construction projects in the Philippines, including roads, bridges, ports, power plants, housing, and water conservancy projects. They have successfully completed the largest power plant project in the Philippines, and are currently involved in the construction of the largest photovoltaic unit in the country. In addition, China has provided assistance in the construction of key infrastructure projects in ASEAN countries, including the National Highway 6 from Phnom Penh to Siem Reap in Cambodia, and the largest solar power project in Southeast Asia, the 500 MW Dau Tieng Solar Power Plant in Vietnam.

Box 4-1 Project Achievements of China's Assistance to ASEAN

1. The Jakarta-Bandung High-Speed Railway Drives Indonesian Social Development[a, b]

The Jakarta-Bandung High-Speed Railway is the first high-speed railway in Southeast Asia and the first overseas project completely built with China's high-speed railway technology. It connects the two major cities of Jakarta and Bandung in Indonesia, with a total length of approximately 142 kilometers and a maximum design speed of 350 kilometers per hour. This means that the travel time between the two cities will be shortened to just 40 minutes. In May 2023, the high-speed railway began connected commissioning and testing, taking an important step toward its full opening and operation. It will inject new momentum into Indonesia's accelerated development. The Jakarta-Bandung High-Speed Railway has already created 51,000 jobs in Indonesia. Once it is fully operational, it is expected to create an additional 30,000 jobs in related supporting industries each year. This will be a boon to the Indonesian economy and help improve the livelihoods of its people.

2. China-Laos Railway Injects Vitality into Lao Tourism[c, d]

The China-Laos Railway was officially opened on December 3, 2021, serving as a new channel connecting China and Laos to develop together. As of December 2022, the railway had transported 8.5 million passengers, including 7.2 million passengers in the Chinese section and 1.3 million passengers in Laos, and 11.2 million tons of goods, including over 1.9 million tons of cross-border goods. The China-Laos Railway has also created jobs in Laos. Since its opening, it has recruited over 3,500 Lao employees and indirectly created over 100,000 jobs in logistics, transportation, commerce, and tourism. Phakhasith Phomchlueth, Consul General of the Laotian Consulate in Shanghai, said that the opening of the railway has changed the way people travel in northern Laos and has promoted trade, cultural exchanges, and transportation. The railway has become an important force in driving the socio-economic development and human resources improvement of Laos.

3. Cambodia Enters "Expressway Era" [e, f]

On October 1, 2022, Cambodia's first expressway, the Phnom Penh-Sihanoukville Expressway, was officially opened to traffic. It is an important achievement under the framework of Cambodia-China cooperation and the Belt and Road Initiative. US$2 billion was invested to build the 187-kilometers-long expressway. During the construction period, the project adhered to the concept of win-win cooperation by creating a localized supply chain, which purchased construction materials, equipment, and services from local sources in Cambodia. The project spent a cumulative amount of over US$246 million on local goods and services. It has vigorously promoted local employment, with local employees accounting for over 82.3% of the workforce during peak periods. Over 11,000 local workers were hired in the project on a cumulative basis. In June 2023, Cambodia's second expressway, the Phnom Penh-Bavet Expressway, was set to break ground. During the construction period, it is expected to directly hire more than 5,000 Cambodian workers and create nearly 10,000 jobs for the local area on a cumulative basis. During the 50-year operation period, the project will also provide over 1,000 jobs in Cambodia every year. The construction and operation of the expressways have promoted the development of Cambodia's economy, improved the professional literacy of local employees, and driven technological progress in Cambodia's infrastructure industry.

Sources: a. "Jakarta-Bandung High-Speed Railway Starts Connected Commissioning", released on the official website of China's Belt and Road Initiative on May 23, 2023.

b. "Jakarta-Bandung High-Speed Railway: Shining 'Golden Business Card' of China's High-Speed Railway", published on People's Daily on December 7, 2022.

c. "China-Laos Railway Hands in Results Showing Booming Passenger and Freight Transportation after One Year of Opening", released on the official website of the State Council of the People's Republic of China on December 2, 2022.

d. The remarks made by Foreign Ministry Spokesperson Mao Ning at the regular press conference on May 25, 2023.

e. "Construction of China-Invested Phnom Penh-Bavet Expressway Commences", released on the website of the Regional Comprehensive Economic Partnership (RCEP) on June 8, 2023.

f. "The First Cambodian Expressway Invested by China Communications Construction Opens to Traffic", released by the State-owned Assets Supervision and Administration Commission of the State Council on October 9, 2022.

Both sides expanded cooperation areas in the new situation. For a long time, China has actively engaged in cooperation with ASEAN countries in various fields, with a particular focus on providing economic and technological assistance to low-income ASEAN countries. This support aims to help ASEAN countries narrow their internal development gaps. Facing the new international situation, both sides are steadily expanding investment cooperation in sectors such as manufacturing, agriculture, infrastructure, high and new technology, and digital economy. During the 19th China-ASEAN Expo, China and ASEAN countries jointly signed 267 investment cooperation contracts on site, with a total investment of RMB413 billion. These projects cover a wide range of industries, including high-end metallic materials, green and environmental protection, light industry and textiles, health and wellness, cultural tourism and sports, as well as green chemical materials and machinery and equipment manufacturing[1]. By the end of 2021, China has organized over 800 agricultural technology training courses for ASEAN countries. It has also established agricultural cooperation demonstration zones in Cambodia and Laos. In addition, China has implemented projects for crop variety trial stations in countries such as Vietnam, Laos, Cambodia, Indonesia, and Myanmar, aiming to promote the cultivation of superior crop varieties[2]. In addition, both sides have launched multiple cooperative projects in areas such as smart cities, 5G, artificial intelligence, e-commerce, big data, blockchain, and telemedicine. They have also applied digital technologies to pandemic prevention and control, creating a series of innovative digital application scenarios and sharing digital solutions for pandemic prevention and control.

China and ASEAN jointly built a road to common prosperity. 2023 marks the tenth anniversary of the proposal of the Belt and Road Initiative. Over the past decade, China has provided assistance to ASEAN in various infrastructure projects that have empowered regional development, such as the Jakarta-Bandung High-Speed Railway, the China-Laos Railway, the Penh-Sihanoukville Expressway, and the China-Myanmar Economic Corridor.

---

1 See: https://www.gov.cn/xinwen/2022-09/16/content_5710313.htm.
2 See: //www.mfa.gov.cn/web/wjbxw_673019/202201/t20220105_10479078.shtml.

Additionally, there have been smaller-scale projects that focus on improving people's well-being, enhancing the sense of satisfaction and happiness among the local population in the region. By 2023, China and all ten ASEAN countries have signed multiple cooperative agreements for jointly implementing the Belt and Road Initiative. Over the past decade, China has put forward more than 160 important cooperation initiatives during the China-ASEAN Summits, with an implementation rate exceeding 99.5%. China has been promoting strategic alignment between the Belt and Road Initiative and various initiatives such as Indonesia's "Global Maritime Fulcrum", Vietnam's "Two Corridors and One Economic Circle", Thailand's "Thailand 4.0" strategy, and Cambodia's "Rectangular Strategy", which has further unlocked policy dividends.

Box 4-2　"Small and Beautiful" Projects Help ASEAN Countries Reduce Poverty [a,b]

The joint implementation of many "small and beautiful" projects along the Belt and Road has effectively improved the people's livelihood of relevant countries and become an important way to quickly enhance the sense of gain of the people in the partner countries as they meet the urgent needs of local residents and are highly recognized by the local communities.

In the past, drinking clean water and taking a shower every day was a luxury for many Cambodians. In 2017, construction commenced for the first phase of the rural water supply project with assistance from China in Cambodia. The project built 846 new deep water wells and nearly 80 community ponds in six provinces of Cambodia. In 2019, the construction commenced for the second phase of the project, which built 54 community ponds and 964 deep water wells in 10 provinces of Cambodia. The rural water supply project has effectively solved the drinking and production water problems of local villagers and accelerated the process of poverty alleviation in rural Cambodia.

Louang Namtha Provincial High School, located in northern Laos, is the only provincial high school in Nanta Province and has over 2,000 teachers and students. For a long time, the school's teachers and students had been troubled by domestic sewage discharge. In 2018, China donated a set of integrated sewage treatment equipment with a daily treatment capacity of 50 tons to the school. This equipment, along with a sewage collection system and a reclaimed water reuse system, has not only solved the problem of uncontrolled sewage discharge but also met the needs of greening and achieved the separation of rainwater and sewage within the campus. It has effectively improved the sewage treatment capacity of the school and surrounding communities.

Sources: a. "'Small and Beautiful' livelihood projects promote people-to-people bonds and enhance the sense of gain of the people in the Countries along the Belt and Road", released on the official website of the State Council of the People's Republic of China on January 23, 2022.

b. "China-ASEAN Environmental Cooperation over the Past Decade: Building a Beautiful Homeland with the People as the Center", released by China-ASEAN Environmental Protection Cooperation Center on October 14, 2022.

4.3.1 Experience sharing for poverty reduction

China's poverty reduction experience has played a positive role in the development of ASEAN countries. China has conducted numerous forums and exchange activities with ASEAN to facilitate the sharing of poverty reduction experience. On October 2007, the inaugural China-ASEAN Forum on Social Development and Poverty Reduction was held in Nanning, China. As of 2023, this forum has been successfully organized for 17 sessions (see Table 4-1). From 2005 to 2020, China actively conducted poverty reduction training for ASEAN countries. A total of 54 training sessions were organized, including the Lancang-Mekong poverty reduction cooperation capacity enhancement program. In addition, since 2014, China has initiated six East Asia poverty reduction demonstration projects in Laos, Cambodia, and Myanmar. These projects have been recognized as the "benchmark for poverty reduction cooperation"[1]. In 2019, Thailand learned from China's experience in targeted poverty alleviation and implemented the "paired-up assistance program", which has produced remarkable results. In November 2022, the 6th Joint Working Group Meeting on Poverty Reduction for Lancang-Mekong Cooperation (LMC) was held online. Representatives from participating countries discussed and adopted the Guideline of the Lancang-Mekong Cooperation on Poverty

---

1 Data from *Facts and Figures about China-ASEAN Cooperation: 1991-2021* released by Ministry of Foreign Affairs of the People's Republic of China.

Reduction (2023-2027), aiming to make positive contributions to promoting regional cooperation and achieving common development in the Lancang-Mekong region.

Table 4-1　　　Previous sessions of ASEAN-China Forum on Social Development and Poverty Reduction and their themes

No.	Time	Place	Theme
17th session	June 26-29, 2023	Beihai, China	Deepening Regional Cooperation and Promoting Poverty Reduction and Rural Development
16th session	June 28-July 1, 2022	Online	Strengthening Exchanges on Poverty Reduction and Jointly Building a Prosperous Homeland
15th session	June 22, 2021	Online	ASEAN-China Cooperation: Promoting Rural Development and Sustainable Poverty Reduction
14th session	July29, 2020	Online	Joining Hands & Fighting against COVID-19, Promoting Poverty Alleviation
13th session	June 26-28, 2019	Nanning, China	ASEAN-China Cooperation on Poverty Reduction towards SDGs
12th session	June 27-29, 2018	Manila, the Philippines	Enhancing Poverty Reduction Partnerships for an ASEAN-China Community with a Shared Future
11th session	July 25-27, 2017	Siem Reap, Cambodia	China and ASEAN: Innovation and Practices on Poverty Reduction
10th session	June 22-24, 2016	Guilin, China	Belt and Road Initiative and China-ASEAN Cooperation on Poverty Reduction
9th session	July 28-30, 2015	Vientiane, Laos	Financial Innovation and Poverty Reduction
8th session	August 7-9, 2014	Naypyidaw, Myanmar	Deepening China-ASEAN Regional Cooperation on Poverty Reduction
7th session	August 21-23, 2013	Fangchenggang, China	Poverty Reduction and Inclusive Development in Urbanization
6th session	September 26-27, 2012	Liuzhou, China	China and ASEAN: Inclusive Development and Poverty Reduction

Continued

No.	Time	Place	Theme
5th session	September 14-16, 2011	Jakarta, Indonesia	Quality of Growth and Poverty Reduction
4th session	July 13-15, 2010	Guilin, China	Free Trade and Poverty Reduction
3rd session	September 28-30, 2009	Ha Noi, Vietnam	The Impact of the Global Economic Slowdown on Poverty and Sustainable Development in Asia and the Pacific Asia
2nd session	November 4-6, 2008	Nanning, China	Regional Cooperation to Achieve the Millennium Development Goals, Improve Food Safety, and Resist Natural Disasters
1st session	October 30-November 2, 2007	Nanning, China	Participating in and Promoting Regional Social Development and Poverty Reducti on Exchanges and Cooperation

Box 4-3   China Shares Poverty Reduction Experience

1. China-aided Laos Poverty Reduction Demonstration Cooperation Technical Assistance Project[a]

Ban Xor Village in Vientiane City, Laos is a demonstration village in the China-aided Laos Poverty Reduction Demonstration Cooperation Technical Assistance Project. In the past, it was an unknown and impoverished small village. In 2016, the project was implemented in Ban Xor Village. Considering the actual conditions and development needs of the village, the project team planted organic vegetables in greenhouses and organic rice, provided technical training, and established a village-level activity center for the local community. The project's implementation has significantly improved the public service facilities in the village and improved the production and living conditions of the local residents. Now, Ban Xor Village has become a well-known vegetable base, attracting a large number of dealers to purchase vegetables in the village. It has developed its own characteristic industry, pillar industry, and wealth creation industry. The effect of the China-aided Laos Poverty Reduction Demonstration Cooperation Technical Assistance Project has been recognized and praised by all levels of government and local people in Laos with wide influence.

2. Thailand Has Improved Poverty Reduction Path by Drawing Inspiration from China's Poverty Alleviation Models[b, c]

In 2001, the Thai government launched the "One Village, One Product" plan to promote traditional handicrafts and characteristic agricultural products. As of the end of 2020, the plan had covered more than 5,000 townships nationwide, with at least 1.2 million farmers engaged in related handicraft and industrial activities. To drive agricultural production, the Thai government has been implementing the "Rural Fund" program since 2007. Over 70,000 villages across the country have received approximately THB1 million in development funds. In 2019, officials from Khon Kaen Province visited China to learn about the poverty alleviation experience in China. After returning to Thailand, they developed a "paired-up assistance" project adapted to local conditions. As of October 2020, 79% of poor households had been lifted out of poverty, and in the future, the entire population will break free from the poverty line of THB38,000 for annual per capita income. Officials from the Thai Ministry of the Interior noted that the model would be promoted throughout the country once it becomes fully successful.

Sources: a. "Collection of Lancang-Mekong Cooperation Poverty Reduction Demonstration Projects" released by the International Poverty Reduction Center in China on April 14, 2021.

b. "Thailand Has Achieved Significant Results by Learning from China's Poverty Alleviation Models", released on People's Daily on November 19, 2020.

c. "Thailand Accelerates the Pace of Poverty Alleviation", released on People's Daily on December 11, 2020.

4.3.2   Strengthen economic and trade exchanges

China and ASEAN have kept promoting economic and trade cooperation between them. In the past three years, China and ASEAN have been each other's largest trading partner. In 2022, the import and export between the two sides reached RMB6.52 trillion, a year-on-year increase of 15%[1].

China and ASEAN are both each other's important market for agricultural trade. From 2010 to 2019, along with the overall growth of trade volume, the proportion of agricultural trade remained around 15% of the total trade. The proportion of agricultural trade increased in most years and declined between 2012-2013 and 2016-2017. From different trade directions, China's absolute

---

1   Based on the information released by Economic and Commercial Office of the Mission of the People's Republic of China to the Association of Southeast Asian Nations.

export volume of agricultural products to ASEAN showed an upward trend, and the proportion also significantly increased, from 15.26% in 2010 to 23.67% in 2019, an increase of over 8 percentage points, though the proportion slightly decreased in a few years. As for imports, China's agricultural product imports from ASEAN showed constant fluctuations between 2012 and 2017, and the proportion also showed a slight decline between 2011 and 2013. From 2014 to 2019, it remained fluctuating between 12% and 14%. Therefore, for China, the agricultural product trade with ASEAN is an important component of China's agricultural product trade market, with the export side subject to the impact to a greater extent (see Figure 4-1).

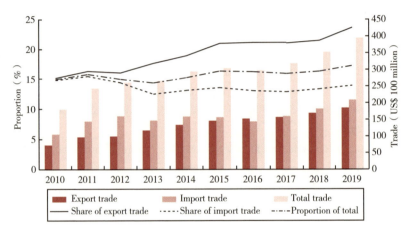

Figure 4-1   The proportion of agricultural products trade between China and ASEAN in China's agricultural products trade, 2010-2019

Source: UN Comtrade; the results are obtained by calculation.

The proportion of agricultural trade between China and ASEAN in ASEAN's agricultural trade remained between 10%-20% between 2010 and 2019. As for the trend, the proportion of agricultural trade between China and ASEAN in total trade volume increased from 10.95% in 2010 to 15.97% in 2019, an increase of over 5 percentage points. However, it experienced a decline between 2015 and 2017, but this trend was not always consistent with the trend of the total trade. The proportion of exports increased from 10.45% in 2010 to 14.96%, an increase of approximately 4.5 percentage points, while the proportion of imports increased from 11.76%

in 2010 to 17.28%, an increase of approximately 5.5 percentage points. The proportion of both exports and imports experienced a decline between 2015 and 2017. Only the absolute volume of import trade showed a decline. This reflects the difference in the trend between absolute and relative trade values (see Figure 4-2).

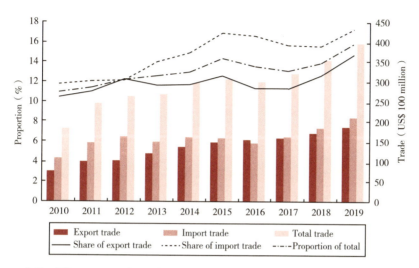

Figure 4-2   The proportion of agricultural products trade between China and ASEAN in ASEAN's agricultural products trade, 2010-2019

Source: UN Comtrade; the results are obtained by calculation.

4.3.3   Joint response to the pandemic and other challenges

China and ASEAN have been working together to fight the pandemic and overcome other difficulties. Health is an important area of cooperation between the two sides. Since the cooperation in the prevention and control of the Severe Acute Respiratory Syndrome (SARS) in 2003, health cooperation between the two sides has steadily developed. Since the outbreak of the pandemic, China and ASEAN countries have set an example of global cooperation in combating the virus. They have strengthened information sharing, health security, and emergency response, thereby promoting knowledge sharing and talent development. During the pandemic, China actively provided vaccines, anti-epidemic supplies, and dispatched medical expert teams to support ASEAN countries. In March 2020, China dispatched its first medical team to Cambodia as part of the anti-pandemic efforts in ASEAN countries. In November 2021, President Xi Jinping announced during the Special Summit to Commemorate the

30th Anniversary of ASEAN-China Dialogue Relations that China would provide an additional 150 million doses of COVID-19 vaccines to ASEAN countries as gratuitous assistance, and contribute an additional US$5 million to the COVID-19 ASEAN Response Fund[1]. Furthermore, China has pledged to provide US$1.5 billion in development assistance to ASEAN over a period of three years starting from 2022. This assistance aims to support ASEAN's efforts in combating the pandemic and promoting economic recovery. As of 2022, China had already provided over 600 million doses of vaccines to ASEAN countries[2].

Box 4-4　China and ASEAN Countries Fight COVID-19 Together

1. China Assists Myanmar in Fighting COVID-19 to Renew Their Millennia-old Pauk-Phaw Friendship[a, b]

On April 8, 2020, China sent a team of 12 medical experts from the National Health Commission and Yunnan Province to Myanmar. They brought RMB4.34 million worth of materials to help Myanmar fight the COVID-19 pandemic. During their stay in Myanmar, the expert team conducted over 60 sessions of specialized training and technical guidance in more than 40 hospitals and laboratories in Rangoon and Mandalay. They shared their experience with Myanmar medical institutions and experts and introduced China's experience in COVID-19 prevention. They also provided guidance and consultation on case screening, infectious disease prevention and control, case management, clinical diagnosis and treatment, community health management, and laboratory work after studying the prevention and control measures, diagnosis, and treatment of COVID-19 in Myanmar. According to incomplete statistics, in 2020, the Chinese government, local governments, and institutions in Myanmar donated a total of 8.35 million masks, 93,000 sets of protective clothing, 41,000 sets of isolation suits, 180,000 pairs of medical gloves, 128,000 isolation masks, 3,471 thermometers, 17 imaging temperature measuring devices, 38,000 test kits, 35 ventilators, as well as epidemic prevention materials such as ambulances, air conditioners, fans, mattresses, and mobile toilets to Myanmar.

2. China Assists Laos in Fighting COVID-19[c]

When the COVID-19 pandemic broke out, China promptly sent teams of anti-epidemic medical experts to Laos. On March 29, 2020, a Chinese medical expert

---

1　See: https://www.gov.cn/xinwen/2021-11/24/content_5653227.htm.

2　See: https://www.yidaiyilu.gov.cn/xwzx/hwxw/270234.htm.

team arrived in Vientiane with medical supplies worth RMB4.17 million. In just two weeks, the team helped Laos develop a comprehensive plan for the prevention and control of COVID-19, featuring external defense to internal containment. Their work helped improve the scientific and standardized level of Laos' prevention and control of the pandemic. On April 24, 2020, a team of five experts from the Chinese People's Liberation Army arrived in Vientiane to provide guidance and donate anti-epidemic materials such as testing reagents, protective clothing, and masks to Laos.

3. China Helps Thailand Build a Vaccine Barrier[d]

As of June 2022, China had provided a total of 50.9 million doses of vaccines to Thailand, of which 3.4 million doses were provided free of charge to help Thailand establish an effective vaccine barrier. According to incomplete statistics, China has provided Thailand with 3,426,000 masks, 79,400 sets of protective clothing, 176,000 test kits, 104,000 pairs of medical gloves, 12,000 pairs of medical goggles, and 30,000 pairs of medical protective shoes.

Sources: a. "China's Anti-COVID-19 Medical Expert Team to Myanmar Has Completed Tasks and Returned", released by the People's Government of Yunnan Province on April 23, 2020.

b. *Guide for Countrtes and Regions on Overseas Investment and Cooperation: Myanmar (2022)* released by Ministry of Commerce of the People's Republic of China.

c. *Guide for Countries and Regions on Overseas Investment and Cooperation: Laos (2022)* released by Ministry of Commerce of the People's Republic of China.

d. *Guide for Countries and Regions on Overseas Investment and Cooperation: Thailand (2022)* released by Ministry of Commerce of the People's Republic of China.

4.3.4 Enhancement of disaster resilience

China and ASEAN conducted pragmatic cooperation to jointly enhance the capacity for natural disaster prevention and mitigation. China offered assistance to ASEAN countries mainly in coping with both natural and human-caused disasters, with a primary focus on natural disaster relief. Among the ASEAN countries, China places particular emphasis on providing assistance to Indonesia, Cambodia, Myanmar, Laos and the Philippines. China has implemented earthquake monitoring network projects in countries such as Laos, Myanmar, Thailand, and Cambodia. These initiatives have significantly enhanced the local capacity for earthquake disaster monitoring and early warning. China has also dispatched international rescue teams twice to Indonesia for humanitarian relief operations. Additionally, China has assisted in the post-earthquake restoration of cultural relics in Myanmar and provided US$1 million in post-earthquake emergency aid to the Philippines. Since 2016, China and ASEAN have jointly organized four disaster management seminars, two seminars on science, technology, innovation, and typhoon disaster response, one seminar on disaster risk reduction management, and one senior officials' forum on disaster risk reduction and emergency management. In 2021, both sides established the ASEAN-China Ministerial Meeting Mechanism on Disaster Management[1]. On October 14, 2021, the inaugural China-ASEAN Ministerial Meeting on Disaster Management was held via video conference, during which the two side approved the ASEAN-China Work Plan on Disaster Management (2021-2025) was approved and issued a joint statement.

4.3.5 Poverty reduction through science and technology cooperation

China and ASEAN intensified science and technology cooperation to facilitate poverty reduction through science and technology. China has established inter-governmental bilateral mechanisms for technology transfer cooperation with nine ASEAN countries, namely Brunei, Cambodia, Indonesia, Laos, Malaysia, Myanmar, the Philippines, Thailand, and Vietnam. It has also created a collaborative network for technology transfer covering all ten ASEAN countries, with over 2,800 member entities. Furthermore, China has facilitated the establishment of 15 joint laboratories and research centers, including the China-ASEAN Joint Laboratory for International Cooperation in Traditional Medicine Research and the International Research Center on Karst, fostering long-term and stable cooperation between research institutions from both sides. In terms of scientific and cultural exchanges, Guangxi has organized various activities such as the 10+3 Youth Scientists Forum, the Innovation China Tour for ASEAN Outstanding Youths, the China-ASEAN Technology Manager International Training, and specialized technical training

---

1　See: https://www.mfa.gov.cn/web/wjbxw_673019/202201/t20220105_10479078.shtml.

courses. These initiatives have cumulatively trained over 1,300 key personnel in technology and science management from ASEAN countries. In 2021, China proposed the launch of the China-ASEAN Science, Technology and Innovation Enhancing Program and released the China-ASEAN Plan of Action for a Closer Partnership of Science, Technology and Innovation for Future (2021-2025)[1]. This includes projects such as the establishment of agricultural cooperation demonstration zones and the implementation of trial stations for superior crop varieties. China's agricultural plant protection drones have supported agricultural development in Thailand, while the Philippine-Sino Center for Agriculture Technology has promoted the commercialization of hybrid rice on 514,400 hectares of fields, resulting in an increase of 4.821 billion kilograms in grain yield[2].

(1) Framework for agricultural science and technology cooperation at the national level

The 19th National Congress of the Communist Party of China called for making China a country of innovators and making new ground in pursuing opening up on all fronts. It emphasized the importance of pursuing the Belt and Road Initiative as a priority and increasing openness and cooperation in building innovation capacity. In 2012, the Ministry of Science and Technology of China hosted a number of major conferences and activities, including the Inaugural ASEAN-China Ministerial Meeting on Science and Technology, the China-ASEAN Science and Technology Partnership Program, and the 1st Forum on China-ASEAN Technology Transfer and Collaborative Innovation. The China-ASEAN Science and Technology Partnership Program proposes ten key technical areas for in-depth cooperation between China and ASEAN countries. These include policy consultation, technical services, human resource development, cooperative research, and the construction of a China-ASEAN technology transfer platform network. The China-ASEAN subregional cooperation mechanisms include the Greater Mekong Subregional Cooperation Mechanism (GMS), the China-Laos-Myanmar-Thailand "Golden Quadrangle"

---

1   See: https://www.mfa.gov.cn/web/wjbxw_673019/202201/t20220105_10479078.shtml.

2   See: https://www.yidaiyilu.gov.cn/xwzx/hwxw/271921.htm.

Plan, the Lancang-Mekong Cooperation Mechanism, and the Pan-Beibu Gulf Economic Cooperation[1].

Box 4-5   Cases of China-ASEAN Science and Technology Cooperation

1. China (Guangxi)-Laos Fine Crop Varieties Experimental Station[a]

In 2013, the China-Laos Fine Crop Varieties Experimental Station, the first crop variety experiment establishment founded by China in ASEAN, started operation. It covers an area of 40 hectares and integrates the experiment and demonstration of new crop varieties, the promotion of new technologies, and agricultural training. This station has provided strong support for the promotion and application of new agricultural technologies and varieties in Laos. The station has tested the planting of over 300 crop varieties and selected 67 excellent varieties suitable for local cultivation. These excellent varieties have significantly increased the local crop yields after their promotion and application. For example, the hybrid corn variety LC188 promoted and applied in Vientiane, Champasak, Sayabourym, and other places in Laos produces an average yield of 6.26 tons/hectare, which is 18.3% higher than the average yield of 5.29 tons/hectare of local varieties.

2. Chinese Agricultural Drones Contribute to Thailand's Agricultural Development[b]

Agriculture plays a crucial role in Thailand's economic development, with nearly half of the population engaged in agricultural-related activities. In recent years, Thailand's demand for modern agricultural machinery has increased rapidly due to the changes in the agricultural population structure, intensified ageing, and increased labor costs. Agricultural plant protection drones from China have continuously optimized functions for local core operation scenarios, continuously accelerating the development of modern agriculture in Thailand. Local residents noted that using drones can help farmers improve their work efficiency, as manual spraying of pesticides on rice fields cannot exceed 10 rai (equivalent to 24 mu) per day, while drones can spray 40 to 50 rai per day.

Sources: a. "Agricultural Technology Cooperation Has Yielded Fruitful Results", released by the International Poverty Reduction Center in China on March 31, 2023.

b. "Chinese Agricultural Drones Contribute to Agricultural Development in Thailand", released on the official website of China's Belt and Road Initiative on August 11, 2022.

---

1   Quan, Y. and Yin, Z. (2017). Exploration of the Mechanism and Cooperation Model of China-ASEAN Regional and Sub Regional Cooperation. Southeast Asian Studies, (6):15-36,152-153. (in Chinese)

China and ASEAN countries have further strengthened their bilateral dialog mechanisms for agricultural science and technology cooperation since 2013, when China proposed the Belt and Road Initiative. At present, China has signed agricultural science and technology cooperation agreements with Thailand, Vietnam, the Philippines, Malaysia, Myanmar, and Laos and has established joint committees for agricultural science and technology cooperation. These efforts have formed a relatively systematic and complete framework for multilateral and bilateral agricultural science and technology cooperation mechanisms. China and ASEAN countries have also jointly set up multinational joint laboratories and technology transfer centers. In 2016, the First LMC Leaders' Meeting proposed the establishment of an agricultural science and technology cooperation fund. In 2017, the Belt and Road Forum for International Cooperation launched the Belt and Road Science, Technology and Innovation Cooperation Action Plan and decided to set up an ecological and environmental protection big data service platform. In March 2019, the National Development and Reform Commission of China released the Policies and Measures to Support Yunnan Province in Accelerating the Construction of a Center for Connecting South Asia and Southeast Asia, which covers agricultural cooperation and economic and trade cooperation between China (Yunnan) and neighboring countries.

(2) Regional cooperation mechanisms at the provincial and local levels

In 2014, the Guangxi ASEAN Technology Transfer Center was approved and established. This center has become an important carrier for promoting technology demand-supply matchmaking and innovation cooperation between China and ASEAN countries. The Forum on China-ASEAN Technology Transfer and Collaborative Innovation, which is hosted by the Ministry of Science and Technology of China and the People's Government of Guangxi Zhuang Autonomous Region under the framework of the China ASEAN Expo, has become a normalized and important high-level forum. This forum has helped to form a comprehensive innovation network with ASEAN countries, implement bilateral technology transfer cooperation mechanisms, and promote numerous cooperation projects. In 2017, the Agricultural Science and Technology Center Connecting South Asia and Southeast Asia, proposed by the Yunnan Academy of Agricultural Sciences, was founded as a non-governmental, non-profit, open, and international cooperation platform with the voluntary participation and joint initiation of agricultural scientific research institutes, educational institutions, and enterprises interested in agricultural technology exchanges, cooperation, and innovation from South Asian and Southeast Asian countries and regions. The center has established long-term and stable cooperative relationships with relevant institutions in more than 40 countries and more than 20 international organizations. In particular, it has developed competitive and distinctive cooperation with countries in South Asia and Southeast Asia in agricultural science and technology. It has also taken a leading role in establishing and running the platforms such as the Greater Mekong Subregion Agricultural Science and Technology Exchange and Cooperation Group and the China-South Asia Agricultural Science and Technology Exchange and Cooperation Group. However, the technology transfer by the center relies on the Yunnan Academy of Agricultural Sciences and its affiliated research institutes, which mainly transfer the technologies of agricultural disciplines overseas. Currently, its scale of cooperation and influence is limited. The center has not yet generated a strong influence and radiation effect on regional agricultural integration. It lacks the role and function of effectively introducing and exporting technology, carrying out targeted innovation, and actively serving the going global strategy in the agriculture sector[1]. Compared to Yunnan and Guangxi, which mainly cooperate with ASEAN in the field of agricultural science and technology, the global partners with China's developed provinces in agricultural science and technology are mainly located in Eastern Europe, Central and Eastern Europe, South Asia, and other European and America regions[2].

(3) Agricultural technology cooperation projects at other levels

Although the development of agricultural industries and agricultural

---

1   Chen, L. J. (2015). Reflections on the Countermeasures of Yunnan's Accelerating the Construction of South Asia-8 Southeast Asia-Orientated Radiation Center. Journal of Kunming University of Science and Technology (Social Sciences),15(6):17-24. (in Chinese)

2   Wang, Y. (2020). Practice and Refection of Belt and Road Innovation Cooperator and Technology Transfer in Jiangsu. Science and Technology Management Research, 40(7):104-109. (in Chinese)

product trade in the developing countries of ASEAN plays an important role in local economic development and complements China's resource advantages, only a few universities and research institutes are engaged in country-specific agricultural science and technology research in China. Its capabilities are limited in the development of international cooperation platforms and talent teams in agricultural science and technology, as well as the utilization of cross-sector resource advantages, especially strengthening the win-win strategy for overseas diffusion of China's agricultural technology through interdisciplinary research[1]. As of now, the largest international cooperation project in China, "Green Super Rice", has involved enterprises in technology promotion. It mainly focuses on direct transfer and training in scientific research cooperation. Among the 47,000 leading agricultural enterprises above the designated size in China, only 300 are truly globalized ones, most of which are state-owned enterprises.[2] Only over 40 enterprises, mostly small private enterprises, have participated in the Yunnan Agricultural Industrial and Technological Innovation Strategic Alliance for Going Global. China's agricultural technology cooperation with ASEAN countries is mainly focused on research fields, but its development is still slower than that in developed countries in terms of investment scale and cooperation depth.

1   Ni, G. H., Zhang, J., and Zheng, T. F. (2014). Understanding the "Agriculture Going Global" Strategy. World Agriculture, (4):15-18,203. (in Chinese)

2   Qiu, H. G., Chen, R. J., Liao, S. P., and Cai, Y. Q. (2013). Foreign Agricultural investments of China's Agricultural Companies: Current Status, Difficulties, and Policy suggestions. Issues in Agricultural Economy, 34(11):44-50, 111. (in Chinese); Wang, F., Wang, J., and Zhao, W. (2014). Re-examining China's Agricultural "Going Global" in an Open Perspective. World Agriculture, (11):160-164. (in Chinese)

Chapter 5   Outlook on Poverty Reduction in ASEAN Countries

In recent years, ASEAN countries have formulated poverty reduction goals based on their own development situations. For example, in Indonesia, the government hopes to reduce the national poverty rate below 10% and eradicate extreme poverty by 2024 by providing assistance to impoverished families and developing the rural digital economy. In Malaysia, the government has stated that it will continue to focus on low-income groups and reduce regional development disparities in the future. Thailand stated in its Thirteenth National Economic and Social Development Plan (2023-2027) that long-term and intergenerational poverty should be addressed based on the principle of "leaving no one behind". Vietnam clearly aims to reduce the extreme poverty rate by 1%-1.5% annually over the next five years. In the Philippines, the government has established an anti-poverty committee specifically for the implementation of poverty reduction plans. The country is expected to reduce the poverty rate to around 16.2% by 2023 and to around 8.9% by 2028. In Cambodia, the government has stated its intention to reduce the national poverty rate to below 10% by 2023. To achieve this goal, the government has launched a series of comprehensive plans to improve rural economic activities and infrastructure. In Laos, the government promises to successfully help over 200,000 Laos households and 3,104 villages (accounting for approximately 36% of the total number of villages) get out of poverty by 2025. The Myanmar Sustainable Development Plan (2018-2030) emphasizes the need to create an enabling environment that supports diversified and productive economies, including agriculture, industry, and multiculturalism, as a foundation for reducing rural poverty.

5.1   Opportunities for Poverty Reduction and Development in ASEAN

First, ASEAN countries experience strong economic recovery after the pandemic. The international community holds a positive outlook on the overall ASEAN regional economy. Various international organizations have predicted a strong economic recovery for ASEAN countries in the post-pandemic era. Moreover, consumer goods prices in emerging economies and developing countries in the Asian region have remained stable, with inflation indexes projected to remain around 3%. This reflects the resilience and positive recovery situation of the regional economy, including ASEAN countries. For example, Vietnam has benefited from its increasing importance in the global supply chain, while the improvement in foreign tourism will accelerate the economic development of Cambodia and Thailand.

Second, trade and investment liberalization and facilitation enhance the trade and investment potential of ASEAN countries. The current world economy is filled with uncertainties, but the economic cooperation between China and ASEAN is becoming increasingly close. This is especially evident with the establishment and improvement of comprehensive cooperative mechanisms such as the Belt and Road Initiative, the China-ASEAN Free Trade Area, and the Regional Comprehensive Economic Partnership (RCEP). The level of trade liberalization and facilitation between China and ASEAN continues to improve, injecting stability into the economic growth of the Asia-Pacific region.

Third, digital economy becomes an important direction for future economic growth in ASEAN. The e-commerce chapter in the RCEP reached a consensus on issues such as cross-border information transfer and data localization for the first time, providing institutional safeguards for e-commerce cooperation within the region. New opportunities for development are emerging in trade-related sectors such as cross-border e-commerce for agricultural products. China and ASEAN are actively promoting the cooperation of RCEP cross-border e-commerce industry associations. The China-Laos Railway is exploring development models such as "Lancang-Mekong express + cross-border e-commerce", indicating that new business forms and models such as cross-border e-commerce are expected to further expand the development space for agricultural trade within the region.

Fourth, the strengthen of regional cooperation provides support for poverty reduction in ASEAN. China has successfully won the fight against poverty, achieving the poverty reduction targets of the United Nations' 2030 Agenda for Sustainable Development 10 years ahead of schedule. Its accomplishment has made significant contributions to the global poverty reduction cause and human progress. China's poverty reduction practices and experience have inspired developing countries around the world in their determination to eliminate absolute poverty. China has engaged in various exchange activities with ASEAN, including forums and other platforms, where it has shared its poverty reduction experience. This has provided valuable insights and lessons for ASEAN member States in their own development efforts.

5.2 Challenges for Poverty Reduction in ASEAN

ASEAN countries also face several challenges in their poverty reduction efforts. First, the significant disparity in economic development within the region affects the effectiveness of poverty reduction efforts in the area. Varying levels of economic development within the region and the presence of multiple factors such as the COVID-19 pandemic further add to the uncertainties of poverty reduction and overall development. Second, the instability of the international environment affects the economic development of emerging economies and developing countries within ASEAN, indicating the need to enhance economic resilience. Risks such as soaring global food and energy prices, depreciation of currencies against the US dollar, and narrowing output gaps pose challenges to multidimensional poverty reduction. Third, underdeveloped digital infrastructure, digital divide, and talent shortage impact the poverty reduction benefits of the digital economy in ASEAN. The uneven development within the region may make it challenging for some countries to leverage digital technologies to promote economic growth. Unequal competition among global enterprises and unequal individual opportunities may further exacerbate poverty, and increase the risk of vulnerable populations falling back into poverty. Fourth, climate change poses challenges to the economic transformation of developing countries. Fifth, continued efforts are needed to promote gender equality and empower women. In some ASEAN countries, women still face unequal access to assets, services, and opportunities, which requires achieving gender equality and empowering women.

5.3   Priorities for Poverty Reduction in ASEAN in the Future

Synergizing efforts in poverty reduction and development within the region. In the ASEAN region, there is significant variation in economic development and poverty levels among countries. It is important for ASEAN countries to focus on strengthening intervention measures that address multiple inequalities and help reduce regional disparities based on local conditions. Conflicts and insecurity remain major drivers of food crisis and food insecurity. Achieving coordinated development for poverty reduction within the region is an important component in reducing systemic risks and achieving shared development.

Focusing on agricultural modernization industry. The agricultural and food system is a major employment sector. The development of the agricultural industry is crucial for not only food security, but also employment and trade in ASEAN countries. Additionally, it plays a significant role in promoting gender equality and women empowerment. Accelerating the promotion of agricultural modernization and establishing a holistic food system will help speed up economic growth, ensure food security, and promote nutrition and health, among other sustainable development goals, in ASEAN countries.

Promoting poverty reduction by utilizing digital technologies. Against the backdrop of the rapid development of the fourth industrial revolution, the digital economy has emerged as a new engine for supporting economic growth and transformation in countries worldwide. ASEAN is the fastest-growing region in terms of internet development worldwide, and its population structure is characterized by a young demographic. This presents immense potential for the growth of digital lifestyles within the region. The pandemic has accelerated the transformation of user behaviors in the ASEAN market. It has provided an opportunity to leverage the digital economy to create poverty alleviation and wealth-building opportunities for vulnerable groups and small and medium enterprises (SMEs). This, in turn, contributes to the efforts of ASEAN countries in their poverty reduction endeavors.

Further strengthening South-South cooperation. While ASEAN countries have made significant progress in poverty reduction, they still face uncertainties arising from the complex international environment and climate change. It is necessary to continue strengthening South-South cooperation to share poverty reduction experiences, consolidate the existing achievements of poverty alleviation, prevent poverty-returning on a large scale, and accelerate progress towards regional economic sustainable and inclusive growth goals.

5.4 Cooperation and Prospects for Poverty Reduction in ASEAN

First, further strengthening experience sharing in poverty reduction. There are many similarities in poverty reduction experiences between developing countries and regions, like China and ASEAN. Rapid economic growth and social transformation have lifted many people out of poverty in both regions. They also face similar challenges such as inequality and the lack of growth in the agricultural sector. China's experience provides valuable insights for designing and implementing poverty reduction strategies in ASEAN countries. Through further exchange and collaboration, the two sides may enhance communication on poverty reduction mechanisms and policy designs, share approaches and methods in poverty reduction, and exchange experience in selecting poverty reduction strategies.

Second, collaboratively implementing poverty reduction and development projects. In recent years, China and ASEAN countries have supported the construction of "small and beautiful" livelihood projects under the Belt and Road Initiative. These projects have effectively enhanced the living skills and conditions of the local population, with small industries playing a significant role in poverty reduction efforts. For developing countries within the region with varying levels of development, they may strengthen coordinated planning, fully utilize limited advantageous resources, and leverage the effectiveness of foreign aid in "small and beautiful" projects to generate more pragmatic and people-centered initiatives.

Third, deepening cooperation in building poverty reduction capacity. The ASEAN should strengthen regional trade flow, increase participation in the value chains within the region, improve transportation networks, and promote connectivity among ASEAN members. ASEAN countries should take the RCEP as an opportunity to optimize the business environment and attract investment from other member States. At the same time, they should strengthen infrastructure development, enhance trade facilitation, lower market access thresholds and provide more opportunities for foreign enterprises. Efforts should be made to enhance government governance and public sector service capacity. In the current world, the rapid development of the digital economy provides intrinsic impetus for poverty reduction in ASEAN through international cooperation in cultural education and vocational training. It is thus necessary to promote the construction of digital infrastructure in ASEAN, enhance the ability of the digital economy to support economic development in the ASEAN region, and gradually eliminate the digital divide. ASEAN countries should g full play to the function of the digital economy to drive employment, vigorously broaden employment channels, and help the poor groups start businesses and increase income, thus getting out of poverty. They should enhance the level of human capital, promote the development of the digital economy, and strengthen vocational skills training for poor groups to realize self-development. The role of the China-ASEAN Digital Economy Cooperation Mechanism should be give fully play to promote digital capacity building in relatively underdeveloped countries. Active efforts should be made to promote China-ASEAN digital economy talent exchanges. Besides, the China-ASEAN Science, Technology and Innovation Enhancing Program should be fully utilized, and targeted selection of ASEAN young scientists for exchange programs in China should be implemented to establish closer partnerships in scientific and technological innovation

Fourth, promoting the building of a closer China-ASEAN community with a shared future. China and ASEAN countries have maintained close high-level exchanges, which have enriched the comprehensive strategic cooperation between them and effectively promoted regional development. It is now necessary to deepen China-ASEAN cooperation in the field of health and improve multilateral health cooperation mechanisms. Taking the implementation of the China-ASEAN Comprehensive Strategic Partnership Action Plan (2022-2025) as an opportunity, they are striving to enhance the quality and effectiveness of practical cooperation. China will promote strategic alignment between the Belt and Road Initiative and "Global Maritime Fulcrum" concept (Indonesia), Two Corridors and One Economic Circle (Vietnam), "Thailand 4.0" strategy (Thailand), Rectangular Strategy (Cambodia), and other initiatives. They will seize the opportunity of implementing global development initiatives to promote the building of a closer China-ASEAN community with a shared future, so as to inject new impetus into regional and global peace, stability, and prosperity.

Appendix 1　Key Indicators for ASEAN Countries

	Brunei	Cambodia	Indonesia	Laos	Malaysia	Myanmar	Singapore	Philippines	Thailand	Vietnam	Timor-Leste
Economy & Growth[1]											
GDP (current US$ billion)	16.7	29.5	1319.1	15.5	407.0	62.3	466.8	404.3	495.4	408.8	3.2
GDP, PPP (constant 2017 international US$ billion)	26.3	76.0	3418.9	59.8	963.3	230.3	609.0	991.7	1255.2	1119.0	5.3
GDP per capita (current US$)	37152	1760	4788	2054	11993	1149	82808	3499	6910	4164	2389
GDP per capita, PPP (constant 2017 international US$)	58670	4534	12410	7948	28384	4250	108036	8582	17508	11397	3943
Agriculture, value added (% of GDP)	1.1	22.2	12.4	14.9	8.9	22.3	0.0	9.5	8.8	11.9	10.2
Industry, value added (% of GDP)	67.9	37.9	41.4	34.1	39.1	38.2	24.2	29.2	35.0	38.3	53.8
Services, value added (% of GDP)	32.5	33.9	41.8	40.3	50.9	39.4	70.9	61.2	56.2	41.3	37.2
Exports of goods and services (current US$ billion)	14.4	20.2	323.1	7.8	313.2	16.4	870.8	114.8	325.9	384.2	1.8
Imports of goods and services (current US$ billion)	10.1	16.2	275.7	6.1	283.8	16.3	701.6	178.0	337.4	375.1	1.3

Continued

	Brunei	Cambodia	Indonesia	Laos	Malaysia	Myanmar	Singapore	Philippines	Thailand	Vietnam	Timor-Leste
Social Development[2]											
Access to electricity (% of population)	100.0	82.5	99.2	100.0	100.0	72.5	100.0	97.5	100.0	100.0	100.0
Access to basic drinking water services (% of population)	99.9	78.0	94.1	85.5	97.2	82.4	100.0	94.9	100.0	98.0	87.0
Access to basic sanitation services (% of population)	99.5	76.7	88.2	79.5	96.0	74.1	100.0	84.8	99.0	92.2	58.4
Mobile cellular subscriptions (per 100 people)	117.8	116.3	114.9	65.0	141.3	106.7	156.5	144.0	176.3	139.9	110.4
Fixed broadband subscriptions (per 100 people)	20.1	3.0	4.9	2.0	12.4	2.1	37.4	7.6	18.5	21.7	0.0
Individuals using the Internet (% of population)	98.1	60.2	62.1	62.0	96.8	44.0	96.9	52.7	85.3	74.2	39.5
CO_2 emissions (kt)	9588	18653	563197	19179	245139	33875	43705	133471	265479	355323	446
Human Development[3]											
Life expectancy at birth (years)	74.6	69.6	67.6	68.1	74.9	65.7	69.3	82.8	78.7	73.6	67.7
Expected years of schooling (years)	14.0	11.5	13.7	10.1	13.3	10.9	13.1	16.5	15.9	13.0	13.2
Mean years of schooling (years)	9.2	5.1	8.6	5.4	10.6	6.4	9.0	11.9	8.7	8.4	6.0
GNI per capita, PPP (constant 2017 international US$)	644900	4079	11466	7700	26658	3851	8920	90919	17030	7867	2005

Continued

	Brunei	Cambodia	Indonesia	Laos	Malaysia	Myanmar	Singapore	Philippines	Thailand	Vietnam	Timor-Leste
Poverty[4]											
Poverty rate at $2.15 a day (2017 PPP) (%)	–	–	2.5	1.2	0	0.3	0.5	–	0	0.1	28.8
Poverty rate at $3.65 a day (2017 PPP) (%)	–	–	20.3	33	0	20	18	–	1	4	72.9
Poverty rate at $6.85 a day (2017 PPP) (%)	–	–	60.5	71	3	68	55	–	12	19	–
Multidimensional poverty index	–	–	3.0	10.3	0.1	–	4.4	–	0.1	1.2	–
Inequality[4,5]											
Gini index	–	–	37.9	38.8	41.2	30.7	40.7	–	35.1	36.8	28.7
Shared prosperity premium	–	–	1.0	–1.2	–0.4	8.2	2.2	–	1.2	–0.9	–
Growth of the annual median income/consumption per capita	–	–	2.4	2.2	4.5	7.1	1.9	–	1.5	4.9	–

Notes: (1) Data from 2022 for Economy & Growth indicators. data from 2021 for "Exports of goods and services" and "Imports of goods and services" of Laos and Myanmar.

(2) Data from 2022 for Social Development indicators. data from 2021 for "Access to electricity" and "Individuals using the Internet". data from 2020 for "CO_2 emissions".

(3) Data from 2021 for Human Development indicators.

(4) Poverty and Inequality indicators are based on the latest data released by the World Bank: data from 2022 for Indonesia, data from 2018 for Laos and Malaysia, data from 2017 for Myanmar, data from 2021 for the Philippines and Thailand, and data from 2020 for Vietnam.

(5) The shared prosperity premium is the difference between the growth rate of the poorest 40 percent and the growth rate of the entire population.

Sources: The World Bank's database (https://data.worldbank.org); *ASEAN Statistical Yearbook 2022, Human Development Report 2021/22*; the World Bank's Poverty and Inequality Platform; *Multidimensional Poverty Index Report 2022.*

Appendix 2　Policies on Major Poverty Reduction Issues in ASEAN

Region/Country	Policy	Year	Key policy insights	Issues
ASEAN	Joint Media Statement of the 27th Meeting of ASEAN Tourism Ministers	2024	The Meeting focused its discussion on the implementation of activities under the ASEAN Tourism Strategic Plan 2016-2025, as well as other key priorities in 2023-2024 to further support the speedy recovery of the tourism sector. In line with the theme of "Quality and Responsible Tourism: Sustaining ASEAN Future", the Meeting emphasised the importance of forging closer collaboration among the ASEAN Member States in all relevant sectors to ensure the sustainability and resiliency of ASEAN tourism	Economic growth
	Joint Media Statement of the 4th ASEAN Digital Ministers' Meeting and Related Meetings	2024	Building an Inclusive and Trusted Digital Ecosystem The Meeting recognised the good progress made on implementing the ASEAN Digital Masterplan 2025 (ADM 2025), despite the COVID-19 pandemic. The Meeting welcomed the ADM 2025 Mid-Term Review (MTR) which took stock of the ADM 2025's progress in building trusted digital services, preventing consumer harm, and increasing the quality and coverage of fixed and mobile broadband infrastructure	Digital economy
	Joint Statement of the 31st ASEAN Socio-Cultural Community (ASCC) Council	2024	Under "Enhancing Connectivity", four priorities were identified: (1) Integrating and Connecting Economies, (2) Forging an Inclusive and Sustainable Future, (3) Transforming for the Digital Future, and (4) Culture and Arts: Promoting the Role of ASEAN Culture and the Arts for Inclusion and Sustainability	Economic growth, Nutrition and health, Climate change

Continued

Region/Country	Policy	Year	Key policy insights	Issues
	Joint Statement of the 31st ASEAN Socio-Cultural Community (ASCC) Council		Five priorities were identified on "Enhancing Resilience": (1) Development of Strategic Plans to implement the ASEAN Community Vision 2045, (2) Enhancing ASEAN Centrality, (3) Promoting Environmental Cooperation: Climate Change Resilience,(4) Women and Children: Promoting the Role of Women and Children Towards the Transformation of Behaviourism in ASEAN, and (5) Health: Transforming ASEAN Health Development Resilience in a New Context. The Meeting looked forward to the successful outcomes of the Lao's ASEAN Chairmanship to enhance ASEAN's connectivity and resilience, including through the implementation of the ASEAN Outlook on the Indo-Pacific (2019)	Economic growth, Nutrition and health, Climate change
ASEAN	Joint Statement of the 11th ASEAN Finance Ministers' and Central Bank Governors' Meeting (AFMGM)	2024	The Meeting welcomed Lao's theme of "ASEAN: Enhancing Connectivity and Resilience". The theme embodies Lao's vision to strengthen the ASEAN Community, enhance ASEAN cooperation on connectivity and resilience, promote infrastructure connectivity and strengthen ASEAN's relations with external partners while maintaining ASEAN's centrality in the evolving regional architecture. Lao's priorities are anchored on three strategic thrusts of (1) Integrating and Connecting Economies, (2) Forging an Inclusive and Sustainable Future, and (3) Transforming for Digital Future	Economic growth Technological innovation
	The Fifty-Fifth ASEAN Economic Ministers (AEM) Meeting	2023	The theme is "ASEAN Matters: Epicentrum of Growth"	Economic growth
	ASEAN Master Plan on Rural Development 2022 to 2026	2022	Goal 1: Food secure and safe region Goal 2: Economic opportunities continually abound in the region Goal 3: Inclusive community that promotes high quality of life Goal 4: Enhanced and sustained resilience and capacity to contribute to mitigation and adaptation to climate change Goal 5: Venues and platforms in place for the ASEAN Community's voices to be heard Goal 6 Sustained responsible investment in agriculture food systems	Food security, Economic growth, Climate change, Technological innovation

Continued

Region/Country	Policy	Year	Key policy insights	Issues
ASEAN	ASEAN Comprehensive Recovery Framework (ACRF)	2020	ASEAN's recovery efforts will focus on five Broad Strategies that are deemed most impactful to take the region through the recovery process and its aftermath. The Broad Strategies will, in turn, be pursued through several Key Priorities: (1) Enhancing healthcare systems, with priorities including maintaining existing health measures, strengthening critical health services and vaccine safety, and improving the level of healthcare human resources; (2) Strengthening human security, with priorities including enhancing social protection, strengthening food security for vulnerable groups, enhancing human capital through digital technology and education training, engaging in dialogue on labor policies, promoting gender equality, and safeguarding human rights; (3) Maximizing the potential of intra-ASEAN market and broader economic integration, with priorities including enhancing intra-ASEAN trade and investment, strengthening supply chain resilience, maintaining market openness, reducing non-tariff barriers, promoting trade and investment facilitation, enhancing transportation and regional connectivity, and promoting tourism and the development of small and medium-sized enterprises (SMEs); (4) Accelerating inclusive digital transformation, with priorities including developing e-commerce and the digital economy, enhancing e-government services, digital interconnectivity, and information and communication technology levels, promoting digital transformation of SMEs, and ensuring data and cyber security; (5) Advancing towards a more sustainable and resilient future, with priorities including achieving sustainable development in all ASEAN sectors, particularly in investment, energy, agriculture, green infrastructure, disaster management, and sustainable finance	Nutrition and health, Economic growth, Climate change

Continued

Region/ Country	Policy	Year	Key policy insights	Issues
	ASEAN Integrated Food Security (AIFS) Framework	2020	The goal of AIFS Framework is to ensure long-term food security and nutrition, to improve the livelihoods of farmers in the ASEAN region. The specific Strategic Plan of Action on Food Security (SPA-FS) for each period will be developed to create a favorable environment, where AMS can integrate, operate and cooperate in various aspects related to food production, processing and trade. To achieve the goal, the AIFS Framework has the following objectives: (1) To sustain and increase food production; (2) To reduce postharvest losses; (3) To promote conducive market and trade for agriculture commodities and inputs; (4) To ensure food stability and affordability; (5) To ensure food safety, quality and nutrition; (6) To promote availability and accessibility to agriculture inputs; and (7) To operationalize regional food emergency relief arrangements	Food security
ASEAN	Strategic Plan of Action on Food Security in the ASEAN Region (SPA-FS) 2021-2025	2020	The Strategic Plan of Action outlines nine corresponding Strategic Thrusts to the AIFS Framework's Components. (1) Strengthen Food Security, including Emergency/ Shortage Relief Arrangement. (2) Promote conducive food market and trade. (3) Strengthen integrated food security information systems to effectively forecast, plan and monitor supplies and utilization for basic food commodities. (4) Promote sustainable food production. (5) Encourage greater investment in food and agri-based industry to enhance food security. (6) Identify and address emerging issues related to food security. (7) Utilize Nutrition Information to support evidence-based food security and agriculture policies. (8) Identify policies, institutional and governance mechanisms for nutrition enhancing agriculture development in AMS. (9) Develop and strengthen nutrition-enhancing food, agriculture and forestry policies/programs and build capacity for their implementation, monitoring and evaluation	Food security

Continued

Region/ Country	Policy	Year	Key policy insights	Issues
ASEAN	ASEAN Plus Three Emergency Rice Reserve (APTERR)	2011	The ASEAN Plus Three Emergency Rice Reserve (APTERR) is a regional cooperation scheme aimed at strengthening food security and reducing poverty within the ASEAN Member States, the People's Republic of China, Japan, and the Republic of Korea. Strengthen the rice production foundation of the 10+3 contracting countries; prevent losses after rice harvest; improve arrangements to meet emergency rice supply needs through effective national rice storage policies; promote rice price stability; improve consumption and nutrition policies and programs to enhance the consumption and nutrition of vulnerable groups in each contracting country; promote employment opportunities, increase income, especially for small rice farmers in rural areas	Food security, Economic growth
	ASEAN Guidelines on the Utilization of Digital Technologies for ASEAN Food and Agriculture Sector	2021	Guideline 1: Contribute to food security, food safety and nutrition by improving the value chains (production, post production, market access/linkages and value addition). Guideline 2: Support equitable, sustainable, and inclusive economic development in FAS and ensure much-needed investment on infrastructure and related support services (e.g., digital banking, accounting and investment for access to loans, microfinancing, reporting). Guideline 3: Support the generation and diffusion of appropriate digital innovations for resource-efficient, sustainable and safe FAS. Guideline 4: Foster capacity building engagement and empowerment especially for the youth, women, and marginalized groups. Guideline 5: Improve FAS resiliency during disruptions caused by unprecedented events and shocks. Guideline 6: Strengthen regional partnerships/approaches for digital innovations in the FAS	Technological innovation
	ASEAN Strategic Framework for Public Health Emergencies	2020	This Strategic Framework is intended to enhance ASEAN's preparedness, detection, response and resilience to public health emergencies. It aims to strengthen ASEAN's cooperation in enhancing regional health security. The Strategic Framework will identify financial and resource mechanisms to increase support and investments in public health emergency preparedness at all levels, and to effectively mobilize resources in scaling-up response as necessary. Another objective is to initiate the establishment of mechanisms to sustain laboratory and medical surge capacity in the event of public health emergencies and disasters	Nutrition and health

Continued

Region/ Country	Policy	Year	Key policy insights	Issues
ASEAN	ASEAN Plus Three Plan of Action on Education 2018-2025	2018	Reiterate the need for an adaptive and enabling environment with supporting instruments that would facilitate student mobility with quality assurance among APT countries. Reiterate the importance of substantial alignment between the work of the ASEAN Plus Three Plan of Action on Education 2018-2025 and the recently adopted ASEAN Work Plan on Education 2021-2025 with the aim to ensure efficiency and synergies among various ASEAN education cooperation frameworks. Value the contribution of scholarships to social and economic development	Education level
	ASEAN Economic Community Blueprint 2025	2015	The overall vision articulated in the AEC Blueprint 2015 remains relevant. The AEC Blueprint 2025 will build on the AEC Blueprint 2015 consisting of five interrelated and mutually reinforcing characteristics: (1) A Highly Integrated and Cohesive Economy; (2) A Competitive, Innovative, and Dynamic ASEAN; (3) Enhanced Connectivity and Sectoral Cooperation; (4) A Resilient, Inclusive, People-Oriented, and People-Centered ASEAN; and (5) A Global ASEAN	Economic growth
	ASEAN Digital Masterplan 2025 (ADM 2025)	2021	ADM 2025 has specified eight desirable outcomes which the master plan should meet in the next five years. (1) Actions of ADM 2025 prioritized to speed ASEAN's recovery from COVID-19. (2) Increase in the quality and coverage of fixed and mobile broadband infrastructure. (3) The delivery of trusted digital services and the prevention of consumer harm. (4) A sustainable competitive market for the supply of digital services. (5) Increase in the quality and use of e-government services. (6) Digital services to connect business and to facilitate cross border trade. (7) Increased capability for business and people to participate in the digital economy. (8) A digitally inclusive society in ASEAN	Economic growth
	ASEAN Strategic Action Plan for SME Development (2016-2025)	2015	Actions for Strategic Goals: Promote Productivity, Technology and Innovation; Increase Access to Finance; Enhance Market Access and Internationalization; Enhance Policy and Regulatory Environment; Promote Entrepreneurship and Human Capital Development	Economic growth

Continued

Region/Country	Policy	Year	Key policy insights	Issues
ASEAN	ASEAN Plan of Action for Energy Cooperation (APAEC)	2015	The key strategies of the seven Programme Areas of the APAEC Phase II : 2021- 2025 are as follows: (1) To expand regional multilateral electricity trading, strengthen grid resilience and modernization, and promote clean and renewable energy integration; (2) To pursue the development of a common gas market for ASEAN by enhancing gas and LNG connectivity and accessibility; (3) To optimize the role of clean coal technology in facilitating the transition towards sustainable and lower emission development; (4) To reduce energy intensity by 32% in 2025 based on 2005 levels and encourage further energy efficiency and conservation efforts, especially in transport and industry sectors; (5) To achieve aspirational target for increasing the component of renewable energy to 23% by 2025 in the ASEAN energy mix, including through increasing the share of RE in installed power capacity to 35% by 2025; (6) To advance energy policy and planning to accelerate the region's energy transition and resilience; (7) To build human resource capabilities on nuclear science and technology for power generation	Climate change
	ASEAN Vision 2025 on Disaster Management	2021	The strategy outlines institutionalization and communication, financing and resource mobilization, partnerships, and innovation as cornerstones for building a resilient ASEAN and a region capable of taking comprehensive action locally and beyond. Three mutually inclusive strategic elements have been identified to guide the direction of the strategy's implementation until 2025. (1) ASEAN needs to leverage and promote its achievements to make the region a global leader in disaster management and emergency response. (2) post-2015 disaster management and emergency response efforts must explore sustainable and innovative approaches, transforming how funding and resources are mobilized for disaster management and emergency response. (3) ASEAN should consider forming stronger traditional and new non-traditional partnerships	Climate change

Continued

Region/ Country	Policy	Year	Key policy insights	Issues
ASEAN	ASEAN Declaration on One ASEAN, One Response: ASEAN Responding to Disasters as One in The Region and Outside the Region	2016	One ASEAN, One Response is an ASEAN declaration responding to disasters as one in the region and outside the region to achieve faster response, mobilize greater resources and establish stronger coordination to ensure ASEAN's collective response to disasters. That is, having as many relevant stakeholders involved to achieve the envisioned speed, scale and solidarity. It is an open and inclusive platform using ASEAN's mechanisms at its core	Climate change
	ASEAN Joint Disaster Response Plan (AJDRP)	2017	The AJDRP goal is to provide a common framework to deliver a timely, at-scale, and joint response through mobilization of required assets and capacities. This goal will be achieved through the following objectives: (1) Increasing the speed of the ASEAN response by supporting ASEAN Member States in making timely and informed decisions; (2) Expanding the scale of the ASEAN response by strengthening the ASEAN Standby Arrangements; (3) Enhancing the solidarity of the ASEAN response by strengthening coordination and cooperation among ASEAN Member States, ASEAN partners, and other humanitarian actors	Climate change
	ICT Roadmap on Disaster Management for 2025 and Beyond	2020	The ICT Roadmap on Disaster Management for 2025 and Beyond is a guideline to ensure the work programme or initiatives of the ICT function are aligned and relevant with the organization plan and strategic direction. This is a multi-purpose tool that will serve as guidelines for ICT infrastructure and solutions for the AHA Centre and its network with the ASEAN Member States (AMS). This will become an important guideline not only owned by the AHA Centre, but also for all AMS to further enhance the ICT capabilities for the betterment of disaster management of ASEAN region	Climate change

Continued

Region/Country	Policy	Year	Key policy insights	Issues
Lancang-Mekong	Five-Year Plan of Action on Lancang-Mekong Cooperation (2018-2022)	2018	This Plan of Action is formulated in accordance with documents including the Sanya Declaration adopted at the first Lancang-Mekong Cooperation (LMC) Leaders' Meeting, which aims at contributing to the economic and social development of sub-regional countries, enhancing well-being of the people, narrowing the development gap within the region and building a Community of Shared Future of Peace and Prosperity among Lancang-Mekong Countries. By synergizing China's Belt and Road Initiative and the ASEAN Community Vision 2025 as well as the Master Plan on ASEAN Connectivity 2025 and visions of other Mekong sub-regional cooperation mechanisms, the LMC is moving towards a new sub-regional cooperation mechanism with unique features driven by internal strength and inspired by South-South cooperation, which will support the ASEAN Community building and regional integration process, as well as promote the implementation of the UN 2030 Agenda for Sustainable Development	Economic growth
Philippines	National Agriculture and Fisheries Modernization and Industrialization Plan 2021-2030	2022	NAFMIP shall aim to inspire the full range of private and public stakeholders to take coordinated, cohesive, and determined actions toward achieving a common vision and objectives, and to galvanize sector-wide public and private investments and resources to support the shared vision, objectives, and concerted action	Food security
	Philippine Plan of Action for Nutrition (PPAN) 2017-2022	2017	PPAN 2017-2022 has two layers of outcome objectives, the outcome targets and the sub-outcome or intermediate targets. The former refers to final outcomes against which plan success will be measured. The latter refers to outcomes that will contribute to the achievement of the final outcomes	Nutrition and health

Continued

Region/ Country	Policy	Year	Key policy insights	Issues
Philippines	Philippines Innovation Act	2019	The State shall place innovation at the center of its development policies, guided by a clear and long-term set of goals that shall take into consideration the key advantages of the country and the opportunities in the regional and global economic arena. As such, it shall harness innovation efforts to help the poor and the marginalized, enable micro, small and medium enterprises (MSMEs) to be a part of the domestic and global supply chain, and catalyze the growth of Philippine industries and local economies. This ecosystem should facilitate and support innovation efforts including, but not limited to, digitalization, cultivation and development of skills and knowledge in science, technology, engineering, entrepreneurship, and mathematics in all educational levels and intellectual property protection	Technological innovation
Laos	2016-2020 National Nutrition Strategy (NNS)	2016	Strategic directions and objectives: (1) To tackle the immediate causes at the level of the individual and focus on achieving sufficient food consumption and safety, emphasizing the first 1,000 days of life and reducing the prevalence of diseases caused by contaminated food and indirectly transmitted infectious diseases which impair the body's ability to absorb food consumed; (2) To tackle the underlying causes (mostly at household and community levels), which requires improvements to the safety and diversity of food consumed so that people may always have access to food and locations, and moreover, to focus on improving maternal and child health (MCH) practices, clean water, and sanitation and healthy environments and access to health services	Nutrition and health
Myanmar	National Health Plan (2017-2021)	2016	Features of the Plan that are noteworthy include: its focus on ensuring access to essential health services for the entire population; its emphasis on primary health care delivered at township level and below; its consideration for involvement of healthcare providers outside Ministry of Health and Sports; its switch from top-down planning to a more inclusive bottom-up approach; and its recognition of the importance of health systems strengthening from all perspectives	Nutrition and health

Continued

Region/ Country	Policy	Year	Key policy insights	Issues
Myanmar	Myanmar National Education Strategic Plan 2016-2021 (NESP)	2016	The NESP aims to establish an accessible, equitable and effective national education system over the next five years. The NESP roadmap clearly recognizes the vital importance of developing an industry-led and competency-based TVET system able to train a skilled and competitive local workforce to support Myanmar's long-term social and economic growth. In the coming years, Myanmar will need a large number of skilled employees, particularly for the agricultural, energy, manufacturing, infrastructure, livestock, fisheries and tourism sectors	Education level
	Myanmar Climate Change Master Plan (2018-2030)	2019	The Myanmar Climate Change Master Plan (2018-2030) clearly defines a series of high-priority activities, their respective strategic indicators, and the responsibilities of involved stakeholders across six specific sectors prioritized in Myanmar Climate Change Strategy defined as: "climate-smart agriculture, fisheries and livestock for food security, sustainable management of natural resources for healthy ecosystems, resilient and low-carbon energy, transport and industrial systems for sustainable growth, building resilient, inclusive and sustainable cities and towns in Myanmar, managing climate risks for people's health and well-being, and building a resilient Myanmar society through education, science and technology"	Climate change
Vietnam	Supporting the Preschool Education Development in Disadvantaged Areas for the 2022-2030 Period	2022	At least 25% of kindergarten children and 95% of preschool children in disadvantaged areas will be able to go to schools by 2030. 100% of children in pre-school institutions in disadvantaged areas are nurtured, cared for and educated. The program on developing preschool education in disadvantaged areas aims to ensure equal accession to education, narrow the development gap between regions, improve conditions for teachers and the quality of schools in ethnic areas	Education level

Continued

Region/ Country	Policy	Year	Key policy insights	Issues
			Economic targets: (1) The average growth rate of Gross Domestic Product (GDP) in five years is expected to increase by 6.5% - 7%; (2) GDP per capita by 2025 is expected to reach about US$4,700-5,000; (3) The share of the processing and manufacturing industry and the digital economy to GDP is expected to account for over 25% and about 20%, respectively; (4) The contribution of total factor productivity (TFP) to growth is expected to reach about 45%; (5) The average social labor productivity will grow by over 6.5% per annum; (6) The urbanization rate is expected to reach about 45%; (7) State budget deficit to GDP during the period of 2021-2025 will account for 3.7% of GDP on average	Economic growth, Nutrition and health
Vietnam	Socio-economic development plan for 2021-2025	2021	Social targets: (1) The average life expectancy will be about 74.5 years, including at least 67 years of healthy life; (2) The share of agricultural workers to total social labor is expected to reach about 25%; (3) Trained workers are expected to account for 70%, including 28% - 30% of those obtaining professional qualification and certificates; (4) Unemployment rate in urban areas will be below 4%; (5) Multidimensional poverty reduction rate will remain by 1% - 1.5% per annum; (6) The number of doctors and beds will be 10 and 30 per 10,000 people, respectively; (7) The percentage of population participating in health insurance is expected to reach 95%; (8) The rate of communes meeting new rural standards will be at least 80%, including 10% of those meeting advanced new rural standards	

Continued

Region/Country	Policy	Year	Key policy insights	Issues
Vietnam	Vietnamese Strategy for Science, Technology and Innovation Development until 2030	2022	By 2030, science, technology and innovation will be firmly developed, truly become motivation for growth, and make a decisive contribution to the development of Vietnam into a developing country with modern industry and upper-middle income; contribute to the comprehensive development of culture, society and people, the safeguarding of national defense - security, environmental protection, sustainable development and improvement of Vietnam's international stature and reputation. The capacity and level of science, technology and innovation will reach advanced levels in many key areas, making Vietnam one of the best performers among upper-middle income countries. Enterprises' technology and innovation level and capacity will surpass the global average. Some areas of science and technology will reach international level	Technological innovation
	Sustainable Smart City Development Plan (2018-2025)	2018	Under a project to develop smart and sustainable cities during the 2018-2025 period and vision to 2030 approved by the Prime Minister, Vietnam's major cities and provinces have been ramping up efforts with new action plans to realize their smart city dreams	Technological innovation
	National Digital Transformation Programme by 2025	2020	Vietnam recently approved the National Digital Transformation Programme by 2025, with an orientation towards 2030. The initiative will help accelerate digital transformation through changes in awareness, enterprise strategies, and incentives towards the digitalization of businesses, administration, and production activities. The programme will target businesses, cooperatives, and business households that want to adopt digital transformation to improve their production, business efficiency, and competitiveness	Technological innovation
	Vietnam Issues Green Growth Strategy 2021-2030 Vision to 2050	2012	Green growth contributes to promoting economic restructuring associated with growth model innovation, in order to achieve economic prosperity, environmental sustainability, and social justice; towards a green, carbon-neutral economy and contribute to the goal of limiting global temperature rise	Climate change

Continued

Region/Country	Policy	Year	Key policy insights	Issues
Vietnam	National Energy Efficiency Program 2019-2030	2019	Vietnam's economy continues to see strong growth compared to regional and global economies. Developing energy to meet socio-economic growth's demand is inevitable, however, energy development must be consistent with energy security and environmental protection. To achieve this goal, there are two strategic solutions for the energy sector: (1) enhance energy use efficiency, improve energy performance to reduce energy loss; and (2) make changes to the energy source structure towards reducing fossil fuel, promoting efficient use of and increase usage rate of renewable energy in energy production and consumption, reducing greenhouse gas. The Vietnam national energy efficiency program had been implemented during 2006 - 2015 which indicates the energy conservation of over 18 tons of oil equivalent; for 2011- 2015, the efficiency rate is 5.65 percent, which is equivalent to the total energy conservation of 11.8 million TOE for the same period	Climate change
Thailand	New Investment Promotion Strategy (2023-2027)	2022	Under the new scheme, the BOI will shift its focus to three core concepts deemed vital to the country's future economy: (1) technology, innovation, and creativity; (2) competitiveness and adaptability; and (3) inclusiveness (especially in regard to environmental and social sustainability). This is complemented by a new set of investment promotion policy aims that cover, for example, supply chain reinforcement, conversion to smart and sustainable industry, promotion of Thai SMEs with global connections, and so on	Economic growth

Continued

Region/Country	Policy	Year	Key policy insights	Issues
Thailand	Thailand 4.0	2016	The Thai government is working hard to promote "Thailand 4.0" as a new gimmick and economic model aimed at pulling Thailand out of the middle-income trap, and push the country in the high-income range. Thailand 4.0 focuses on a "value-based economy", as the country needs to deal effectively with disparities and the imbalance between the environment and society. The first element aims to enhance the country's standing to become a high-income nation through developing it as a knowledge-based economy. In the second element, Thailand will move toward an "inclusive society" with equitable access to the fruits of prosperity and development. The third element focuses on "sustainable growth and development," in order to achieve economic growth and sustainable development without destroying the environment. The 10 targeted industries are: Aviation and logistics; biofuels and biochemicals; robotics; digital development; next-generation automotive; medical industries; smart electronics; affluent, medical and wellness tourism; agriculture and biotechnology, and food for the future	Technological innovation, Economic growth
	Thailand's Digital Roadmap for 2024	2020	Thailand's Digital Roadmap for 2024 aims to align technological advancements, consumer behavior, and business environments to drive the transformation and rapid growth of Thailand's digital economy, facilitating the country's success in the digital realm over the next 20 years. The roadmap consists of four main components: building a digital technology talent pool, fostering digital economic development, promoting community digital capacity building, and constructing a digital innovation ecosystem through smart cities, big data, and cybersecurity initiatives. Thailand's objective is to become an advanced broadband nation by 2022-2027, which involves narrowing the digital divide, particularly in rural areas, and laying the groundwork for economic and social sustainability	Technological innovation

Continued

Region/Country	Policy	Year	Key policy insights	Issues
Thailand	Plan for driving Thailand with the BCG model, 2021-2027	2022	The Thai government has a policy to drive Thailand toward "Thailand 4.0" by using holistic economic development in a 3D economy. This new economic model is called "BCG," for Bio-Circular-Green, which consists of three interlinking dimensions including bioeconomy, circular economy, and green economy. The plan focuses on several major areas including agriculture and food, health and medical, energy, materials, and biochemicals, tourism and the creative economy and circular economy	Climate change
	Tourism Development Master Plan Siem Reap 2021-2035	2021	The RGC is strongly committed to the development of the tourism in Siem Reap and the surrounding area to be a "quality tourist destination" that has thorough management on the tourism development, and minimizes negative impacts on the Angkor heritage site and natural resources in order to attract revisit tourists, especially up-market tourists in order to increase the incomes of the nation and local people	Economic growth
Cambodia	Cambodia Digital Economy and Society Policy Framework 2021-2035	2021	The framework contains 139 specific measures, aiming to complete Cambodia's "digital transformation" by 2035, with the digital economy accounting for 5% to 10% of GDP. By 2025, urban areas are targeted to achieve 100% high-speed internet coverage, while rural areas are aimed to reach 70%. By 2030, the goal is to achieve digitization of major public services, with a 70% adoption rate of digital technology among private enterprises, and the proportion of employment in related industries to reach 4% of the workforce	Technological innovation

Continued

Region/ Country	Policy	Year	Key policy insights	Issues
			The National STI Policy notably focuses STI priorities on five scientific and technological domains: (1) Agricultural yield increase, produce diversification and agroprocessing; (2) Modern production and engineering; (3) Health and biomedical; (4) Material science and engineering; (5) Services and digital economy, including artificial intelligence and space and spatial technology.	
Cambodia	Cambodia's Science, Technology & Innovation Roadmap 2030	2021	Following the National Innovation System conceptual framework and taking into account the current strengths and weaknesses of the National Innovation System of Cambodia, the STI Roadmap 2030 was designed to guide the implementation of the National STI Policy. (1) Enhancing the governance of the STI system. (2) Build human capital in STI. (3) Strengthening research capacity and quality. (4) Increasing collaboration and networking between different actors. (5) Fostering an enabling ecosystem for building absorptive capacities in firms and attracting investments in STI	Technological innovation
	Long-Term Strategy for Carbon Neutrality (LTS4CN)	2021	This LTS4CN outlines priority mitigation actions for each sector to achieve the country's goal of a carbon neutral economy in 2050. It takes into consideration the balance between emissions reductions, economic growth, social justice, and climate resilience. Economic analysis shows that the investments to be made under this strategy have the potential to create 449,000 additional jobs, and deliver an additional 2.8% of annual GDP growth by 2050 for Cambodia. We can achieve carbon neutrality by 2050 through continued efforts to address the forest sustainability and land use; decarbonize our power sector and pursue higher energy efficiency; as well as promote low-carbon agriculture, industrial processes, and waste management	Climate change

Continued

Region/ Country	Policy	Year	Key policy insights	Issues
	Master Plan of National Research (RIRN) 2017-2045	2015	RIRN is a planning document for national research sector. One of the goals is to increase the contribution of research to national economic growth. Strategy and performance indicators such as macro research groups, priority research areas, number of researchers, research funding in % GDP, number of publications, etc.., are formulated in RIRN. RIRN is currently in the process of approval to become Presidential Decree	Technological innovation
Indonesia	Roadmap Digital Indonesia 2021-2024	2021	The plan covers four strategic areas: digital infrastructure, digital government, digital economy, and digital society, with six strategic directions and ten key industries to achieve inclusive digital transformation. The key industries include digital transformation in tourism, digital trade, digital financial services, digital media and entertainment, digital agriculture and fisheries, digital real estate and urban development, digital education, digital health, industry digitization, and government agency digitization	Technological innovation

Appendix 3　Poverty Reduction Goals of ASEAN Countries

Country	Policy documents, meetings, or speeches	Poverty reduction goals	Specific measures
Laos	9th Five-Year National Socio-Economic Development Plan (2021-2025)	Increase the number of families lifted out of poverty by 204,360 families (from 964,149 to 1,168,509 families); Increase the number of villages lifted out of poverty by 3,104 villages (from 4,792 to 7,896 villages)	In the field of rural development and poverty alleviation, legislation such as the Immigration Law, Central Politburo Decree No. 097, Lao Government Decree on Poverty Alleviation and Development Standards, and Decree No. 348 on the determination of strategies and development priority areas have been enacted
	Prime Minister addressed the Fourth Session of the 9th National Assembly in December 2022.	By developing clean, safe, and sustainable agriculture, ensuring national food security, and building an agricultural production system that makes significant contributions to the national economy in line with industrialization and modernization goals	Utilize domestic resource advantages, improve the agricultural production system, further strengthen agricultural infrastructure, and promote agricultural modernization through technology. Accelerate the development of agricultural integrated enterprises focusing on small and medium-sized enterprises, enabling them to access low-interest loans more conveniently, conduct trade, and access product markets
	10th National Congress of the Lao People's Revolutionary Party	Striving to graduate from least developed country status by 2020 towards becoming a developing upper middle-income country alongside green and sustainable development by 2030	

Continued

Country	Policy documents, meetings, or speeches	Poverty reduction goals	Specific measures
Philippines	Philippine Development Plan 2023-2028	The PDP also aims to bring down the poverty incidence rate to 16 to 16.4 percent this year, 12.9 to 13.2 percent in 2025, 10 to 10.3 percent in 2027, and 8.8 to nine percent by 2028 from 18.1 percent in 2021	Key transformation strategies for the economic or production sector include modernize agriculture and agri-business, revitalize industry, reinvigorate services. For the social and human development sector, strategies include: (1) Promote and improve lifelong learning and education by providing access to high-quality learning opportunities that develop adequate competencies and character qualities; (2) Boost health through interventions leading to healthy schools, communities, workplaces, and lifestyles; (3) Ensure food security and proper nutrition through production and effective supply management; (4) Strengthen the social protection system by integrating safeguards into development interventions and by streamlining contingency financing mechanisms, strengthening the delivery of digital payments of cash transfers, and expanding insurance coverage; (5) Increase income-earning ability of the workforce through skills upgrading and updating, employment facilitation services, including the reintegration of migrant workers back to the domestic economy; (6) Establish livable communities by upgrading and planning human settlements such that an integrated use of space will bring people closer to work, recreation, and transit options
	Philippine Development Plan 2017-2022	Reduce poverty rate to 14% by 2022	The Philippine President signed into law in April last year Republic Act 11291, otherwise known as the Magna Carta of the Poor. The Philippines' Department of Social Welfare and Development is also implementing a conditional cash-transfer program popularly known as Pantawid Pamilyang Pilipino Program (roughly translated as "Enabling Filipino Families to Cross the Threshold"). The program covers more than 42,000 communities and has served more than 4.5 million households. Proof of the success of the program is the voluntary withdrawal from the program of hundreds of recipients for the reason that they are already out of poverty and no longer need the support of the program

Continued

Country	Policy documents, meetings, or speeches	Poverty reduction goals	Specific measures
Philippines	2022 State of the Nation Address	9% or single-digit poverty rate by 2028	To curb inflation, sustain and expand infrastructure development schemes, further drive economic growth and employment; implement reliable fiscal management, enforce tax reforms, increase revenue, enhance expenditure efficiency to promptly address the economic impacts brought about by the pandemic; fully support the introduction of high-tech manufacturing, healthcare, and other emerging strategic industries to promote economic growth beyond the Manila metropolitan area
	Vision 2040	By 2040, the Philippines shall be a prosperous, predominantly middle-class society where no one is poor	
	National Strategic Development Plan (NSDP) 2019-2023	Continue to reduce poverty with rates below 10% by the end of the plan period, with reductions exceeding 1% per year and reducing vulnerabilities and ensuring income security	Utilizing connectivity to enhance rural economic activities, promoting community development through skill development, providing rural credit for entrepreneurship to diversify rural economic activities. Initiating comprehensive plans, with a focus on constructing sustainable and inclusive rural infrastructure
Cambodia	Agricultural Development Policy 2022-2030	Gross Value-Added (GVA) of crop production will increase by 3.1 percent per annum 2030	The overarching goal of policy development is to enhance agricultural growth with high competitiveness and inclusivity by delivering high-quality products that ensure food safety and nutrition, while also prioritizing the sustainable management of land, water, forestry, and fishery resources. To achieve this goal, four strategic policy objectives have been defined for implementation: (1) Enhancing the competitiveness of agricultural value chains; (2) Increasing support for infrastructure in agriculture and agri-business facilitation; (3) Promoting sustainable land, forestry, and fishery resource management; and (4) Strengthening institutional management and regulatory reforms, human resource development, and addressing emerging challenges

Continued

Country	Policy documents, meetings, or speeches	Poverty reduction goals	Specific measures
Vietnam	13th National Congress of the Communist Party of Vietnam	By 2025, the rate of multidimensional poverty reduction shall be maintained at 1% - 1.5% per year	Introduce conditional support policies; strengthen social policies to support impoverished populations, providing social security for those unable to work; implement policies to encourage collaboration between enterprises and cooperatives in production, operation, and consumption, fostering production models involving impoverished and near-impoverished individuals
	National Sustainable Poverty Reduction Plan (2021-2025).	The programme targets to reduce the nationwide poverty rate by 1%-1.5%, by over 3% among ethnic minority households, and by 4%-4.5% in poor districts per year. The number of poor and near-poor households is expected to halve by 2025. The rate of children from poor and near-poor households going to school at the right age will reach 90%	Permanent Deputy Prime Minister Pham Binh Minh signed a decision approving the national target programme on sustainable poverty reduction for the 2021-2025 period with total funding of at least 75 trillion VND (US$3.3 billion), The overall goal of the programme is to achieve multidimensional, inclusive and sustainable poverty reduction . It will be carried out nationwide, with the focus on poor districts and extremely disadvantageous communes in lowland and coastal areas and on islands. Specifically, eligible families will be provided with VND 40 million (US$ 1,700) for building a new house or VND 20 million for home repair
	National New Rural Development Goal Plan (2021-2025)	By 2025, the program targets to have at least 80 percent of the communes recognized as new-style rural areas, with about 40 percent meeting advanced standards and at least 10 percent being model areas	The program is expected to mobilize capital resources of VND 2.45 quadrillion (US$ 105 billion) in the 2021-2025 period. The program focuses on building new-style countryside, improving rural residents' material and spiritual life, promoting gender equality, developing a complete and modern socio-economic infrastructure in rural areas, ensuring a green, clean, beautiful, and safe environment and landscape, and boosting traditional culture preservation, climate change adaptation, and sustainable development in the areas

Continued

Country	Policy documents, meetings, or speeches	Poverty reduction goals	Specific measures
	Indonesian Minister of National Development Planning Suharso Monoarfa's remarks at a development planning meeting held in Jakarta in 2022	The Indonesian Government targets to reduce the poverty rate to 7.5 percent, from 8.5 percent in 2023 by increasing productivity for an inclusive and sustainable economic transformation	First, the mainstreaming of extreme poverty targets will become all parties' intervention, including non-governmental organizations (NGOs) and the business world through the SDGs regional action plans. Second, improving coordination to target the central and local social protection programs. Third, assisting and facilitating access to capital and markets and increasing the productivity of the extreme poor. The last one is the integration of social protection and empowerment programs to increase the self-reliance of the extreme poor
Indonesia	National Mid-Term Development Plan 2020-2024	By 2024, poverty and open unemployment rates are expected to decrease to 6.0%-7.0% and 3.6%-4.3% respective-ly; the Gini coefficient is expected to decrease to 0.360-0.374	Reducing poverty, through: accelerating the strengthening of the family economy, mediating businesses and their social impact, agrarian reforms, community forest management through social forestry schemes
	Indonesia's first Nationally Determined Contribution (NDC) in 2016 and Indonesia's Enhanced NDC in 2022	Reduce the poverty rate to below 4% by 2025	
	Indonesia Vision 2045; 2025-2045 National Long-Term Development Plan (RJPJN)	Reduce the extreme poverty rate to zero percent by 2045	
Thailand	The 13th National Economic and Social Development Plan (2023-2027)	Sustainable Development Goals (SDGs) by basing the development direction on the concept of "leaving no one behind". Remedy chronic poverty and prevent intergenerational poverty	Providing aid and building the capacity of intergenerational poor households to ensure suitable living conditions for child development. Developing local-level mechanisms to address intergenerational transmission of poverty with a focus on enhancing the capacity and increasing the role of regional and local agencies in addressing intergenerational poverty. Supporting intergenerational poor households in providing quality care to children from gestation to early childhood. Boosting opportunities for quality education and professional skills development

Continued

Country	Policy documents, meetings, or speeches	Poverty reduction goals	Specific measures
Thailand	National Strategy (2018-2037)	To become a developed country with security, prosperity and sustainability in accordance with the Sufficiency Economy Philosophy	Exploring value-added agriculture in order to upgrade productivity in terms of quantity and value as well as product diversity within the following sectors including farming that reflects local identity, safe farming, biological farming, processed agricultural products and smart farming. Conducting targeting social investment to provide assistance to poor and underprivileged people
Malaysia	Twelfth Malaysia Plan (2021-2025)	Zero hardcore poverty by 2025; Decent standard of living for all Malaysians irrespective of gender, ethnicity and location; Reduced inequalities among the rakyat, including Bumiputera which constitutes the majority of the poorest group	A more effective mechanism of eliminating hardcore poverty will encompass the following: (1) Establishing dedicated poverty units at Federal and district levels; (2) Formulating poverty policies based on data-driven approach; (3) Integrating and centralizing the database on poverty; (4) Enhancing bottom-up approach programmes; (5) Localizing poverty solution at the grassroot level; (6) Exploring the possibility of introducing dedicated tax as a financing source for poverty alleviation programmes. Zakat and waqf as well as contributions from GLC, private entities and individuals will be considered
	Rural Development Policy (RDP) 2023	To develop a "Prosperous, Inclusive, Sustainable and Holistic Rural Area" by 2030	In response to the poverty reduction challenges after the pandemic, the Malaysian government has made numerous efforts. These efforts include extending discounts and rental waivers for affiliated businesses and selected housing, launching online networking programs for rural entrepreneurs, implementing food basket programs for impoverished families and indigenous residents, as well as providing fee waivers for affiliated kindergartens under the department

Continued

Country	Policy documents, meetings, or speeches	Poverty reduction goals	Specific measures
Myanmar	Myanmar Sustainable Development Plan (2018-2030).	A comprehensive, well-resourced and inclusive social safety net protects against a wide range of risks faced by those living below the poverty line and those hovering close to it, particularly women and youth	Create an enabling environment which supports a diverse and productive economy through inclusive agricultural, aquacultural and polyculture practices as a foundation for poverty reduction in rural areas

Note: (1) The Paris Agreement requires each country to develop and communicate its climate actions after 2020, known as Nationally Determined Contributions (NDCs), and mandates countries to update their NDCs every five years.

(2) Myanmar experienced a military coup in February 2021. The "Myanmar Sustainable Development Plan (2018-2030)" was formulated by the previous government.

Appendix 4 Events of ASEAN-China Poverty Reduction Cooperation

Year	Region/Country	Fields	Events
2012	ASEAN	Technological innovation	China-ASEAN Science and Technology Partnership Program was officially launched
2013	Cambodia	Infrastructure	China aided in the construction of Highway No. 6 in Cambodia
	ASEAN	Economic growth	The Belt and Road Initiative was proposed
	Laos	Technological innovation, Food security	The China-Laos Fine Crop Varieties Experimental Station, the first crop variety experiment establishment founded by China in ASEAN, started operation
2014	Laos, Cambodia, Myanmar	Poverty reduction cooperation, Food security	China proposed the "East Asia Poverty Reduction Cooperation Initiative" and established demonstration sites in Laos, Cambodia, and Myanmar
	ASEAN	Technological innovation	Guangxi ASEAN Technology Transfer Center was approved and established
2015	Laos	Infrastructure	China and Laos governments sign the "Cooperation Agreement on Railway Infrastructure Development between China and Laos and the China-Laos Railway Project"
2016	Lancang-Mekong	Technological innovation, Food security	The First LMC Leaders' Meeting proposed the establishment of an agricultural science and technology cooperation fund
	Laos, Cambodia, Myanmar	Poverty reduction cooperation, Food security	The East Asia Poverty Reduction Demonstration Cooperation Technical Assistance Project was launched as a pilot program in Laos, Cambodia, and Myanmar. The initial phase of the project had a funding amount of RMB100 million
2017	Cambodia	Infrastructure, Nutrition and health	Construction commenced for the first phase of the rural water supply project with assistance from China in Cambodia
	ASEAN	Technological innovation	Belt and Road Initiative Science and Innovation Action Plan

Continued

Year	Region/Country	Fields	Events
2017	ASEAN	Technological innovation, Food security	Yunnan Academy of Agricultural Sciences proposed the establishment of the "South Asia-Southeast Asia Agricultural Technology Radiation Center"
	Indonesia	Infrastructure	The groundbreaking ceremony for the iconic project of Belt and Road construction and pragmatic cooperation between China and Indonesia-the Jakarta-Bandung High-Speed Railway
	Laos	Nutrition and health	China donated set of integrated sewage treatment equipment with a daily treatment capacity of 50 tons to a high school in Laos
2018		Climate change	China-ASEAN seminar on disaster risk reduction management
	ASEAN	Technological innovation	China-ASEAN Innovation Year launch ceremony and China-ASEAN Innovation Forum
		Technological innovation	Joint Statement on China-ASEAN Science and Technology Innovation Cooperation was released in the 21st China-ASEAN Leaders' Meeting
2019	Vietnam	Infrastructure	China Energy Construction's 500MW photovoltaic project in Vietnam's Datu completed
	Cambodia	Infrastructure	Jingang Expressway officially commences construction
	Thailand	Poverty reduction cooperation	Thai officials visited Guangxi, China to inspect poverty alleviation projects
		Climate change	China-ASEAN High-Level Forum on Disaster Reduction and Emergency Management
	ASEAN	Economic growth	The National Development and Reform Commission of China released the Policies and Measures to Support Yunnan Province in Accelerating the Construction of a Center for Connecting South Asia and Southeast Asia
2020	Philippines	Infrastructure	China aided in the construction of the Davao River Bridge project in the Philippines
	Cambodia	Nutrition and health	China dispatched a medical team to Cambodia for COVID-19
	Myanmar	Nutrition and health	China dispatched a medical team to Myanmar for COVID-19
	Laos	Nutrition and health	China dispatched a medical team to Laos for COVID-19

Continued

Year	Region/Country	Fields	Events
2021	ASEAN		China and ASEAN joint released the Plan of Action to Implement the ASEAN-China Strategic Partnership for Peace and Prosperity (2022-2025) and announced a comprehensive strategic partnership between the two sides
		Nutrition and health	China would provide an additional 150 million doses of COVID-19 vaccines to ASEAN countries as gratuitous assistance, and contribute an additional US$5 million to the COVID-19 ASEAN Response Fund
		Climate change	China-ASEAN establishes the Ministerial Meeting Mechanism on Disaster Management
		Climate change	The "China-ASEAN Disaster Management Work Plan (2021-2025)" was released
		Education level, Technological innovation	China proposed the launch of the China-ASEAN Science, Technology and Innovation Enhancing Program and provided ASEAN with 1000 advanced and applicable technologies and would support 300 ASEAN young scientists to exchange in China in the next five years
		Technological innovation	China-ASEAN Plan of Action for a Closer Partnership of Science, Technology and Innovation for Future (2021-2025) was released
		Infrastructure	Philippine Mishandao Substation Transformation Project
	Philippines	Infrastructure	Southern Power Grid International wins the bid for the Philippine power project
		Infrastructure	The Philippines' Chico River Irrigation Project, funded by the Chinese government and constructed by China Gezhouba Group, is officially completed
2022	ASEAN	Economic growth	During the 19th China-ASEAN Expo, China and ASEAN countries jointly signed 267 investment cooperation contracts on site, with a total investment of RMB413 billion. These projects cover a wide range of industries, including high-end metallic materials, green and environmental protection, light industry and textiles, health and wellness, cultural tourism and sports, as well as green chemical materials and machinery and equipment manufacturing

Continued

Year	Region/ Country	Fields	Events
2022	Lancang-Mekong	Poverty reduction cooperation	The 6th Joint Working Group Meeting on Poverty Reduction for Lancang-Mekong Cooperation (LMC) was held online. Representatives from participating countries discussed and adopted the Guideline of the Lancang-Mekong Cooperation on Poverty Reduction (2023–2027), aiming to make positive contributions to promoting regional cooperation and achieving common development in the Lancang-Mekong region
	ASEAN	Economic growth	China has pledged to provide US$1.5 billion in development assistance to ASEAN over a period of three years starting from 2022
	Myanmar	Infrastructure	China aids in the repair of the Zhou Enlai Pavilion in Bagan, Myanmar, and the restoration of the Thabinpey Pagoda project
2023	Cambodia	Infrastructure	The groundbreaking ceremony for the second expressway in Cambodia – the Kimba Expressway – invested and constructed by China Road and Bridge Corporation – is officially held